European Yearbook of International Economic Law

EYIEL Monographs - Studies in European and International Economic Law

Volume 7

Series Editors
Marc Bungenberg, Saarbrücken, Germany
Christoph Herrmann, Passau, Germany
Markus Krajewski, Erlangen, Germany
Jörg Philipp Terhechte, Lüneburg, Germany
Andreas R. Ziegler, Lausanne, Switzerland

EYIEL Monographs is a subseries of the European Yearbook of International Economic Law (EYIEL). It contains scholarly works in the fields of European and international economic law, in particular WTO law, international investment law, international monetary law, law of regional economic integration, external trade law of the EU and EU internal market law. The series does not include edited volumes. EYIEL Monographs are peer-reviewed by the series editors and external reviewers.

More information about this series at http://www.springer.com/series/15744

Elza Reymond-Eniaeva

Towards a Uniform Approach to Confidentiality of International Commercial Arbitration

 Springer

Elza Reymond-Eniaeva
Lausanne, Switzerland

ISSN 2364-8392   ISSN 2364-8406   (electronic)
European Yearbook of International Economic Law
ISSN 2524-6658   ISSN 2524-6666   (electronic)
EYIEL Monographs - Studies in European and International Economic Law
ISBN 978-3-030-19002-6   ISBN 978-3-030-19003-3   (eBook)
https://doi.org/10.1007/978-3-030-19003-3

This Springer imprint is published by the registered company Springer Nature Switzerland AG.
The registered company address is: Gewerbestrasse 11, 6330 Cham, Switzerland

To my parents
Jean-Marc, Charles Kirsan and Marie
Tsagan

Acknowledgements

I would like to express my profound gratitude to Professor Andrea Bonomi, supervisor of this thesis, for sharing his extensive knowledge and for his continuous support. His guidance contributed greatly to the drafting and finalization of this work.

I would also like to extend my gratitude to the other members of the PhD defense committee, Professors Sébastien Besson, Eva Lein, Philippe Meier and Christoph Müller, for their insightful and valuable comments.

I am also very grateful to my friends and colleagues who supported me in their own way, whether by reviewing my drafts or providing emotional support, during the challenging period of writing this thesis: my colleagues from Sidley Austin LLP, in particular, Marc Palay, Tanya Landon, Victor Libet and Nicola Rylatt, my colleagues from Sedlex Avocats, in particular, Mathias Burnand and Yvan Guichard, the Director and staff of the Swiss Institute of Comparative Law, and my friends Jorun Baumgartner, Annie-Fabienne Pillionnel and Lia Meyer.

Finally, I could not have accomplished my work without the endless love and support of my family, in particular, my mother, my husband Jean-Marc and our children Charles Kirsan and Marie Tsagan. I dedicate this book to them and in memory of my late father.

Contents

Abbreviations

AAA	American Arbitration Association
ABA	American Bar Association
Abu Dhabi Rules	Abu Dhabi Procedural Regulations of Arbitration
ACICA Rules	Arbitration Rules of Australian Centre for International Commercial Arbitration
AIAA	Australian International Arbitration Act 1974
ATF	Decision of the Swiss Federal Court
CC	Swiss Civil Code
CIArb Code of Ethics	Code of Professional and Ethical Conduct for Members of the Chartered Institute of Arbitrators
CISG	UN Convention on Contracts for the International Sale of Goods
CO	Swiss Code of Obligations
DIAC Rules	Dubai International Arbitration Centre Arbitration Rules
DIS Rules	Arbitration Rules of the German Institution of Arbitration
ECHR	European Convention on Human Rights
European Convention	European Convention on International Commercial Arbitration
EEA	European Economic Area
EFTA	European Free Trade Association
EU	European Union
HKIAC Rules	Hong Kong International Arbitration Centre Administered Arbitration Rules 2018
IBA Rules on Evidence	International Bar Association Rules on the Taking of Evidence in International Arbitration

ICAC Rules	Rules of Arbitration of International Commercial Disputes of the International Commercial Arbitration Court at the Chamber of Commerce and Industry of the Russian Federation
ICC Rules	International Chamber of Commerce Arbitration and ADR Rules
ICDR Rules	Canadian Dispute Resolution Procedures of the International Center for Dispute Resolution
ICSID	International Center for Settlement of Investment Disputes
Inter-American Convention	Inter-American Convention on International Commercial Arbitration
JCAA Rules	Commercial Arbitration Rules of the Japan Commercial Arbitration Association
LCIA Rules	London Court of International Arbitration Rules
LLCA	Loi fédérale sur la libre circulation des avocats/Swiss Law on the Freedom of Movement for Lawyers
LTF	Swiss Federal Supreme Court Act
Milan Guidelines	Guidelines for the Anonymous Publication of Arbitral Awards of the Milan Chamber of Arbitration
Milan Rules	Arbitration Rules of the Milan Chamber of Arbitration
Model Law	UNCITRAL Model Law
New York Convention	New York Convention on the Recognition and Enforcement of Foreign Arbitral Awards
NZAA	New Zealand Arbitration Act of 1996
Oslo Rules	Rules of the Arbitration and Dispute Resolution Institution of the Oslo Chamber of Commerce
PECL	Principles of European Contract Law
SCC Rules	Arbitration Rules of the Arbitration Institute of the Stockholm Chamber of Commerce
SIAC Rules	Arbitration Rules of the Singapore International Arbitration Center
Swiss Rules	Swiss Rules of International Arbitration
Swiss PILA	Swiss Federal Law on Private International Law Act
UNCITRAL	United Nations Commission on International Trade Law
UNCITRAL Notes	UNCITRAL Notes on Organizing Arbitral Proceedings
UNIDROIT Principles	UNIDROIT Principles of International Commercial Contracts 2010
UNCITRAL Rules	UNCITRAL Arbitration Rules
U.S.	United States of America
VIAC Rules	Vienna International Arbitral Centre Rules
WIPO Rules	World Intellectual Property Organization Arbitration Rules

Chapter 1
Introduction

Confidentiality is the opposite of publicity. It can be defined as an *'obligation to*   **1**
protect information that is not generally known and to use or disclose it only to
approved persons, for agreed purposes'.[1] Thus, the purpose of confidentiality is to
prevent disclosure to third parties, but not the use of the information between the
same parties. This definition also implies that a complete confidentiality cannot be
achieved as, in some cases, the confidential information will have to be disclosed.

Confidentiality is also one of the most controversial issues in international   **2**
commercial arbitration. On the one hand, it is widely recognised that confidentiality
is an important advantage of international commercial arbitration, contributing to
its attractiveness.[2] On the other hand, there is no uniform regulation in national
legislations, arbitration rules, and other relevant sources as to the scope or even to the
existence of a duty of confidentiality.[3] Moreover, there is currently an ongoing
doctrinal debate over the existence of an implied duty of confidentiality—in the
absence of a legal or contractual basis for such a duty.

Despite all the uncertainty, however, confidentiality has long been considered an   **3**
inherent feature of international arbitration. As pointed out by Serge Lazareff: '[t]*he*
inseparable link between arbitration and confidentiality derives from the very
origins of arbitration as a method of dispute resolution, from its raison d'être and
the manner in which it has been practiced over the centuries'.[4] In addition, since

---

[1]Pattenden (2003), para 1.16.

[2]See, for example, Ashford (2014), p. 217; Bührung-Uhle (2006), p. 108; Pryles (2014), p. 109; Queen Mary University of London in partnership with White & Case 2015 International Arbitration Survey, 6.

[3]See, for example, para 31 of the UNCITRAL Notes: 'It is widely viewed that confidentiality is one of the advantageous and helpful features of arbitration. Nevertheless, there is no uniform answer in national laws as to the extent to which the participants in an arbitration are under the duty to observe the confidentiality of information relating to the case.'

[4]Lazareff (2009), p. 81.

© Springer Nature Switzerland AG 2019
E. Reymond-Eniaeva, *Towards a Uniform Approach to Confidentiality of
International Commercial Arbitration*, European Yearbook of International
Economic Law 7, https://doi.org/10.1007/978-3-030-19003-3_1

arbitral hearings are traditionally held *in camera* and arbitral awards are published only sporadically (in contrast with court proceedings and court judgments), there have been no reasons in the past to believe that arbitral proceedings are not confidential.

4   Thus, confidentiality was an assumed presumption, at least until 1995, when the High Court of Australia in *Esso/BHP etc. v. Plowman* issued a decision that came as a shock for most of arbitration scholars and practitioners.[5] In this case, the Australian Supreme Court held that a distinction needs to be made between privacy of hearings and confidentiality of arbitration proceedings. It ruled, in particular, that unless the parties had specifically agreed on a confidentiality provision, there was no obligation of confidentiality regarding the information obtained in the course of the arbitration, and that such information could thus be disclosed to third parties. When commenting on this decision, Jan Paulsson stated:

> The recent decision of the High Court of Australia in *Esso/BHP* v. *Plowman* casts severe doubts on the question whether, as a general legal principle, international commercial arbitration is 'confidential'. It is a dramatic decision, with significance far beyond the shores of Australia.[6]

5   Today, no one challenges the fact that privacy of hearings does not automatically imply confidentiality of arbitration proceedings. The debate on confidentiality is, however, far from over. As referred to above, the main current controversy surrounding the issue of confidentiality is whether an implied duty of confidentiality exists in the absence of an express contractual or legal basis. There are also other unsettled issues. The most important one concerns publication of arbitral awards, but debate also continues on the extension of a confidentiality duty.

6   The purpose of this thesis is to find a way to a uniform approach to confidentiality of international commercial arbitration. For this, we need to identify the areas of convergence and divergence in regulation of a confidentiality duty. We will see that many issues regarding confidentiality, such as a general duty of confidentiality owed by arbitrators, arbitration institutions and counsel, or confidentiality with respect to hearings, are not controversial.

7   Finally, we will see that the two main areas of divergence are: (i) the existence of parties' duty of confidentiality in the absence of an express legal and contractual basis; and (ii) publication of arbitral awards. We will attempt to understand whether divergence on these two issues can be reconciled so that a uniform approach can be adopted. As a result of our research and analysis, we will propose a solution aiming at harmonization of the rules on confidentiality.

8   Transparency is a general trend in today's society and it also affects arbitration. Indeed, many authors argue for more transparency in arbitration. We agree that transparency can and should be increased, but it should not be an obstacle to maintaining confidentiality of arbitration.

---

[5]Esso Australia Resources Ltd. and Others v. Sidney James Plowman and Others, Arbitration International, Volume 11 No. 3, 1995, 235.

[6]Paulsson (1995), Esso/BHP v. Plowman, 231–234.

As to the scope of our research, we will examine *confidentiality of international*   **9**
commercial arbitration. We will not extend our research to the problems of domestic
arbitration, and we will not analyse the problem of confidentiality regarding investment or sport arbitration. Thus, when referring to *arbitration* or *arbitration pro-*
ceedings, we will generally mean international commercial arbitration, unless
otherwise specified.

In addition, we will examine only information and documents which are confi-   **10**
dential due to the fact that they became available because of arbitration. We will not
address the problem of information and documents which are confidential by their
nature, particularly because they contain know-how, trade secrets, state secrets, etc.

We will not confine our analysis to the regulation of certain pre-determined   **11**
jurisdictions, but will extend it to the laws where we could find the most interesting
examples of the regulation. The Swiss law will, however, be very frequently used
since it is the home jurisdiction of the author of the present thesis.

Given the complexity of issue, we will adopt a systematic approach for examining   **12**
the problem of confidentiality. First, we will survey the existing sources of confidentiality obligations. Second, we will examine the duty of confidentiality owed by
different persons involved in arbitration proceedings, such as parties to an arbitration, arbitrators, the arbitration institution, counsel, and third parties. Third, we will
examine the different aspects composing the duty of confidentiality: information
subject to the duty of confidentiality, confidentiality regarding documents exchanged
in the course of arbitral proceedings, confidentiality regarding arbitral awards and
orders, and confidentiality in respect of hearings. Fourth, we will set out exceptions
to the duty of confidentiality. Fifth, we will review remedies and sanctions in case of
confidentiality breach. Finally, we will discuss the possibility of a uniform approach
on confidentiality and will propose some rules on confidentiality which could be
introduced into national arbitration laws.

Chapter 2
Sources

2.1 Introduction

The purpose of the present section is to set out a list of existing sources for **13** confidentiality obligations in international commercial arbitration. While we will discuss them in greater detail in subsequent sections, in this section we will provide a short explanation as to the place and role of each source.

It is also important to determine the hierarchy of the sources and their interaction. **14** Subject to public policy and mandatory legal requirements, an express agreement of the parties will always prevail.[1] In the absence of an express agreement, or as a supplement to an express agreement, rules of an arbitration institution—or another set of rules containing provisions on confidentiality—will apply if adopted by the parties. Generally accepted arbitration practices might also be a guide in the absence of more specific applicable rules.

The rules of a national applicable law can become relevant in the absence of an **15** express agreement on confidentiality. They can also supplement an agreement of the parties or even prevail if the parties' agreement violates public policy and/or mandatory legal requirements. The relevant applicable law might include international conventions ratified by the state, national arbitration law, other relevant national laws and case law. However, international conventions, such as the New York Convention, the European Convention, or the Inter-American Convention, do not provide any rules on confidentiality.[2] Therefore, we will focus on national legislation and case law.

First, we will discuss parties' agreements on confidentiality and will see that they **16** have the advantage that the parties can tailor the confidentiality regime according to

---

[1]See, for example, Art. 30.1 LCIA Rules: 'Unless the parties expressly agree in writing to the contrary [...]'.

[2]Born (2014), p. 2783.

© Springer Nature Switzerland AG 2019
E. Reymond-Eniaeva, *Towards a Uniform Approach to Confidentiality of International Commercial Arbitration*, European Yearbook of International Economic Law 7, https://doi.org/10.1007/978-3-030-19003-3_2

their needs (Sect. 2.2). Second, we will present an overview of the regulation on confidentiality provided by some institutional arbitration rules (Sect. 2.3). Third, we will review regulation provided by national law and domestic state courts (Sect. 2.4). Fourth, we will briefly examine confidentiality orders (Sect. 2.5). Fifth, we will review arbitral practice as another source of the confidentiality obligation (Sect. 2.6). Finally, we will analyse the situations where different sources can overlap (Sect. 2.7).

2.2 Parties' Agreement

17   The parties' autonomy regarding the confidentiality of their arbitral proceedings will generally be recognised in most developed legal systems.[3] This is an application of the broader contractual and procedural autonomy of the parties.[4]

18   The parties can exercise their autonomy not only by expressly agreeing on a duty of confidentiality, but also by choosing the applicable substantive law and the seat of the arbitration, as well as by adopting institutional or non-institutional arbitration rules and possibly procedural rules or guidelines. These choices might have a direct influence on how confidentiality of the arbitral proceedings will be regulated as by making one of the above-mentioned choices, the parties will generally adhere to the provisions on confidentiality that the applicable law and selected rules/guidelines might contain.

19   Expressly agreeing on a specific confidentiality clause is a more tailored approach. This can be done in anticipation of arbitration proceedings, at the commencement of arbitration or at any time thereafter. The parties can add a provision on confidentiality into the arbitration agreement. The confidentiality agreement can also be entered into by a separate agreement at any time before or after the dispute arose.

20   The underlying contract may also contain a broader confidentiality provision applying to all parties' contractual obligations, and covering by extension arbitration proceedings related to the contract.[5] Whether the main contract contains a confidentiality provision applicable to the relevant arbitration proceeding is a question of interpretation of the parties' agreement.[6] Thus, the benefits of an express agreement, in terms of predictability, are self-evident.

21   Here is the language proposed for an express agreement on confidentiality by the authors of the Handbook of ICC Arbitration:

> Unless the parties expressly agree in writing to the contrary, the parties undertake to keep confidential all awards and orders in the present arbitration, together with all materials in the proceedings created for the purpose of the arbitration and all other documents produced by

---

[3]Born (2014), p. 2787.

[4]Born (2014), p. 2787.

[5]Smeureanu (2011), pp. 9–10.

[6]Haas and Kahlert (2015), para 27.

any party in the proceedings, save to the sole extent that disclosure may be required of a party by a legal duty, to protect or pursue a legal right, or to enforce or challenge an award in bona fide legal proceedings before a State Court or other judicial authority.[7]

Unless it violates public policy or is in contradiction with mandatory legal   **22** requirements, a confidentiality agreement will be valid and enforceable.[8] However, confidentiality agreements will be enforceable against the parties, but will not bind third parties, such as witnesses, experts, interpreters, etc.[9] Indeed, the doctrine of privity (*effet relatif du contrat*) provides that a contract cannot confer rights or impose obligations arising under it on any other person or agent except the parties to it. Thus, a separate agreement can be entered into with the witnesses, experts, interpreters and other persons having access to confidential information.

If the parties impose a duty of confidentiality on arbitrators in their confidentiality   **23** agreement, the arbitrators will be bound by such a duty once they accept to serve as arbitrators. Another possibility would be to insert a specific provision on confidentiality in the Terms of Reference.

The UNCITRAL Notes, the purpose of which is to '*assist arbitration practi-*   **24** *tioners by listing and briefly describing questions on which appropriately timed decisions on organizing arbitral proceedings may be useful*', propose a detailed list of issues that might be covered by an agreement on confidentiality.[10]

In its Guidelines for Drafting International Arbitration Clauses, the International   **25** Bar Association recommended that the parties address the issue of confidentiality in their arbitration clause. The parties are, however, advised to '*avoid absolute require-ment because disclosure may be required by law, to protect or pursue a legal right or to enforce or challenge an award in subsequent judicial proceedings*'. It should also be anticipated that the preparation of the case might require disclosure of confidential information to third parties (for example, witnesses and experts).[11]

Here is the proposed text imposing the confidentiality obligation upon the parties: **26**

The existence and content of the arbitral proceedings and any rulings or award shall be kept confidential by the parties and members of the arbitral tribunal except (i) to the extent that disclosure may be required of a party to fulfil a legal duty, protect or pursue a legal right, or enforce or challenge an award in bona fide legal proceedings before a state court or other judicial authority, (ii) with the consent of all parties, (iii) where needed for the preparation or presentation of a claim or defense in this arbitration, (iv) where such information is already in the public domain other than as a result of a breach of this clause, or (v) by order of the arbitral tribunal upon application of a party.[12]

---

[7]Webster and Bühler (2014), para 23–64.

[8]Born (2014), p. 2791.

[9]Born (2014), p. 2789; Lew (2011), The Arbitrator and Confidentiality, 3.

[10]UNCITRAL Notes, para 32.

[11]IBA Guidelines for Drafting International Arbitration Clauses, para 61.

[12]IBA Guidelines for Drafting International Arbitration Clauses, para 64.

27   The International Commercial Arbitration Committee of the International Law Association in its Report and Recommendations on 'Confidentiality in International Commercial Arbitration' came to the conclusion that the best way to ensure confidentiality or non-confidentiality across multiple jurisdictions was to make an express agreement before or during the arbitration.[13] The Committee has proposed the following model arbitration clauses for confidentiality:

Model Arbitration Confidentiality Clause

[A]. The parties, any arbitrator, and their agents or representatives, shall keep confidential and not disclose to any non-party the existence of the arbitration, all non-public materials and information provided in the arbitration by another party, and orders or awards made in the arbitration (together, the 'Confidential information').

[B]. If a party or an arbitrator wishes to involve in the arbitration a non-party—including a fact or expert witness, stenographer, translator or any other person—the party or arbitrator shall make reasonable efforts to secure the non-party's advance agreement to preserve the confidentiality of the Confidential information.

[C]. Notwithstanding the foregoing, a party may disclose Confidential information to the extent necessary to: (1) prosecute or defend the arbitration or proceedings related to it (including enforcement or annulment proceedings), or to pursue a legal right; (2) respond to a compulsory order or request for information of a governmental or regulatory body; (3) make disclosure required by law or by the rules of a securities exchange; (4) seek legal, accounting or other professional services, or satisfy information requests of potential acquirers, investors or lenders, provided that in case of any disclosure allowed under the foregoing circumstances (1) through (4) where possible the producing party takes reasonable measures to ensure that the recipient preserves the confidentiality of the information provided. The arbitral tribunal may permit further disclosure of Confidential information where there is a demonstrated need to disclose that outweighs any party's legitimate interest in preserving confidentiality.

[D]. This confidentiality provision survives termination of the contract and of any arbitration brought pursuant to the contract. This confidentiality provision may be enforced by an arbitral tribunal or any court of competent jurisdiction and an application to a court to enforce this provision shall not waive or a in a way derogate from the agreement to arbitrate.[14]

28   This model clause is rather extensive. Also, provision D is an added value to the confidentiality clause as it provides clarification on its scope of application in time and on the competence of arbitral tribunal and state courts to enforce the provision on confidentiality.

---

[13]De Ly et al. (2012), pp. 381–383.
[14]De Ly et al. (2012), p. 381.

It might be, however, that the parties do not wish to be bound by a confidentiality   **29**
duty. In this case, they can expressly agree on a non-confidentiality clause. The IBA
Guidelines for Drafting International Clauses propose the following text for such a
non-confidentiality clause:

> The parties shall be under no confidentiality obligation with respect to arbitration hereunder
> except as may be imposed by mandatory provisions of law.[15]

The International Commercial Arbitration Committee of the International Law   **30**
Association has also proposed a text of model arbitration non-confidentiality clause:

Model Arbitration Non-Confidentiality Clause
Save to the extent required by any applicable law and by any other obligations to
which a party may otherwise be bound, the parties shall have no obligation to keep
confidential the existence of the arbitration or any information or document relating
thereto.[16]

The advantage of agreeing on a confidentiality (or non-confidentiality) clause is   **31**
clear: the parties can tailor the confidentiality regime according to their needs. There
may, however, be some downsides as well. For example, if the parties agree on
confidentiality terms in anticipation of a dispute, they might change their mind
between the time when the confidentiality agreement is drafted and the time when
an issue with confidentiality arises in an arbitration proceeding.[17] Another problem
is the enforceability of the confidentiality agreement. According to Yves Derains and
Eric Schwartz, in order to ensure continued protection of confidentiality, an appropriate judicial and/or arbitral recourse should be provided for.[18]

2.3 International Arbitration Rules

2.3.1 Introduction

A significant number of arbitration rules contain provisions on the confidentiality of   **32**
arbitral proceedings. These include, for example, Art. 44(1) of the Swiss Rules, Art.
30.1 of the LCIA Rules, Art. 44.1 of the DIS Rules, Art. 75(a) of the WIPO Rules,
Art. 22.2 of the ACICA Rules, Art. 8(1) of the Milan Rules, Art. 33 of the Abu Dhabi
Rules, Art. 39(1) of the SIAC Rules, Art. 41(1) of the DIAC Rules, Art. 38(2) of the
JCAA Rules and Art. 12 of the Oslo Rules.

The purpose of the present section is to give an overview of the regulation on   **33**
confidentiality provided in arbitration rules. While we will compare in further

---

[15]IBA Guidelines for Drafting International Arbitration Clauses, para 65.
[16]De Ly et al. (2012), p. 383.
[17]Lew (2011), The Arbitrator and Confidentiality, 4.
[18]Derains and Schwartz (2005), p. 286.

sections how arbitration rules regulate specific issues, it appears important to start with the analysis focused on a few selected rules to demonstrate how arbitration rules generally regulate the issue of confidentiality.

34   We will first examine provisions on confidentiality contained in the UNCITRAL Rules, which are non-institutional arbitration rules. We will then review regulation on confidentiality provided by a few selected institutional rules, such as the LCIA, Swiss, ICC, WIPO and Oslo Rules.

2.3.2   UNCITRAL Rules

35   The UNCITRAL Rules do not impose a duty of confidentiality regarding arbitral proceedings. This absence of regulation is deliberate; the issue was discussed during the 46th session of the Working Group, but the members of the Working Group decided that the issue of confidentiality should rather be addressed by the parties and the arbitrators on a case-by-case basis.[19] Although a concern was raised that the users might expect that the UNCITRAL Rules guarantee confidentiality, the arguments against inclusion of a general provision on confidentiality prevailed in the end.[20] Thus, it was, in particular, argued that inclusion of a general confidentiality provision would run counter the current trend towards more transparency, that it would leave no flexibility to accommodate evolving law and practices, and that it would be problematic to regulate such issues as when the confidentiality duty arose and ended, whether that duty extended to persons other than the parties, and what should be the exceptions to that duty.[21]

36   This is why the revised 2010 UNCITRAL Rules regulate only some aspects of confidentiality, such as privacy of the hearings and publication of the award, but contain no general provision on confidentiality of the arbitration proceedings. According to Art. 28(3) of the UNCITRAL Rules, hearings are to be held in private. This provision is not mandatory, however, so the parties can agree on a different approach. Art. 34(5) UNCITRAL Rules provides that the award may be published with the consent of all the parties involved or

> '*if disclosure is required of a party by legal duty, to protect or pursue a legal right or in relation to legal proceedings before a court or other competent authority*'.

---

[19]Report of the Working Group on Arbitration and Conciliation on the work of its forty-sixth session, paras 127–133.

[20]Report of the Working Group on Arbitration and Conciliation on the work of its forty-sixth session, paras 127–133.

[21]Report of the Working Group on Arbitration and Conciliation on the work of its forty-sixth session, paras 129–131.

2.3.3 LCIA Rules

The 1998 LCIA Rules were revised in 2014, and an updated version became **37** effective in October of that year. In the new version, however, no substantive changes were made to the provisions on confidentiality. Art. 19.4 contains provisions on the privacy of hearings, and Art. 30 contains specific provisions protecting confidentiality of arbitration proceedings. This article was introduced in the 1998 edition of the LCIA Rules.[22] LCIA was the first institution to introduce such a detailed and sophisticated provision on confidentiality.[23] Art. 30 protects the confidentiality of an arbitration proceeding by regulating three aspects: parties' duty of confidentiality, secrecy of the deliberations of the tribunal, and the publication of arbitral awards.[24]

First, Art. 30.1 of the LCIA Rules provides that, as a general principle, the parties **38** are bound to keep confidential all materials in the proceedings created for the purpose of the arbitration and all other documents produced by another party in the proceedings provided that they are not in the public domain. Art. 30.1 also contains several exceptions to the general principle of confidentiality. The parties are allowed to disclose the above-mentioned documents if disclosure is

> *'required of a party by legal duty, to protect or pursue a legal right or to enforce or challenge an award in bona fide legal proceedings before a state court or other legal authority'*.

Second, according to Art. 30.2 of the LCIA Rules, members of the arbitral **39** tribunal must keep their deliberations confidential from any person outside of the arbitral tribunal, including the LCIA and the parties themselves.[25] The only exceptions are when an arbitrator's refusal or inability to participate in deliberations hinders the tribunal's work and therefore needs to be disclosed and if the disclosure is required by the applicable law. *Third*, in accordance with Art. 30.3, the LCIA will only publish the award with prior written consent of all the parties and the arbitral tribunal.

2.3.4 Swiss Rules

Although based on the UNCITRAL Rules, the Swiss Rules contained explicit and **40** detailed provisions on confidentiality in their 2004 edition.[26] These provisions were

---

[22]Nesbitt and Darowski (2015), p. 558.

[23]Dimolitsa (2009), Obligation of Confidentiality on Parties, 9.

[24]Nesbitt and Darowski (2015), p. 558.

[25]Nesbitt and Darowski (2015), p. 558.

[26]See under letter (b) of Introduction to the former Swiss Rules on International Arbitration of 2004.

introduced to '*promote the confidential nature of arbitration by making sure that the parties and the arbitrators would be efficiently protected.*'[27] The Swiss Rules were revised in 2012, but no major substantive changes were made to the relevant provisions. The only change—other than to the number of the article—was to the provision on the publication of the award,[28] which now allows, provided the required conditions are met,[29] publication of the orders of the tribunal and not only of awards, as was previously the case. Art. 44 of the Swiss Rules, like the LCIA Rules, protects the confidentiality of the arbitration proceedings in three ways.

41   *First*, Art. 44(1) of the Swiss Rules imposes a duty of confidentiality on the parties, arbitrators, tribunal-appointed experts, secretary of the arbitral tribunal, members of the board of directors of the Swiss Chambers' Arbitration Institution, members of the Court and the Secretariat, and the staff of the individual Chambers. This duty of confidentiality covers awards and orders of the arbitral tribunal as well as materials submitted by the parties which are not already in the public domain.[30] Disclosure of confidential materials is allowed, according to Art. 44(1) of the Swiss Rules, when such disclosure is required to exercise a legal duty, to protect or pursue a legal right, or to enforce or challenge an award in court proceedings. Art. 44(1) is not a mandatory provision, but the parties need to agree on its non-application in writing.[31]

42   *Second*, according to Art. 44(2) of the Swiss Rules, deliberations of the arbitral tribunal are confidential. This means that the arbitrators cannot disclose any information concerning deliberations of the arbitral tribunal, including their position during the deliberations, outside of the arbitral tribunal.[32]

43   *Third*, Art. 44(3) of the Swiss Rules provides that an award or order may be published if the following three requirements are met: (a) the Secretariat has received a request for publication; (b) references to the parties' names are deleted; and (c) there is no objection from the parties within the time limit provided by the Secretariat.

44   *Finally*, the Swiss Rules, like most other institutional rules, provide that the hearings are to be held in camera (Art. 25(6)).

2.3.5 ICC Rules

45   The ICC Rules guarantee the confidential character of the work of the Court and its Secretariat.[33] There is also a practice within the ICC Secretariat to consistently

---

[27]Rohner and La Spada (2013), Commentary of Art. 44 of the Swiss Rules, para 1.

[28]Currently, Art. 44(3) Swiss Rules.

[29]Art. 44(3) Swiss Rules.

[30]Rohner and La Spada (2013), Commentary of Art. 44 of the Swiss Rules, para 10.

[31]Rohner and La Spada (2013), Commentary of Art. 44 of the Swiss Rules, para 17.

[32]Rohner and La Spada (2013), Commentary of Art. 44 of the Swiss Rules, para 20.

[33]Art. 6 of the Appendix I and Art. 1 of the Appendix II to the ICC Rules.

inform arbitrators prior to their appointment about their duty to respect the confidentiality of the arbitration proceedings.[34]

The ICC Rules, however, do not impose a general duty of confidentiality on the parties, arbitrators, counsel and other persons involved in arbitration proceedings.[35] Drafters of the 1998 ICC Rules could not reach a consensus on this issue, which explains the absence of rules on confidentiality obligations.[36] When the 2012 ICC Rules were discussed, the issue of confidentiality was raised again. The debates were, however, not in favour of introducing a general duty of confidentiality. Instead, it was argued that the confidentiality issue should be addressed by the involved parties and the arbitral tribunal depending on specific circumstances of the case.[37] **46**

Art. 22(3) of the 2012 ICC Rules contains a provision entitling the arbitral tribunal to issue orders concerning the confidentiality of the arbitration proceedings upon the request of any party. These confidentiality orders may be issued in relation to specific documents, such as pleadings, witness statements, documentary evidence, or the award.[38] They can also relate to the very existence of the arbitration or to any other information relating to the arbitration (see below Sects. 2.5 and 6.2.1 on confidentiality orders).[39] **47**

2.3.6 WIPO Rules

Compared to other arbitration rules, the WIPO Rules contain probably the most comprehensive and complete regulation on confidentiality.[40] Unlike most provisions on confidentiality, the WIPO Rules provide, as a general principle, that even the existence of the arbitration is to be kept confidential: **48**

Confidentiality of the Existence of the Arbitration

Article 75

(a) Except to the extent necessary in connection with a court challenge to the arbitration or an action for enforcement of an award, no information concerning the existence of an arbitration may be unilaterally disclosed by a party to any third party unless it is required so by law or by a competent regulatory body, and then only:

---

[34]Calvo Goller (2012), p. 337.

[35]Fry et al. (2012), para 3-807.

[36]Derains and Schwartz (2005), p. 285; Müller (2005), p. 222.

[37]Fry et al. (2012), para 3-807.

[38]Fry et al. (2012), para 3-808; Derains and Schwartz (2005), p. 286.

[39]Fry et al. (2012), para 3-808; Derains and Schwartz (2005), p. 286.

[40]Smeureanu (2011), p. 17.

(i) by disclosing no more than what is legally required; and

(ii) by furnishing to the Tribunal and to the other party, if the disclosure takes place during the arbitration or to the other party alone, if the disclosure takes place after the termination of the arbitration, details of the disclosure and an explanation of the reason for it.

(b) Notwithstanding paragraph (a), a party may disclose to a third party the names of the parties to the arbitration and the relief requested for the purpose of satisfying any obligation of good faith or candor owed to that third party.

49   Another particularity of the WIPO Rules is that they contain separate provisions on the confidentiality of disclosures made during the arbitration proceedings and on the confidentiality of the arbitral award:

Confidentiality of Disclosures Made During the Arbitration

Article 76

(a) In addition to any specific measures that may be available under Article 54,[41] any documentary or other evidence given by a party or a witness in the arbitration shall be treated as confidential and, to the extent that such evidence describes information that is not in the public domain, shall not be used or disclosed to any third party whose access to that information arises exclusively as a result of its participation in the arbitration for any purpose without the consent of the parties or order of a court having jurisdiction.

(b) For the purposes of this Article, a witness called by a party shall not be considered to be a third party. To the extent that a witness is given access to evidence or other information obtained in the arbitration in order to prepare the witness's testimony, the party calling such witness shall be responsible for the maintenance by the witness of the same degree of confidentiality as that required of the party.

Confidentiality of the Award

Article 77

The award shall be treated as confidential by the parties and may be disclosed to a third party if and to the extent that;

(i) the parties consent; or

(ii) it falls into the public domain as a result of an action before a national court or other competent authority; or

(iii) it must be disclosed in order to comply with a legal requirement imposed on a party or in order to establish or protect a party's legal rights against a third party.

---

[41]Art 54 WIPO deals with specific measures with regard to disclosure of trade secrets and other confidential information.

2.3.7 Oslo Rules

Article 12 of the Oslo Rules provides that the arbitration proceedings and the arbitral   **50**
award are *not* subject to confidentiality. Such a provision is quite unusual, given that
the idea of arbitration proceedings being confidential is most frequently accepted.
　　Further, Art. 13 regulating the arbitration procedure provides that   **51**

> *'it must be clarified by the parties as to whether the arbitration proceedings and
> the decisions of the Tribunal shall be subject to confidentiality'.*

Although the purpose of the provision is not entirely explicit in the language, it
likely serves to indicate that confidentiality is subject to the parties' agreement.
Absent such an agreement, Art. 12, which provides that the arbitration proceedings
and the arbitral award are not confidential, will apply.
　　Note that Art. 12 of the Oslo Rules is consistent with the provision of the   **52**
Norwegian Arbitration Act on the duty of confidentiality which will be discussed
below (see Sect. 2.4.1).

2.3.8 Intermediary Conclusions

While we will further analyse regulation on the confidentiality of arbitration pro-   **53**
ceedings below, it is already clear at this stage that the legal framework established
by different arbitration rules varies considerably. Thus, the ICC Rules provide
almost no regulation on confidentiality of arbitral proceedings. The UNCITRAL
Rules deal only with the issues related to the publication of the award and the privacy
of the hearings. The LCIA Rules and the Swiss Rules go further: they also contain
provisions on the confidentiality of the arbitral tribunal's decisions, the confidentiality of the materials submitted by the parties in the arbitration, and the confidentiality of the deliberations of the arbitral tribunal.
　　Overall, however, most rules containing regulation on confidentiality provide, as   **54**
a general principle, that arbitration proceedings are confidential. As mentioned
above, the Oslo Rules are an exception. They propose an unusual regulation
establishing, as a general principle, that arbitration proceedings are not subject to
confidentiality. The parties can nevertheless derogate from this rule.
　　Looking ahead, rule-making is tending towards introducing at least some regu-   **55**
lation on the confidentiality of arbitration proceedings. But overall consensus on
many aspects of confidentiality seems to be far off, which is why the UNCITRAL
and ICC Rules have no regulation on many issues regarding confidentiality. However, as will be discussed below, we think that reaching consensus on confidentiality
of arbitration proceedings is possible.

2.4 National Legislation and Case Law

2.4.1 National Arbitration Laws

56   Today, many national legislations are silent on the confidentiality of international arbitration.[42] The UNCITRAL Model Law, which influenced a significant number of national arbitration laws,[43] does not contain rules on confidentiality.[44] The question was intentionally left open, at least with regard to publication of arbitration awards, in order to avoid regulation of an overly controversial issue.[45] According to certain authors, confidentiality should be dealt with in arbitration rules rather than in the Model Law.[46] Some very insightful observations appear in the 1981 Report of the Secretary-General on Possible Features of a Model Law on International Commercial Arbitration:

> On peut douter que la loi type doive traiter de la question de la publication des sentences. Bien que cette question soit épineuse, sachant le nombre d'arguments que l'on peut invoquer soit pour, soit contre cette publication, la décision pourrait être laissée à la discrétion des parties ou aux règles d'arbitrage que celles-ci adopteront. Si, cependant, une disposition à cet effet devait être incorporée à la loi type, le compromis le plus acceptable serait vraisemblablement de stipuler que la sentence ne peut être rendue publique qu'avec le consentement exprès des parties.[47]

57   Not surprisingly, countries which have closely followed the Model Law do not have provisions on confidentiality in their arbitration laws.[48] Absence of express provisions in the national laws may also be explained by the contractual nature of the arbitration and the willingness of legislators to keep statutory interference to a minimum.[49] Indeed, the parties can exercise their autonomy by agreeing on a confidentiality clause tailored to their needs or choose ready-made institutional rules already containing a confidentiality clause.

58   Some countries, such as England and Wales, France, Sweden, Singapore and Switzerland do not have express provisions on confidentiality in their arbitration

---

[42]See, for example, Swiss Private International Law Act, Swedish Arbitration Act of 1999, English Arbitration Act of 1996, Russian Law On International Commercial Arbitration of 1993, USA Federal Arbitration Act.

[43]By 2005, some 50 states adopted the UNCITRAL Model Law (Sanders 2005, p. 443).

[44]Sanders (2005), p. 456.

[45]Rapport du Secrétaire général sur les éléments éventuels de la Loi type sur l'arbitrage commercial international, Annuaire de la Commission des Nations Unies pour les droit commercial international, Volume XII, 1981, deuxième partie, 95–96.

[46]Sanders (2005), p. 456, 476; Dimolitsa, Obligation of Confidentiality on Parties, 13.

[47]Rapport du Secrétaire général sur les éléments éventuels de la Loi type sur l'arbitrage commercial international, Annuaire de la Commission des Nations Unies pour les droit commercial international, Volume XII, 1981, deuxième partie, 95–96.

[48]Dimolitsa (2009), Obligation of Confidentiality on Parties, 13.

[49]See, for example, for Switzerland: Jolles and Canals de Cediel (2004), p. 93; Bucher and Tschanz (1988), para 115.

laws, but the principles related to confidentiality are established by case law and practice. For example, an obligation of confidentiality is not included in the English Arbitration Act of 1996. When such an inclusion was discussed, the Departmental Advisory Committee on Arbitration Law advised against it, considering that such a codification would be premature because of an important number of possible exceptions to the general principle of confidentiality. Therefore, it was decided to leave the issue to be developed over time by the common law.[50] In Singapore, the absence of an express provision was explained as follows by the High Court:

> Certainly the obligation of confidentiality does not find expression in the statutes because of its somewhat amorphous scope and exceptions as well as its elusive juridical basis.[51]

However, in several countries, there is a tendency towards introducing more or less elaborate rules on confidentiality to national arbitration laws. These countries have decided to address the issue of privacy and/or confidentiality of the arbitral proceedings in their legislations. For example, the arbitration laws of Australia, Costa Rica, Ghana, Hong Kong, Hungary, New Zealand,[52] Norway, Philippines, Portugal, Scotland, Slovakia and Spain have specific provisions dealing with confidentiality.[53]   **59**

Some of these countries, such as Australia and New Zealand, have chosen to have very detailed provisions on confidentiality. Before 2015, the Australian regulation was distinctive in that its confidentiality provisions applied only if the parties had specifically agreed to their application.[54] The amendments introduced by the Civil Law and Justice Legislation Amendment Act 2015 reversed the situation: the AIAA confidentiality provisions apply in the proceedings arising from all arbitration agreements concluded from 14 October 2015 onwards, unless the parties decide to 'opt-out'.[55] If the parties 'opt-out' from these provisions, the common law rules will apply.[56]   **60**

Similarly to the AIAA regulation, the confidentiality provisions of the NZAA (Arts 14A to 14I NZAA) apply unless the parties decide to 'opt-out'.[57] Art. 14 NZAA provides as follows: **61**

---

[50]Report on the Arbitration Bill, in Merkin and Flannery (2014), pp. 433–444.

[51]AAY and others v AAZ AS, High Court, Suit [Y], Case No. [2009] SGHC 142, 15 June 2009, 54.

[52]Arts 14A ff NZAA.

[53]This list is not exhaustive; it is mainly based on the 'Privacy and Confidentiality in Arbitration Smart Charts' (www.smartcharts.wolterskluwer.com, last updated in November 2016).

[54]Arts 22 (3), 23C, 23D, 23E, 23F, 23G before the 2015 amendment of the AIAA.

[55]Art, 22(2) AIAA; Nottage (2017), pp. 1–2; Shirlow (2015), p. 2.

[56]Sam Luttrell, Isuru Devendra in their report on Australian regulation in 'Privacy and Confidentiality in Arbitration Smart Charts' (www.smartcharts.wolterskluwer.com, last updated in November 2016).

[57]Art. 14 NZAA.

Except as the parties may otherwise agree in writing (whether in the arbitration agreement or otherwise), sections 14A to 14I apply to every arbitration for which the place of arbitration is, or would be, New Zealand.

Although the text of Art. 14 is rather explicit, some authors question whether all provisions on confidentiality can be 'opted-out'.[58]

62   As already mentioned, the Norwegian Arbitration Act also regulates confidentiality in a rather distinctive and unusual way. Contrary to the widely admitted idea that arbitration proceedings are confidential, Art. 5(1) of the Norwegian Arbitration Act provides that the arbitration proceedings and arbitral award are *not* subject to a duty of confidentiality unless the parties have agreed otherwise. As to the privacy of hearings, it is still to be maintained unless the parties agree otherwise (Art. 5(2)). These provisions are relatively recent; they were introduced along with the Norwegian Arbitration Act of 2004. The initial idea was to make arbitral proceedings more transparent by publishing awards, but the final text went even further, stipulating non-confidentiality of arbitral proceedings as a general principle.[59]

63   It should be noted that Art. 12 of the Oslo Rules is consistent with Art. 5(1) of the Norwegian Arbitration Act as it provides that the arbitration proceedings and the arbitral award are not confidential, unless the parties agreed otherwise. These provisions on confidentiality confirm the intent of the Norwegian lawmakers to grant autonomy to the parties regarding confidentiality of the arbitration proceedings and of the arbitral award. In the absence of an agreement between the parties, the lawmakers chose not to impose confidentiality obligations regarding the arbitration proceedings and the arbitral award.

64   Other countries have opted for rather general clauses declaring confidentiality as one of the principles governing arbitral proceedings.[60] For example, the Law of the Republic of Kazakhstan on International Arbitration of 2004 has established a duty of confidentiality for arbitrators as one of the principles of arbitral proceedings:

[C]onfidentiality meaning that arbitrators shall not disclose information, which became known to them in the course of arbitral proceedings, without prior consent of the parties or their legal successors, and may not be interrogated as witnesses with respect to circumstances that became known to them in the course of arbitral proceedings, save in the cases where the law explicitly provides for the duty of a citizen to report information to a relevant body.[61]

---

[58]Kawharu (2008), p. 406.

[59]Nisja (2008), p. 190.

[60]*See, e.g.*, Art. 24(2) of Spanish Arbitration Act 60/2003.

[61]Art. 4(5) of the Law of the Republic of Kazakhstan on International Arbitration of 2004.

2.4.2   Case Law of National Courts

A lack of express provisions in national legislation does not automatically imply the   **65**
absence of regulation. Domestic courts in many countries have already had opportunities to rule on different aspects of confidentiality. The role and legal consequences of state court decisions will obviously vary, depending, in particular, on
whether the court is in a civil law or a common law country.[62]

State courts in several countries have established very important—but diver-   **66**
gent—principles of confidentiality. For example, the confidentiality obligations
upon the parties involved in international arbitration proceedings have been
recognised by the English Courts in the *Dolling-Baker v. Merrett, Ali Shipping*,
and *Emmott cases*.[63] The opposite position was taken by Australia's High Court in
the famous *Esso/BHP etc. v. Plowman* case, which established that, in the absence of
a specific regulation and express agreement, there was no implied duty of
confidentiality.

The parties to an arbitration must therefore be vigilant with regard to different   **67**
principles regarding confidentiality obligations in different jurisdictions. Both the
parties and the arbitral tribunal have to consider these varying principles, in particular, in anticipation of a possible court proceeding.

2.4.3   Other Potentially Relevant Rules of National Law

National law rules not originally intended for application in international arbitration   **68**
are another important source of confidentiality obligation. Depending on the specific
confidentiality problem at issue, rules from multiple areas of law can become
relevant. We will provide a further analysis of such rules below, when dealing
with the persons bound by a duty of confidentiality and remedies in case of
confidentiality breach (see Chaps. 3 and 6.). Below, we provide only a few examples
as a starting point.

One category of national rules that can come into play is statutory or   **69**
non-statutory rules that impose confidentiality obligations on certain professions.
The most obvious example are rules on the lawyer's professional duty of confidentiality (see below Sect. 3.5.4). Another example is the set of national laws regulating
the relations between the parties and the arbitrators. Since such relations are most
likely to have a contractual basis, it would be necessary to check national rules

---

[62]See more developments on the role and importance of case law in international arbitration in
Besson (2016a), Evolution of Case Law, 46–50.
[63]Dolling-Baker v. Merrett [1990] 1 WLR 1205; Ali Shipping v. Shipyard Trogir [1997] EWCA
Civ 3054; Emmott v. Wilson & Partners Limited [2008] EWCA Civ 184.

applicable to the contract with the arbitrator, which will likely impose a duty of confidentiality on the arbitrator.[64]

2.5 Confidentiality Orders

70   A confidentiality obligation can also find its source in a confidentiality order. Such an order can be granted by an arbitral tribunal or by a state court. For example, a party can ask the arbitral tribunal or a state court to prohibit the other party from disclosing certain information and documents if there is a real risk that such disclosure will reveal confidential information regarding the arbitration. The ICC Rules contain an express provision granting powers to the arbitral tribunal to issue such orders:

> Upon the request of any party, the arbitral tribunal may make orders concerning the confidentiality of the arbitration proceedings or of any other matters in connection with the arbitration and may take measures for protecting trade secrets and confidential information.[65]

The arbitral tribunal, however, does not need an express provision in applicable arbitration rules or arbitration laws granting it powers to issue a confidentiality order. The arbitral tribunal's competence to decide on confidentiality issues in international arbitration is generally admitted.[66] Confidentiality orders can also be issued by state courts in the form of an injunctive relief.

71   We will examine confidentiality orders as a legal remedy in the section dealing with the remedies against the confidentiality breach (see Sect. 6.2.1 below). Notably, confidentiality orders can also be issued by an arbitral tribunal even when there is no real risk of disclosure. This can happen, for example, when a tribunal orders a party to produce documents containing sensitive information, but will assure confidentiality of these documents by issuing a procedural order prohibiting the other party to disclose these documents. An arbitral tribunal can also order the parties to maintain confidentiality of all documents that any party will mark in the proceedings as confidential. An example of such a confidentiality order issued in an ICC arbitration between two European parties in 2006 was reported by Yves Derains:

> Documents or information furnished by one party to the other before or during this arbitration and designated by that party as confidential may not be disclosed to any third party;

---

[64]In Switzerland, Arts 394 ff CO on the Agency Contract apply to a contract between the parties and the arbitrators; for more details, see below Sect. 3.3.2.1.2.

[65]Art. 22(3) of the ICC Rules.

[66]See, for example, Born (2014), p. 2813; Tjio (2009), pp. 14–15; Hwang and Chung (2010), Confidentiality in arbitration, 1 [of the electronic version].

Documents or information furnished by one party to the other before the start of this arbitration and not designated as confidential at the time when it was furnished will not become confidential if and when it is submitted in this arbitration.[67]

2.6 Arbitral Practice

2.6.1 Introduction

When faced with the problem of confidentiality, the competent authority can also be **72** inspired by generally accepted arbitration practice.[68] When invoking generally accepted arbitration practice, we refer to a set of principles or procedures that are commonly recognised by professionals working in the field of international arbitration, whether legal scholars or practitioners. These principles can be found, in particular, in prior arbitral awards, legal literature and can sometimes be codified. If this arbitration practice is reflected in a set of codified rules, such as the IBA Rules on Evidence, and the parties adopt them, these rules can have a binding effect. In the present section, we will examine whether a duty of confidentiality can find its source in (i) arbitral jurisprudence, (ii) *lex mercatoria* and (iii) codified rules.

2.6.2 Arbitral Jurisprudence

In the present thesis, we mainly had to rely on the decisions of state courts rather than **73** on arbitral jurisprudence, because very few arbitral awards on the issue of confidentiality are publicly available. The reason for that is that arbitral awards are not systematically published. This absence of systematic publication also partly explains the fact that the role of 'arbitral jurisprudence' or 'arbitral precedent' is not clearly defined in international commercial arbitration.

A survey of several hundred awards from commercial arbitration cases reported **74** by Gabrielle Kaufmann-Kohler showed that there was no uniform practice regarding the effect of prior awards.[69] Another survey focused on the ICC awards, as part of the same study, demonstrated that out of the 190 reviewed awards only about 15% cited other arbitral decisions.[70] Among these 15%, most arbitral awards were used as a reference on the issues of jurisdiction and arbitral procedure.[71]

Gabrielle Kaufmann-Kohler argues that although past arbitral decisions do not **75** have a binding effect *per se*, arbitrators have a moral obligation to follow precedents

---

[67]Derains (2009), Evidence and Confidentiality, 67–68.

[68]Lew (2011), The Arbitrator and Confidentiality, 3.

[69]Kaufmann-Kohler (2007), p. 362.

[70]Kaufmann-Kohler (2007), p. 363.

[71]Kaufmann-Kohler (2007), p. 363.

where it is necessary to secure the predictability of the legal environment.[72] The necessity for the existence of binding rules through arbitral decisions would logically be desirable in the areas where the law is not yet well developed.[73] With regard to commercial arbitration, this author states that:

> [T]here is no need for developing consistent rules through arbitral awards because the disputes are most often fact and contract-driven. The outcome revolves around a unique set of facts and upon the interpretation of a unique contract that was negotiated between private actors to fit their specific needs. Unsurprisingly, awards are published only sporadically in this context, unlike sports and investment arbitration, where publication has become the rule.[74]

76   While Gabrielle Kaufmann-Kohler seems to treat commercial, investment and sports arbitrations differently when discussing the issue of precedent, Gary Born tends to take a more universal approach when discussing the role of precedent in international arbitration:

> In practice, and like the application of concepts of *stare decisis* by most national courts, arbitral tribunals have adopted nuanced approaches towards the question of precedent. Tribunals afford varying degrees of precedential authority to past arbitral awards, based on the number of decisions adopting a particular analysis, the nature of the tribunal(s), the quality of the tribunal's reasoning and similar factors. As with most national courts, there is no absolute rule of binding precedent, but instead a pragmatic analysis that gives effect to the underlying values served by the doctrine of precedent, while permitting change, evolution and correction in the law. That is consistent with, and mandated by, the basic objectives and aspirations of the international arbitral process.[75]

77   Both authors, therefore, recognise that while prior arbitral awards do not have a binding effect, they might influence arbitrators' decisions. Given the importance of past arbitral awards, many authors argue in favour of a systematic publication of the awards. Indeed, the difficulty of establishing a uniform arbitral practice is due in particular to the fact that the arbitral awards are not systematically published.

78   The existence of 'arbitral jurisprudence' is closely linked to publication of arbitral awards. The creation of a uniform arbitral case law would require publication of the most important arbitral awards so that the arbitrators could take decisions consistent with the ones previously rendered. Publication of arbitral awards will be examined in greater detail below in the section dealing with confidentiality of arbitral tribunals' decisions (see below Sect. 4.4).

---

[72]Kaufmann-Kohler (2007), p. 374.

[73]Kaufmann-Kohler (2007), p. 378.

[74]Kaufmann-Kohler (2007), pp. 375–376.

[75]Born (2014), p. 3827.

2.6.3   Lex Mercatoria

The next question to be considered is whether the *lex mercatoria* could be basis of   **79**
confidentiality obligations. In this context, we mean by the *lex mercatoria* not an
autonomous legal order, but a set of transnational rules and principles of law which
prevailed through their consistent application in a large number of domestic law
systems.[76] Here are a few examples of such rules: *pacta sunt servanda, force
majeure*, good faith, *venire contra factum proprium, in favorem validitatis*, mitiga-
tion of damages.[77]

Emmanuel Gaillard criticizes the use of '*lex mercatoria*' term arguing that it   **80**
might be misleading.[78] He prefers the terms '*general principles of law*' and '*transnational rules*' which can be used interchangeably and by which are meant the rules
'*rooted in national legal systems and identified through a comparative law analysis*'.[79] Since the '*lex mercatoria*' is still commonly used, we will use this term
keeping in mind that a different terminology can be employed to refer to the same
legal concept.

In international arbitration, some rules and principles were recognised by practi-   **81**
tioners as *lex mercatoria* because of their systematic application. These principles
are, for example, impartiality and independence of the arbitrators, powers of the
arbitrators to determine the applicable law in the absence of the parties' agreement,
the competence-competence principle,[80] a party autonomy in matters of procedure
and due process.[81] The question is whether duty of confidentiality regarding arbitration proceedings could become one of such principles.

One could argue that a duty of confidentiality can be recognised as an autonomous   **82**
lex mercatoria principle applicable in arbitration proceedings. This is, however, not
possible because, as we will see below, there is no consensus on the existence of a duty
of confidentiality in the absence of applicable rules and express agreement.[82] By
contrast, we will see that such issues as privacy of hearing and secrecy of deliberations
of arbitral tribunal are not subject to any controversy.[83] Therefore, they could be
recognised, in our opinion, as autonomous *lex mercatoria* principles.

---

[76]*See, e.g.*, Perret (2007), p. 28, with further references.

[77]Kaufmann-Kohler (2007), p. 364; Paulsson (1990), Lex mercatoria, 81–93; Berger (2010), Lex
Mercatoria, 14, 128, 142, 169.

[78]Gaillard (2011), p. 161.

[79]Gaillard (2011), p. 162.

[80]Paulsson (1990), Lex mercatoria, 78–81.

[81]Kaufmann-Kohler (2003), p. 1321.

[82]See below Sect. 3.2.3.

[83]See below Sects. 4.5 and 3.3.3.2.

2.6.4   Codified Rules

83   Arbitral practice can also be codified in a set of non-binding rules, as was the case with
the IBA Rules. The IBA Rules adopted in 1999 and revised in 2010 contain a set of
rules regarding the taking of evidence in international arbitration. These rules can be
used as procedural guidelines, leaving a wide flexibility and discretion to the arbitrators.[84] The parties can also choose to give a binding force to the IBA Rules on
Evidence if they adopt them at any time before or after the dispute arose.[85] The IBA
Rules contain, in particular, an obligation of confidentiality concerning all documents
submitted or produced in the arbitration. Art. 3.13 IBA Rules provides the following:

> Any Document submitted or produced by a Party or non-Party in the arbitration
> and not otherwise in the public domain shall be kept confidential by the Arbitral
> Tribunal and the other Parties, and shall be used only in connection with the
> arbitration. This requirement shall apply except and to the extent that disclosure
> may be required of a Party to fulfil a legal duty, protect or pursue a legal right, or
> enforce or challenge an award in bona fide legal proceedings before a state court
> or other judicial authority. The Arbitral Tribunal may issue orders to set forth the
> terms of this confidentiality. This requirement shall be without prejudice to all
> other obligations in the arbitration.

84   Therefore, if the parties choose to give a binding force to the IBA Rules on
Evidence, Art. 3. 13 on confidentiality of documents will apply in their arbitration
proceedings. An arbitral tribunal can also use this provision as procedural guidelines
on the issue of confidentiality regarding documents. We will discuss regulation
provided in the IBA Rules on Evidence in the section dealing with confidentiality
regarding documents exchanged in the course of arbitral proceedings (see below
Sect. 4.3).

2.7   Overlap Between the Sources

85   As we have seen above, there are a number of sources regulating the confidentiality
of arbitral proceedings: express agreement on confidentiality (in the arbitration
agreement or in the underlying contract), institutional or non-institutional arbitration
rules, national arbitration laws and national case law. Confidentiality orders would
usually be issued after the start of the arbitration proceedings. They should take into
account the applicable rules and regulations and the existing agreement, if any, to
reduce to the minimum the risk of a conflicting decision. Arbitral 'jurisprudence',
codified rules of non-binding nature and *lex mercatoria* principles are 'soft law

---

[84]Lew et al. (2003), p. 553.
[85]Forword to IBA Rules on Evidence.

instruments' and, as such, should not cause any conflicts when overlapping with other sources.

When several sources regulating the confidentiality apply, in most cases they will **86** complement each other without creating conflicts. In other cases, however, different sources can contain conflicting provisions with regard to confidentiality. We will make several hypothetical assumptions of the situations when several sources apply and will analyse possible outcomes. To simplify our examples, we will discuss only the parties' obligation of confidentiality and will not examine the scope of such duty.

In the first example, we will assume that Chapter 12 of Swiss PILA (the Swiss law **87** on arbitration) and the Swiss Rules apply and that the parties did not reach an express agreement on confidentiality. Chapter 12 of Swiss PILA does not have an express provision on confidentiality. The Swiss Rules provide in Art. 44(1) that

> *'[u]nless the parties expressly agree in writing to the contrary, the parties undertake to keep confidential all awards and orders as well as all materials submitted by another party in the framework of the arbitral proceedings'.*

Since the parties did not reach an agreement on the confidentiality, the parties are bound by a duty of confidentiality in accordance with Art. 44(1) of the Swiss Rules.

In the second example, there is also no express agreement on confidentiality. **88** Chapter 12 of the Swiss PILA and the Oslo Rules apply to the arbitration proceeding. The Oslo Rules provide in Art. 12:

> *'Unless otherwise agreed by the parties, both the arbitration proceedings and the Tribunal's decision will not be subject to confidentiality'.*

Since there is no express agreement on confidentiality and Chapter 12 of Swiss PILA does not contain relevant provisions, the parties are not bound by confidentiality obligations with regard to their arbitration proceedings.

In the third example, the Norwegian Arbitration Act and the Oslo Rules apply, **89** but the parties expressly agreed in the arbitration agreement to be bound by a duty of confidentiality. The Norwegian Arbitration Act provides in Art. 5:

> *'Unless the parties have agreed otherwise, the arbitration proceedings and the decisions reached by the arbitration tribunal are not subject to a duty of confidentiality'.*

The Oslo Rules, as we have seen before, have a similar provision allowing the parties to reach an agreement on the confidentiality (Arts 12 and 13). Although both the Norwegian Arbitration Act and the Oslo Rules provide that the arbitration proceedings are not confidential, they allow the parties to reach agreement on an opposite solution. In this situation, there is no conflict between the sources and the parties do have a duty of confidentiality as their agreement prevails.

In the fourth example, the parties have reached an agreement providing that they **90** would not be bound by confidentiality obligations in relation to their arbitration proceedings. The arbitration proceedings are governed by the Norwegian Arbitration Act and the Swiss Rules apply. As we have seen above, the Norwegian Arbitration Act stipulates in Art. 5 that the arbitration proceedings are not subject to a duty of confidentiality. The Swiss Rules provide in Art. 44(1) that the parties are to keep confidential all materials submitted by another party in the framework of the arbitral proceedings. Although these provisions provide a contradictory solution, they both stipulate that it is the agreement of the parties that prevails. Therefore, in this case the parties are not bound by the confidentiality obligations in accordance with their agreement.

91   What, however, if the same provisions of the Swiss Rules and of the Norwegian Arbitration Act apply, but there is no express agreement of the parties on the issue of confidentiality? The situation is more complicated as we have contradictory applicable provisions in the absence of an express agreement. Art. 44(1) of the Swiss Rules should, in our opinion, prevail because Art. 5 of the Norwegian Arbitration Act is not a mandatory provision while the parties specifically agreed on the application of the Swiss Rules.

92   In practice, the situations are more complex and nuanced. The above-described examples demonstrate nevertheless that as long as national arbitration laws and institutional or non-institutional arbitration rules do not have mandatory provisions on confidentiality, there will be no conflict with the parties' agreement as the latter will prevail.

2.8   Intermediary Conclusions

93   Confidentiality obligations can originate from a number of different sources, such as an express agreement, international arbitration rules, domestic statutes or case law. The parties' autonomy with regard to determining the existence and the scope of confidentiality of their arbitral proceedings is very important. The most obvious tool is an express agreement, which has the benefit of being tailor-made. The only limit to the parties' autonomy would be the applicable legal mandatory requirements and the public policy rules.

94   Depending on their needs, the parties can also adhere to the confidentiality obligations contained in international arbitration rules or in a set of other rules, such as the IBA Rules on Evidence, for example, or can combine such rules with an express agreement. The parties can also exercise their autonomy by choosing the seat of arbitration and the law applicable to their disputes.

95   Although the ICC and the UNCITRAL Rules still do not impose a duty of confidentiality regarding arbitration proceedings on the parties, there are many arbitration rules containing specific provisions on confidentiality. These are, for example, Swiss Rules, LCIA Rules, DIS Rules, WIPO Rules, ACICA Rules, Milan Rules, Abu Dhabi Rules, SIAC Rules, DIAC Rules, JCAA Rules and Oslo Rules. Most arbitration rules containing regulation on the confidentiality provide as a general principle that arbitration proceedings are confidential. Oslo Rules, however, unusually provide that arbitration proceedings are not subject to confidentiality.

Legislators in such jurisdictions as Australia and New Zealand have chosen to   **96**
have very detailed provisions on confidentiality. In most jurisdictions, however,
arbitration laws remain silent on confidentiality of arbitration. Some landmark court
decisions greatly influenced the current regime applicable to confidentiality in
international commercial arbitration. While the English Courts recognised a general
principle of confidentiality of arbitration, the Australian High Court denied the
existence of an implied duty of confidentiality in the absence of a specific regulation
and express agreement.

In our opinion, the existence of a general duty of confidentiality cannot be   **97**
recognised as an autonomous *lex mercatoria* principle applicable in the arbitration
proceedings because there is no consensus on this issue. By contrast, such issues as
privacy of hearing and secrecy of deliberations of arbitral tribunal are not subject to
any controversy and thus could be recognised, in our view, as autonomous *lex
mercatoria* principles.

Given a large diversity of the regulation on confidentiality, it is advisable for the   **98**
parties seeking for some predictability and consistency to carefully choose the seat of
the arbitration, the law applicable to the contract, the applicable procedural rules and
the rules of an arbitration institution. In addition, the parties can also enter into a
tailor-made agreement on confidentiality, which will in most cases prevail given the
general principle of the party's procedural autonomy.

As to the overlap of different sources regulating confidentiality of arbitration   **99**
proceedings, we have shown that as long as national arbitration laws and institutional or non-institutional arbitration rules do not have mandatory provisions on
confidentiality, there is unlikely to be a conflict with the parties' agreement.

Chapter 3
Persons Subject to the Duty of Confidentiality

3.1 Introduction

Once the sources of confidentiality obligations have been identified, it is important to catalogue the persons who can be bound by the duty of confidentiality and to determine the scope of their duty. The main addressees of the duty of confidentiality are the parties with their representatives, the arbitrators and the relevant arbitration institution. Although the circle of persons involved in arbitration proceedings is usually limited, there will inevitably be other natural and legal persons, who will have access to the information relating to the arbitration proceedings. **101**

The following persons/groups of persons will potentially have access to at least some of the arbitration materials through the life of the proceedings: (i) the parties, (ii) the arbitrators, (iii) members and employees of the arbitration institution, (iv) counsel, (v) fact and expert witnesses as well as (vi) other third parties (third party funders, interpreters, court reporters, etc.). **102**

In the present section, we will examine the basis of the duty of confidentiality, if there is any, for each group and will attempt to define the scope of the obligation. First, we will analyse the parties' duty of confidentiality, which is the core issue of our thesis. Second, assuming that the parties' obligation of confidentiality exists, we will examine the confidentiality duty of other persons involved in arbitration proceedings. **103**

© Springer Nature Switzerland AG 2019
E. Reymond-Eniaeva, *Towards a Uniform Approach to Confidentiality of International Commercial Arbitration*, European Yearbook of International Economic Law 7, https://doi.org/10.1007/978-3-030-19003-3_3

3.2   Parties' Duty of Confidentiality

3.2.1   Introduction

104   The parties' obligation of confidentiality is at the core of our research. Sometimes regulation of the parties' duty of confidentiality is provided for in arbitration laws or rules—in particular, many arbitration rules impose an obligation of confidentiality on the parties. The parties can also agree on an express contractual confidentiality clause regarding the information and documents from the arbitration proceedings.

105   In the absence of an express provision on confidentiality in the applicable law, rules or in the parties' agreement, the question is whether an implied duty exists. Regulation of the existence of the parties' implied duty of confidentiality varies depending on the jurisdiction. Sometimes, there is no consensus even within a single jurisdiction.

106   In the present section, we will first review how the parties' obligation of confidentiality is regulated in arbitration rules and arbitration laws (Sect. 3.2.2). Second, we will focus on the existence of the parties' duty of confidentiality in the absence of an express agreement and rules (Sect. 3.2.3). Third, we will examine the main interests involved and will analyse arguments for and against confidentiality (Sect. 3.2.4). Finally, we will examine the problem of the applicable law (Sect. 3.2.5). As for the scope of the parties' obligation of confidentiality, we will examine this issue in the section dealing with the content of the confidentiality duty (Sect. 3.4) and in the section addressing the exceptions to the duty of confidentiality (Sect. 3.5).

3.2.2   Express Rules and Agreement on the Parties' Obligation of Confidentiality

107   As discussed above,[1] the parties can indirectly agree to be bound by confidentiality obligations contained in the relevant arbitration rules or the arbitration law applicable to their proceedings. They can do so, for example, by adopting specific arbitration rules or through their designation of the seat in their arbitration agreement.

108   A significant number of arbitration rules contain provisions on the confidentiality of arbitral proceedings and, in particular, on the parties' obligation of confidentiality. These include, for example, Art. 44(1) of the Swiss Rules, Art. 30.1 of the LCIA Rules, Art. 44.1 of the DIS Rules, Art. 75(a) of the WIPO Arbitration Rules, Art. 22.2 of the ACICA Rules, Art. 8(1) of the Milan Rules, Art. 33 of the Abu Dhabi Rules, Art. 39(1) of the SIAC Rules, Art. 41(1) of the DIAC Rules, and Art. 38(2) of the JCAA Rules.

---

[1]See above Sect. 2.2.

There are fewer national arbitration laws that expressly impose an obligation of **109** confidentiality on parties. Such examples include Art. 23C(1) AIAA, Art. 14B NZAA and Rule 26 of the Scottish Arbitration Act of 2010.

If there is no express agreement or applicable provision on the parties' obligation **110** of confidentiality, the question is whether the parties are still bound by an obligation of confidentiality. This was the controversial issue raised by the High Court of Australia in *Esso/BHP etc. v Plowman*, a key case that we will discuss in detail below.[2] We will further examine the approaches taken by different jurisdictions to this issue, and we will see that approaches vary significantly.

3.2.3 Confidentiality As an Implied Obligation

3.2.3.1 Introduction

In our thesis, when we refer to an 'implied obligation' we mean a term that was not **111** agreed by the parties and which does not result from express statutory provisions of the relevant legal system. Therefore, in this section we will discuss whether a competent authority can infer the existence of a confidentiality obligation on the parties in the absence of an express agreement or specific regulation.

It is important to explain, however, what an 'implied term' can mean in certain **112** common law jurisdictions. Under English law, an 'implied term' is a legal notion that designates a term of the contract on which the parties did not expressly agree, but which the courts add by implication.[3] These terms are implied into a contract: (i) as a result of custom; (ii) by law, whether statute or common law; (iii) from the fact of the particular contract; or (iv) to give effect to the parties' presumed intentions.[4] For the purpose of our research, we do *not* use the term 'implied' within the meaning given to 'implied term' under English law. The reason is that this notion of 'implied term' was developed in the common law and does not exist in civil law jurisdictions. Thus, unless discussing English law or other common law jurisdictions, we will mean by 'implied' obligation a term that was not agreed by the parties and which does not result from statutory provisions of the relevant legal system.

National courts of several countries have had to deal with this issue, but have **113** reached rather contradictory decisions. The approach taken towards the duty of confidentiality varies widely across jurisdictions. In England and Singapore, for example, an implied duty of confidentiality is considered well established, whereas the opposite is true in other common law jurisdictions such as Australia and the United States. Similarly, Swedish law does not recognise the existence of an implied duty of confidentiality. The question remains open in France and Switzerland.

---

[2]See below Sect. 3.2.3.4.
[3]Chen-Wishart (2018), p. 414.
[4]Chen-Wishart (2018), p. 414; O'Sullivan and Hilliard (2012), pp. 167–173.

114   Originally, the prevailing opinion in most jurisdictions was in favour of the existence of an implied obligation of confidentiality.[5] The confidentiality duty was simply assumed without any real questioning of its origins. Then came the unexpected decision rendered in 1995 by the High Court of Australia in *Esso/BHP etc. v Plowman*.[6] The High Court of Australia confirmed the privacy of arbitration hearings, but it rejected the principle of confidentiality of arbitral proceedings, which was considered as a separate issue. The High Court decided that unless the parties had specifically agreed on a confidentiality regime, there was no obligation of confidentiality covering the information obtained in the course of the arbitration.

115   The *Esso/BHP etc. v Plowman* decision overtly questioned the confidential nature of arbitration proceedings. Following this decision, two opposing theories have been developed. There are those who think that an arbitration agreement includes an implied obligation of confidentiality, and those who consider that unless there is a legal or contractual basis for confidentiality, no such obligation applies to the parties in an arbitration.

116   We will now examine the case law on the parties' duty of confidentiality from the national courts of several jurisdictions. We will also discuss, where relevant, legal scholars' opinions on the existence of an implied duty of confidentiality.

3.2.3.2   England

117   English courts have had several occasions to deal with the issue of confidentiality of arbitral proceedings and have made a major contribution to the development of jurisprudence in this area. In *Dolling-Baker v. Merrett*[7] and several subsequent cases, English courts elaborated a general principle of confidentiality in arbitration. As a result, it is today well established under English law that in arbitrations the parties are under an implied duty to maintain the confidentiality of the information and documents disclosed and generated during the arbitral proceedings, even in the absence of an express agreement. The obligation of confidentiality is, however, not without limitations. These are to be determined on a case-by-case basis.[8] Below we will examine in greater detail exceptions to the rule of confidentiality (see below Sect. 3.5).

118   In 1990, in the *Dolling-Baker v. Merrett*[9] case, the English Court of Appeal established that the parties to an arbitration are bound by an implied obligation not to

---

[5]See, for example, Dolling-Baker v. Merrett [1990] 1 WLR 1205; Shearson Lehman Hutton Incorporated and Another v. Maclaine Watson & Co. Ltd. [1988] 1 WLR 948; G. Aïta v. A. Ojjeh, Cour d'appel de Paris (1ère Chambre suppl.), 18 February 1986; Bucher (1988), Le nouvel arbitrage international en Suisse, para 205; Bucher and Tschanz (1988), para 169.

[6]Esso Australia Resources Ltd. and Others v. Sidney James Plowman and Others, Arbitration International, Volume 11 No. 3, 1995, 235.

[7]Dolling-Baker v. Merrett [1990] 1 WLR 1205.

[8]Blackaby et al. (2015), para 2.169.

[9]Dolling-Baker v. Merrett [1990] 1 WLR 1205.

disclose documents prepared for and used in the arbitration. As to the origins of this implied obligation, the Court of Appeal held that it arises out of the nature of the arbitration itself:

> What is relied upon is, in effect, the essentially private nature of an arbitration, coupled with the implied obligation of a party who obtains documents on discovery not to use them for any purpose other than the dispute in which they were obtained. As between parties to an arbitration, although the proceedings are consensual and may thus be regarded as wholly voluntary, their very nature is such that there must, in my judgment, be some implied obligation on both parties not to disclose or use for any other purpose any documents prepared for and used in the arbitration, or disclosed or produced in the arbitration or transcripts or notes of the evidence in the arbitration or award – and indeed not to disclose in any other way what evidence had been given by any witness in the arbitration – save with the consent of the other party, or pursuant to an order or leave of the court. That qualification is necessary, just as it is in the case of the implied obligation of secrecy between banker and customer.

> It will be appreciated that I do not intend in the foregoing to give a precise definition of the extent of the obligation. It is unnecessary to do so in the present case. It must be perfectly apparent that, for example, the fact that a document is used in an arbitration does not confer on it any confidentiality or privilege which can be availed in subsequent proceedings. If it is a relevant document, its relevance remains. But that the obligation exists in some form appears to be abundantly apparent. It is not a question of immunity or public interest. It is a question of an implied obligation arising out of the nature of arbitration itself.[10]

Three years later, in *Hassneh Insurance v Mew*,[11] the Queen's Bench of the **119** English High Court had to rule on the disclosure of an arbitral award and other documents from an arbitration in a subsequent court proceeding. The Court assumed that there was at least an implied term in every arbitration agreement that the arbitration is to be held privately. It considered that this privacy should in principle extend to the documents created for the purpose of the hearing.[12]

In 1997, in the *Ali Shipping* case,[13] the Court of Appeal confirmed the existence **120** of an implied duty of confidentiality and found that the nature of the duty was an implied term of the arbitration agreement. According to the Court of Appeal, this implied term[14] should be 'regarded as attaching as a matter of law', i.e. as '*a term which the law will necessarily imply as a necessary incident of a definable category of contractual relationship*'.[15]

In 2008, the Court of Appeal reconfirmed the existence of an implied duty of **121** confidentiality in the *Emmott* case,[16] but stated that this duty originates in substantive law rather than in the arbitration agreement.

---

[10]Dolling-Baker v. Merrett [1990] 1 WLR 1205.

[11]Hassneh Insurance Co v Mew [1993] 2 Lloyd's Rep 243.

[12]Hassneh Insurance Co v Mew [1993] 2 Lloyd's Rep 243.

[13]Ali Shipping v. Shipyard Trogir [1997] EWCA Civ 3054.

[14]See Sect. 3.2.3.1 explaining the notion of an implied term under English law.

[15]Ali Shipping v. Shipyard Trogir [1997] EWCA Civ 3054.

[16]Emmott v Wilson & Partners Limited [2008] EWCA Civ 184.

122   Analysis of the above-mentioned cases demonstrates that the existence of an implied duty of confidentiality in international commercial arbitration is well established under English law. Only the nature (contractual or non-contractual) and the scope of this duty are still being questioned.

3.2.3.3 Singapore

123   Singapore is a common law jurisdiction. It is therefore unsurprising that, following English law, the existence of an implied obligation of confidentiality is also well established under Singapore law. In the *AAY and others v. AAZ AS* case,[17] the Singapore High Court is very explicit about the implied obligation of confidentiality and its meaning. The High Court explains that, in any arbitration with a seat in Singapore, the obligation of confidentiality will apply absent a parties' express agreement to the contrary:

> [A]s a principle of arbitration law at least in Singapore and England, the obligation of confidentiality in arbitration will apply as a default to arbitrations where the parties have not specified expressly the private and/or confidential nature of the arbitration. While parties anticipating international arbitration would remain well advised to agree prospectively on the obligation of confidentiality, there is no need to do so where Singapore is to be the seat of the arbitration because confidentiality will apply as a substantive rule of arbitration law, not through the IIA [International Arbitration Act] or the AA [Arbitration Act], but from the common law [. . .].[18]

124   As to the nature of this confidentiality obligation, the High Court begins by extensively discussing the English and Australian authorities on the obligation of confidentiality in arbitration. Regarding English case law, it makes some interesting observations:

> It thus appears that discussion has come almost a full circle, the obligation having been characterized in turn as an implied term based on custom or the officious bystander test,[19] then as an implied term in law, and finally as a substantive rule of arbitration law masquerading as an implied term, whose scope, nature and application must be determined in the context of each case and the nature of the information or documents at issue.[20]

125   Finally, the High Court concludes that the confidentiality obligation is a substantive rule of arbitration law finding its origins in the common law (as opposed to

---

[17] AAY and others v AAZ AS, High Court, Suit [Y], Case No. [2009] SGHC 142, 15 June 2009.

[18] AAY and others v AAZ AS, High Court, Suit [Y], Case No. [2009] SGHC 142, 15 June 2009, 55–56.

[19] Here is a proposed definition of the 'officious bystander test' from uk.practicalllaw.com: The proposed terms will be implied if it is so obvious that if an officious (interfering) bystander suggested to the parties that they include it in the contract, 'they would testily suppress him with a common 'oh of course''. In other words, the proposed term must be so obvious that it goes without saying.

[20] AAY and others v AAZ AS, High Court, Suit [Y], Case No. [2009] SGHC 142, 15 June 2009, at 54.

arbitration statutes). It is also suggested that the common law, as compared to statutory provisions, is better suited to deal with the confidentiality obligation because of '*its amorphous scope and exceptions as well as its elusive juridical bases*'.[21]

3.2.3.4   Australia

Australia was the first jurisdiction to decide, in the famous High Court decision in the **126** *Esso/BHP etc. v. Plowman* case,[22] that there is no implied duty of confidentiality in arbitration proceedings in the absence of a specific regulation or express agreement.

Although the text of the decision is publicly available,[23] given the importance of **127** this decision, we will review not only the main legal arguments, but also the relevant factual circumstances of the case. It is important to understand what prompted the High Court of Australia to take this 'revolutionary' approach denying the existence of an implied duty of confidentiality. The Court had to dispose, in particular, of the question of whether a party to an arbitration proceeding is under a duty of confidentiality in relation to documents and information disclosed in, and for the purposes of, an arbitration.

The dispute originated in two agreements for the sale of natural gas by Esso **128** Australia Resources Ltd. (and other entities) to two public utilities, the Gas and Fuel Corporation of Victoria (GFC) and the State Electricity Commission of Victoria (SEC) ('Sales Agreements'). The sellers and appellants in this case were referred to as 'Esso/BHP'. Each of the Sales Agreements contained a clause providing that the price payable for the gas was to be adjusted by taking into account changes in royalties and taxes imposed on gas production or supply. In the event of such an adjustment, the sellers were to provide to the buyers '*details of the increase or decrease and the method and distribution of such royalties, taxes, rates, duties or levies*'. In November 1991, Esso/BHP sought an increase in the price, using the imposition of a new tax as a justification. After GFC and SEC refused to pay, Esso/BHP commenced an arbitration proceeding.

Prior to initiation of the arbitration, Esso/BHP refused to provide the '*details of* **129** *the increase or decrease and the method and distribution of such royalties, taxes, rates, duties or levies*' as required by the contracts. They justified this refusal by citing the commercial sensitivity of this information. They agreed, however, to disclose the information required by GFC and SEC provided that these entities

---

[21]AAY and others v AAZ AS, High Court, Suit [Y], Case No. [2009] SGHC 142, 15 June 2009, at 54.

[22]Esso Australia Resources Ltd. and Others v. Sidney James Plowman and Others, Arbitration International, Volume 11 No. 3, 1995, 235.

[23]Esso Australia Resources Ltd. and Others v. Sidney James Plowman and Others, Arbitration International, Volume 11 No. 3, 1995, 235.

contractually agreed not to disclose the requested information to any person, including the Minister, the Government and the general public.

130   On 1 June 1992, the Ministry for Energy and Minerals (Ministry), supervisor of GFC and SEC, brought an action before the first instance Court against Esso/BHP. The Ministry sought the following declarations from the Court:

> (i) GFC and SEC are not restricted from disclosing to the Minister and third persons information provided to it by Esso/BHP on details of the price increase or decrease and the method and distribution of royalties, taxes, rates, duties or levies.

> (ii) There are no express or implied terms in the Sales Agreements that restrict disclosure to the Minister and third persons of information obtained by GFC and SEC in the course of or by reason of the arbitration.

> (iii) GFC and SEC are not restricted from disclosing information to the Minister and third persons by reason only that the information was obtained from Esso/BHP in the course of or by reason of the arbitration and that the information has not otherwise been published.

> (iv) In case GFC and SEC obtain from Esso/BHP the required information justifying the price increase, they are under a statutory duty to disclose this information to the Ministry.

131   In the first instance proceedings, the Court ordered Esso/BHP to provide the information required by GFC and SEC justifying the price increase, and made the declarations the Ministry sought in its requests for relief.

132   Esso/BHP appealed to the Appeal Division of the Supreme Court of Victoria. The Appeal Division set aside the orders for Esso/BHP to provide the information justifying the price increase and overturned most of the declarations made by the first instance judge. Only the following declaration was maintained:

> GFC and SEC are not restricted from disclosing information to the Minister and third persons by reason only that the information was obtained from Esso/BHP in the course of or by reason of the arbitration and that the information has not otherwise been published.

Thus, the Appeal Division ruled in favour of a confidentiality duty by deciding that GFC and SEC could not disclose to the Minister and third persons information provided to it by Esso/BHP. It considered, however, that this confidentiality duty was not due to the fact that the information was obtained by reason of the arbitration.

133   Esso/BHP filed a further appeal to the High Court of Australia. The decision was rendered by five judges of the High Court of Australia. The judges needed to decide on two main issues: the privacy of the hearing and the confidentiality of the arbitration. The judges chose to uphold the privacy but questioned the confidentiality of the arbitration; they then remitted the matter back to the Supreme Court of Victoria so that the declarations sought by the Ministry could be reformulated. Although the decision to remit was unanimous, the judges disagreed on the reasons for doing so. Justice Toohey provided a dissenting opinion on the issue of the implied duty of confidentiality, which we will discuss in some detail.

Chief Justice Mason confirmed that an arbitration hearing is to be held in private **134** in the sense that it should not be open to the public.[24] He did not agree that privacy was an implied term, but described privacy '*as something that inheres in the subject-matter of the agreement to submit disputes to arbitration rather than attribute that character to an implied term*'.[25]

When discussing the issue of confidentiality, Chief Justice Mason referred in **135** particular to the arguments provided by the Ministry, which claimed that a distinction must be made between the privacy of the hearing and the confidentiality of the arbitration. The Ministry had argued in particular that:

(i) In Australia and the United States there were no decided cases supporting the existence of a confidentiality duty.
(ii) Arbitration practitioners expressed conflicting views on the issue.
(iii) If a confidentiality obligation '*had formed part of the law, one would have expected it to have been recognised and enforced by judicial decision long before Dolling-Baker*'.[26]

Moreover, Chief Justice Mason maintained that, for various reasons, complete **136** confidentiality cannot be achieved in arbitration proceedings. Thus, witnesses are not bound by the confidentiality duty; the arbitration award may be subject to judicial review; and there are other circumstances allowing a party to disclose information regarding the arbitration to a third party.[27]

Further, Chief Justice Mason questioned the source of an obligation not to **137** disclose. He held that, in the absence of an express agreement, it was not justified to conclude that confidentiality was an essential characteristic of a private arbitration.[28] For this reason, he rejected the appellants' argument that an agreement to arbitrate contains an implied term restricting the parties from disclosing the information provided in and for the purposes of the arbitration.[29]

Chief Justice Mason admitted confidentiality obligations of the parties regarding **138** the documents produced by a party compulsorily pursuant to an order from the arbitral tribunal. He noted that the same principle applied in English and Australian

---

[24]Esso Australia Resources Ltd. and Others v. Sidney James Plowman and Others, Arbitration International, Volume 11 No. 3, 1995, 241.

[25]Esso Australia Resources Ltd. and Others v. Sidney James Plowman and Others, Arbitration International, Volume 11 No. 3, 1995, 242.

[26]Esso Australia Resources Ltd. and Others v. Sidney James Plowman and Others, Arbitration International, Volume 11 No. 3, 1995, 243–244. The Ministry referred to a case adjudicated by the English High Court: Dolling-Baker v. Merrett [1990] 1 WLR 1205; see Sect. 3.2.3.2 discussing this case.

[27]Esso Australia Resources Ltd. and Others v. Sidney James Plowman and Others, Arbitration International, Volume 11 No. 3, 1995, 244.

[28]Esso Australia Resources Ltd. and Others v. Sidney James Plowman and Others, Arbitration International, Volume 11 No. 3, 1995, 245.

[29]Esso Australia Resources Ltd. and Others v. Sidney James Plowman and Others, Arbitration International, Volume 11 No. 3, 1995, 245–246.

state court proceedings, and he saw no reason why this should be regulated differently in arbitration.[30] He maintained, however, that:

> The existence of this obligation does not provide a basis for the wide-ranging obligation of
> confidentiality which the appellants seek to apply to all documents and information provided
> in and for the purposes of an arbitration.[31]

139   As for the declarations sought by the Ministry which would allow GFC and SEC
to disclose information obtained from Esso/BHP in the course of the arbitration to
the Minister and third persons, Chief Justice Mason ruled that these declarations
should be maintained but reformulated by the Supreme Court of Victoria in order to
render their scope of application more specific.[32] His reasoning and conclusions
were supported by a majority of the court.

140   The decision of the High Court of Australia in the *Esso/BHP* case came as a shock
to the international arbitration community. Confidentiality—a pillar of international
arbitration and long considered one of its main advantages—was cast in doubt. The
decision challenged mainstream opinion that there was an implied duty of confidentiality resulting from the arbitration agreement.

141   Importantly, however, Justice Toohey produced a dissenting opinion. This opinion shows that there was another way for the High Court to resolve the issue of the
confidentiality of arbitral proceedings. It also demonstrates the reasoning the judges
could have used to support the decision in favour of an implied duty of confidentiality. Justice Toohey agreed with the other judges that the matter should be remitted
to the Supreme Court of Victoria, but opined that the appeal of Esso/BHP should be
allowed and declarations allowing GFC and SEC to disclose information obtained
from Esso/BHP in the course of the arbitration to the Minister and third persons
should be set aside.

142   Justice Toohey confirmed the existence of at least some confidentiality obligation
regarding the documents and information emanating from an arbitration. He stated
that confidentiality is a '*term implied as a matter of law in commercial arbitration
agreements*'. He further argued:

> The term is implied from the entry by the parties into a form of dispute resolution which they
> choose because of the privacy they expect to result. If this is said to confuse privacy and
> confidentiality, the answer is that they are not distinct characteristics.[33]

143   In his dissent, Justice Toohey also referred to one of the important decisions on
confidentiality from England, the *Hassneh* decision. Justice Toohey agreed with the

---

[30]Esso Australia Resources Ltd. and Others v. Sidney James Plowman and Others, Arbitration
International, Volume 11 No. 3, 1995, 247–248.

[31]Esso Australia Resources Ltd. and Others v. Sidney James Plowman and Others, Arbitration
International, Volume 11 No. 3, 1995, 248.

[32]Esso Australia Resources Ltd. and Others v. Sidney James Plowman and Others, Arbitration
International, Volume 11 No. 3, 1995, 248.

[33]Esso Australia Resources Ltd. and Others v. Sidney James Plowman and Others, Arbitration
International, Volume 11 No. 3, 1995, 254–262.

reasoning in *Hassneh*[34] and, in particular, with the idea of comparing disclosure to a third party to opening the door of the arbitration room to third parties. He argued:

> Any aspect of disclosure to third parties must infringe the privacy of the arbitration. Thus, if one party is free to disclose to a newspaper or media outlet the progress of an arbitration and the evidence adduced in its course, the notion of privacy is meaningless. There must be an underlying principle, significantly qualified in accordance with these reasons, that a party to an arbitration is under a duty not to disclose to a third party documents and information obtained by reason of the arbitration.

In addition, Justice Toohey stated that it was easier to express a principle of **144** non-confidentiality as there appeared to be many exceptions to the principle of confidentiality:

> In terms of formulation, it is easy enough to express a principle of non-confidentiality. In effect, that is what the Minister has done in declarations 6C and 6F which he seeks to uphold. But it is much harder to express a principle of confidentiality which accepts, as it must, that there are significant exceptions. And this has been the appellants' difficulty from the outset of this litigation. A principle of confidentiality, expressed to be subject to 'all exceptions' or the like, is a principle so nebulous as to be hardly a principle at all.[35]

Notwithstanding the difficulty to formulate a general principle of confidentiality subject to many exceptions, Justice Toohey expressed his firm position in favour of confidentiality.

As we will see below,[36] no rule on the confidentiality of arbitration was intro- **145** duced into the English Arbitration Act of 1996 precisely because there were so many potential exceptions to the duty. Could the difficulty in formulating exceptions to the principle of confidentiality also explain the decision of the majority of Justices of the High Court of Australia in the *Esso/BHP* case? Probably not, at least not entirely, since in this specific case there were important factual circumstances which could justify the decision.

In particular, GFC and SEC were public utilities supplying gas and electricity to **146** the general public, and the Minister for Energy needed to know the reasons for the price increases imposed on the two entities it was supervising. Therefore, although the judges focused their arguments on the issue of confidentiality of international arbitration, the rationale for this decision, in our opinion, was the fact that the public interest called for disclosure of information justifying the price increase. In other words, the justification for the price increase imposed by ESSO/BHP on GFC and SEC (or lack thereof) was an issue of public interest because it would influence the price charged by the two public utilities to consumers of gas and electricity in Victoria.[37]

---

[34]Hassneh Insurance Co v Mew [1993] 2 Lloyd's Rep 243. We will further discuss this decision in Sects. 4.3.4 and 4.5.2.1.

[35]Esso Australia Resources Ltd. and Others v. Sidney James Plowman and Others, Arbitration International, Volume 11 No. 3, 1995, p. 259.

[36]See Sect. 5.1.

[37]Tweeddale (2005), p. 61, with further references.

147   In addition, it was not some random third party who requested the disclosure of information from the arbitration, but the Minister for Energy, a supervising authority to GFC and SEC, the parties in the arbitration. Thus, there appear to be strong arguments in the *Esso/BHP* case justifying the denial of the existence of an implied duty of confidentiality under the specific circumstances of the case.

148   Notwithstanding the unexpected approach to the issue of confidentiality, the decision has since been followed by the Australian courts. In 2010, however, provisions providing for confidentiality in international arbitration on an opt-in bases were added to the AIAA.[38] Thus, the parties could opt for confidentiality, but if they were silent, the common law rules providing no confidentiality were to apply. In 2015, the Australian legislators went even further towards greater confidentiality in international commercial arbitration. According to the 2015 amendments, the AIAA confidentiality provisions will apply in the proceedings arising from all arbitration agreements concluded from 14 October 2015 onwards, unless the parties decide to 'opt-out'.[39] Thus, although the Australian common law denies the existence of an implied duty of confidentiality, the parties will be bound by an obligation of confidentiality in accordance with the AIAA confidentiality provisions.

3.2.3.5 United States

149   The Federal Arbitration Act governing international arbitrations in the Unites States is silent on the issue of confidentiality.[40] However, the issue was indirectly examined in *United States v. Panhandle Eastern Corp.*[41] In this case, Panhandle Eastern Pipe Line Co. (PEPL) resisted production of documents from an earlier arbitration. The U.S. Court of Appeals, Third Circuit (Delaware District) ordered PEPL to produce them. In its decision, the Court did not directly discuss the existence of an implied duty of confidentiality, but it did question the legal or contractual basis for the existence of a duty of confidentiality that would discharge PEPL from producing documents from its earlier arbitration with a party not involved in the relevant court proceedings.

150   The background of the *Panhandle* case is as follows. PEPL and Sonatrach, the Algerian National Oil and Gas Company, were engaged in an ICC arbitration seated in Geneva (Sonatrach Arbitration). The U.S. Federal Government brought an action before the U.S. District Court of Delaware, requesting PEPL to produce certain documents from the Sonatrach Arbitration.[42]

151   PEPL filed a motion for a protective order to preserve the 'confidentiality of documents'. The Court rejected PEPL's motion based on both substantive and

[38]Nottage (2017), p. 1; 2010 version of Art. 22(3) AIAA.

[39]Art. 22(2) AIAA; Nottage (2017), pp. 1–2; Shirlow (2015), p. 2.

[40]Hargrove (2009), p. 51.

[41]United States v Panhandle Eastern Corporation 118 FRD 346 (D Del 1988).

[42]United States v Panhandle Eastern Corporation 118 FRD 348 (D Del 1988).

procedural grounds. The procedural ground for denying the motion was that it had not been filed timely. The substantive arguments are analysed below.

Referring to *Cipollone v. Liggett Group, Inc.*[43] and *Zenith Radio Corp. v. Matsushita Elec. Indus. Co.*,[44] the Court recalled the standards for issuing a protective order under Rule 26(c) of the Federal Rules of Civil Procedure. First, Rule 26(c) places the burden of persuasion on the party seeking the protective order. Second, according to the same rule, *'the party seeking the protective order must show good cause by demonstrating a particular need for protection'* and *'must provide specific examples of the hardship that will be suffered because of the disclosure of information'*.[45] The Court found that these criteria were not met by PEPL.   **152**

As the only support for its motion, PEPL provided an affidavit from the lead counsel for PEPL in the Sonatrach Arbitration. The affidavit presented the argument that the applicable ICC Rules required the Sonatrach Arbitration documents to be kept confidential. But the Court found that the affidavit failed to establish the basis of the confidentiality obligation. As already mentioned,[46] the ICC Rules impose an obligation of confidentiality only on the ICC Court and its Secretariat, but not on the parties. The U.S. District Court of Delaware correctly pointed to this fact, stating that the provisions of the ICC Rules cited in the affidavit were not applicable to the parties.[47]   **153**

As another basis for the confidentiality obligation, the affidavit referred to *'a general understanding [. . .] that the pleadings and related documents in the Arbitration would be kept confidential'* that had been allegedly reached by counsel at the outset of the Sonatrach Arbitration. According to the Court, this allegation was insufficient to meet the stringent requirement of Rule 26(c), because, among other things, the affidavit did not present evidence of any actual agreement on confidentiality.[48]   **154**

Further, the Court, even assuming that an understanding of confidentiality existed, found that the affidavit failed to provide specific examples of the hardship that would befall PEPL upon disclosure. The argument that disclosure would be prejudicial to a possible settlement of the Sonatrach Arbitration was rejected, since the settlement had already taken place. The Court was also not convinced by PEPL's allegation that the disclosure would prejudice future business negotiations of a new contract between the relevant companies. It found that broad allegations of economic injury were insufficient to show 'good cause'.[49] Referring to *Zenith Radio Corp.*   **155**

---

[43]Cipollone v. Liggett Group, Inc., 785 F.2d 1108 (3d Cir.).

[44]Zenith Radio Corp. v. Matsushita Elec. Indus. Co., 529 F.Supp. 866, 891 (E.D.Pa.1981).

[45]United States v Panhandle Eastern Corporation 118 FRD 349 (D Del 1988).

[46]See above Sect. 2.3.5.

[47]United States v Panhandle Eastern Corporation 118 FRD 349-350 (D Del 1988).

[48]United States v Panhandle Eastern Corporation 118 FRD 350 (D Del 1988).

[49]United States v Panhandle Eastern Corporation 118 FRD 350 (D Del 1988).

v. Matsushita Elec. Indus. Co.,[50] the Court recalled that the standard of '*good cause*' required showing that the '*disclosures will work a clearly defined and serious injury*'.[51]

156   *United States v. Panhandle Eastern Corp*[52] is the most frequently cited U.S. court decision on confidentiality in arbitration proceedings. In line with this decision, legal scholars generally admit that there is no implied duty of confidentiality under U.S. law.[53] Notably, however, the U.S. Court of Delaware did not examine whether a confidentiality duty could exist as an implied term, in the absence of a specific agreement and applicable rules on the confidentiality obligations. It is not clear whether this was due to the failure by PEPL to raise this argument or whether the Court chose not to address it directly.

3.2.3.6   Sweden

157   The Swedish courts were obliged to examine the existence of an implied duty of confidentiality in the famous *Bulbank* case.[54] A.I. Trade Finance (AIT), which was opposed to Bulgarian Foreign Trade Bank Ltd. (Bulbank), provided the text of the partial award rendered in this arbitration (through its counsel) to an American periodical Mealey's International Arbitration Report. The partial award was published.

158   After Bulbank and the Arbitral Tribunal learned of the publication of the partial award, Bulbank requested that the Arbitral Tribunal declare the arbitration agreement invalid and that it cancel the final hearing. Bulbank's request was rejected, and the final arbitral award was issued on 22 December 1997.

159   The final award then became subject to review by the Swedish courts at three levels: the Stockholm City Court, the Svea Court of Appeal and the Supreme Court of Sweden. First, Bulbank filed an appeal to the Stockholm City Court against the final award. Bulbank claimed that by entering into an arbitration agreement, AIT undertook a duty of confidentiality regarding the arbitration proceedings. Bulbank's case was that AIT, by breaching its duty of confidentiality, was in fundamental breach of the arbitration agreement, which, as a result, became invalid.

160   The Stockholm City Court agreed with this reasoning and declared the arbitration agreement invalid, and consequently the final award as well.[55] This ruling was

---

[50]Zenith Radio Corp. v. Matsushita Elec. Indus. Co., 529 F.Supp. 866, 891 (E.D.Pa.1981).

[51]United States v Panhandle Eastern Corporation 118 FRD 350 (D Del 1988).

[52]United States v Panhandle Eastern Corporation 118 FRD 346 (D Del 1988).

[53]Born (2014), p. 2800; Brown (2001), p. 976; Hargrove (2009), p. 3; Raymond (2005), p. 494.

[54]Judgment of the Supreme Court of Sweden rendered in 2000 in Case N T 1881-99: The Bulbank Case, in: Stockholm Arbitration Report, Volume 2, 2000, 137–160. See below Sect. 6.2.3 for more discussion on this case.

[55]Judgment of the Supreme Court of Sweden rendered in 2000 in Case N T 1881-99: The Bulbank Case, in: Stockholm Arbitration Report, Volume 2, 2000, pp. 139–140.

nearly as revolutionary as the decision of the High Court of Australia in the *Esso/ BHP etc. v. Plowman* case, although for the opposite reason. It meant that even in the absence of an express legal provision or express agreement, both parties were bound by a duty of confidentiality and that a breach of this duty of confidentiality could be grounds for declaring an arbitration agreement void.

The decision of the Stockholm City Court was, however, overturned by the Svea **161** Court of Appeal and by the Supreme Court of Sweden. The latter court concluded that there was no clear and well-founded view on the duty of confidentiality either in Sweden or elsewhere. It upheld the final judgment of the Svea Court of Appeal declaring the arbitral award valid:

> Against the background of that stated, the Supreme Court considers that a party to arbitration proceedings cannot be deemed to be bound by a duty of confidentiality, unless the parties have concluded an agreement concerning this.

> It consequently follows that AIT has not committed a breach of contract by allowing the publication of the decision that the arbitration panel issue during the proceedings. Therefore, Bulbank did not have grounds for revoking the arbitration agreement and Bulbank's application for a declaration of invalidity of revocation of the arbitral award can therefore not be granted.[56]

As a consequence of this decision, and since there is no provision on the **162** obligation of confidentiality in the Swedish Arbitration Act, Swedish authors generally admit that, under Swedish law, parties to arbitral proceedings are not bound by a duty of confidentiality unless they have specifically agreed on such a duty.[57]

3.2.3.7 France

In France, the issue of an implied duty of confidentiality is not clear-cut. At first **163** sight, the position of the French Courts regarding the existence of an implied duty of confidentiality does not seem to be entirely consistent. Thus, in two French Court decisions, *G. Aïta v. A. Ojjeh* and *Bleustein et autres v. Société True North et Société FCB International*, the existence of an implied duty of confidentiality was affirmed. However, in a later decision, *Société National Company for Fishing and Marketing 'Nafimco' v. Société Foster Wheeler Trading Company AG,*[58] the Paris Court of Appeal took a different position and questioned the basis for the confidentiality obligation in French international arbitration law. However, as we will see below, the factual circumstances in these cases were very different, which probably explains the apparent lack of consistency.

---

[56]Judgment of the Supreme Court of Sweden rendered in 2000 in Case N T 1881-99: The Bulbank Case, in: Stockholm Arbitration Report, Volume 2, 2000, p. 147.

[57]Brocker and Löf (2013), p. 201; Heuman (2003), p. 14; Shaughnessy (2006), pp. 316–317; Madsen (2007), p. 194.

[58]Société National Company for Fishing and Marketing 'Nafimco' v. Société Foster Wheeler Trading Company AG, Cour d'appel de Paris (1ère Ch. C), 22 January 2004.

164   In the *G. Aïta v. A. Ojjeh* case,[59] the award was rendered by an arbitral tribunal
seated in London. The claimant, Mr. Aïta, challenged the award before the Paris
Court of Appeal. Since the award was rendered in England and there was no
application for an *exequatur* in France, the French authorities did not have jurisdiction
to set aside the award.

165   According to the Paris Court of Appeal, the claimant sought to bypass this lack of
jurisdiction by invoking the arbitration agreement at clause 14 of the underlying
contract which stated the following: '*this agreement will be governed by the English
law and the procedures in relation to its validity and execution can only be initiated
in England, France and Switzerland*'. The claimant argued that this provision was
intended to extend jurisdiction for setting aside the award to the English, French and
Swiss Courts. The Court of Appeal did not accept this interpretation. It stated, in
particular, that clause 14 of the agreement applied to the conditions of the arbitration
agreement's validity, but not to the validity of the arbitral award. The Court of
Appeal considered that the claim was frivolous as filed before a manifestly incompetent
authority and held that the defendant had suffered damages as a result of this
public disclosure. Therefore, it ordered the claimant to pay FF 200,000 in damages,
as well as court costs.

166   When deciding on this case, the Paris Court of Appeal affirmed the principle of
confidentiality of arbitral proceedings and stated that it is in the very nature of
arbitral proceedings that they ensure the highest degree of discretion in the resolution
of private disputes.[60] By this ruling, the Paris Court of Appeal confirmed, in
particular, that: (i) arbitral proceedings should ensure the highest degree of confidentiality;
(ii) this confidentiality finds its origins in the very nature of arbitration;
(iii) by submitting their dispute to arbitration, parties expect the proceedings to be
confidential.

167   The Paris Commercial Court expressed a similar view in *Bleustein et autres
v. Société True North et Société FCB International*, where it was requested to decide
whether a party to an arbitration was in breach of its confidentiality obligations.[61]
The defendant, True North, had issued an official press release through a news
agency on the existence of its dispute with the claimant Publicis, announcing that the
dispute was subject to an arbitration proceeding.[62] The Court found that True North
had breached its confidentiality obligations, but did not explain what the legal basis
of the duty of confidentiality was; it simply stated that '*arbitration is a private
proceeding of a confidential nature*'.[63]

---

[59]G. Aïta v. A. Ojjeh, Cour d'appel de Paris (1ère Chambre suppl.), 18 February 1986, in: Rev. Arb.
1986, 583. Also see below Sects. 5.3.2.2 and 6.2.2 discussing this case.

[60]G. Aïta v. A. Ojjeh, Cour d'appel de Paris (1ère Chambre suppl.), 18 February 1986.

[61]Bleustein et autres v. Société True North et Société FCB International, Tribunal de commerce de
Paris (Ord. réf.), 22 February 1999. See below Sect. 4.2.2.3 for more details on this case.

[62]Bleustein et autres v. Société True North et Société FCB International, Tribunal de commerce de
Paris (Ord. réf.), 22 February 1999.

[63]Bleustein et autres v. Société True North et Société FCB International, Tribunal de commerce de
Paris (Ord. réf.), 22 February 1999.

However, the Paris Court of Appeal took a different position in its decision in **168** *Société National Company for Fishing and Marketing 'Nafimco' v. Société Foster Wheeler Trading Company AG*.[64] The Court considered that Société Foster, which was seeking relief for a breach of confidentiality, did not prove the existence and foundation of an implied duty of confidentiality in French international arbitration law. On its face, this reasoning is not consistent with the two previously-mentioned decisions suggesting that a duty of confidentiality is inherent in international arbitration proceedings, even absent a specific legal or contractual basis.

However, the facts of the *Nafimco* case may explain this apparent inconsistency in **169** the reasoning of the court. The background of *Nafimco* is very different from that of *G. Aïta v. A. Ojjeh*. In the *Nafimco* case, information about the arbitration was disclosed when one party legitimately initiated a court proceeding, whereas in the *G. Aïta v. A. Ojjeh* case, the initiation of the proceeding was frivolous and abusive. In other words, in both cases a party sought damages from the other party for breaching its duty of confidentiality as a result of an appeal against the arbitral award filed to a state court, but the appeal and the party's claim were frivolous in the *G. Aïta v. A. Ojjeh* case and legitimate in the *Nafimco* case. As we will see below in the section dealing with exceptions to the duty of confidentiality,[65] a party is, in principle, allowed to disclose information from an arbitration, i.e., the award and, if necessary, other arbitration materials, to a state court in order to challenge the arbitral award. It is only when a party's claim is frivolous and does not pursue a legitimate goal that such an action can be considered to be in breach of confidentiality.

Thus, it is understandable that, in *Nafimco*, the Court of Appeal found no breach **170** of confidentiality due to the filing of the appeal. Indeed, the mere fact of initiating a court proceeding in order to challenge an arbitral award cannot be regarded as a violation of confidentiality duties, unless an abuse of process is found. This may be the reason why the Court of Appeal invited Foster to prove the existence and foundation of the duty of confidentiality in French international arbitration law.

Changes to France's domestic and international arbitration law were adopted in **171** 2011 (Décret N 2011-48 of 13 January 2011). Under the new law, the issue of confidentiality is treated differently in domestic and international arbitrations. While domestic arbitration proceedings are subject to confidentiality according to Art. 1464 of the Décret N 2011-48, this is not the case for international arbitration proceedings.[66] Indeed, contrary to domestic arbitration, there is no express provision on confidentiality in the section dealing with international arbitration.[67] In addition, Art. 1506 of the French Code of Civil Procedure, which lists the provisions on domestic arbitration which also apply to international arbitration, excludes application of the

---

[64]Société National Company for Fishing and Marketing 'Nafimco' v. Société Foster Wheeler Trading Company AG, Cour d'appel de Paris (1ère Ch. C), 22 January 2004.

[65]See below Sect. 3.5.

[66]Loquin (2015), para 323.

[67]French Code of Civil Procedure, Articles 1504 to 1527.

last paragraph of Art. 1464 of the Décret N 2011-48 containing the provision on confidentiality.[68]

172   Some legal scholars consider that the French legislator intended to leave the issue of confidentiality in international arbitrations to the parties (via an express agreement) by declining to provide a provision on confidentiality applying to international arbitrations. According to this view, absent such an agreement, international arbitral proceedings are not deemed to be confidential in France.[69]

3.2.3.8 Switzerland

173   Chapter 12 of the Swiss Private International Law Act does not contain any provisions on the confidentiality of arbitration proceedings. Moreover, there is no reported case law on the existence of an implied duty of confidentiality. Some Swiss legal commentators contend that the parties have an implied obligation to respect the confidentiality of the arbitration, but others assert the contrary.

174   In the late 1980s–early 1990s, arbitration proceedings were generally considered confidential and the parties were thought to be bound by an implied duty of confidentiality originating from the arbitration agreement.[70] The following citation from the treatise of Andreas Bucher published in 1988 reflects the contemporaneous predominant view on the confidentiality being an essential feature of the arbitration:

> Confidentiality is an essential element of the arbitration. The parties are often concerned about confidentiality because publicity in relation to an arbitration proceeding might cause moral and financial damages. Observance of confidentiality principle is an obligation inherent in an arbitration agreement. It should be admitted therefore that an arbitral tribunal has competence to order a party to refrain from any publication with regard to the arbitration, and in particular if a party presents a one-sided account outside of the arbitration proceeding.[71]

175   At the same period, Andreas Bucher and Pierre-Yves Tschanz argued that the parties had an implied obligation under the arbitration agreement to respect the confidentiality of arbitration.[72] In addition, according to these two legal scholars, in certain cases, when disclosure of information from the arbitration had already resulted or could result in expanding or aggravating the dispute, the confidentiality

---

[68]Loquin (2015), para 323.

[69]Gaillard and de Lapasse (2011), p. 184.

[70]See, for example, Bucher (1988), para 205; Bucher and Tschanz (1988), para 169.

[71]Bucher (1988), para. 205, with other references. Loose translation from French, here is the citation of the original: 'La confidentialité est un aspect essentiel de l'arbitrage. Les parties y sont en general très sensibles, car une publicité relative au contentieux arbitral est susceptible de leur causer un prejudice moral et économique. Le respect du principe de la confidentialité constitue une obligation inhérente à la convention d'arbitrage. L'on doit donc admettre la competence du tribunal arbitral d'ordonner qu'une partie s'abstienne de toute publication relative au differend, notamment losqu'elle tend à presenter unilatéralement son point de vue en dehors de l'instance arbitrale.'

[72]Bucher and Tschanz (1988), para 169.

obligation could originate from the principle of good faith.[73] According to this principle, the parties have an obligation to refrain from taking any action that could worsen the dispute or provoke any undue delay of the arbitration proceeding.[74]

However, during the same period, and already before the *Esso/BHP* case, Thomas **176** Rüede and Reimer Hadenfeldt opined that a confidentiality duty cannot be derived from the private nature of arbitration proceedings.[75]

Today there is still no consensus among Swiss scholars. This lack of consensus is **177** stated, for example, in a collective study by Jolles, Stark-Traber and de Cediel, in which the authors lay out the existing controversy on confidentiality:

> It is, however, controversial among authors whether an arbitration agreement that is silent on the question of confidentiality may be supplemented by the arbitrators either according to the parties' hypothetical intent or with a rule determined by the arbitrators in the manner of a legislator (*modo legislatoris*).[76]

The authors specify that the former prevailing view that parties are bound by an implied obligation of confidentiality arising out of the arbitration agreement is now questioned.[77]

The majority of Swiss legal scholars still favour the existence of an implied **178** obligation of confidentiality. Thus, besides Andreas Bucher, Jean-François Poudret and Sébastien Besson also defend the existence of an implied duty of confidentiality, arguing that it flows from the arbitration agreement.[78] They admit, however, that the mere existence of an arbitration agreement does not allow one to define the scope of its confidentiality obligations.[79] Marco Stacher generally agrees with this opinion, arguing that an arbitration agreement implies, to a limited extent, the existence of a confidentiality duty relating to the arbitration proceedings.[80]

Bernhard Berger and Franz Kellerhals consider that, in the absence of an express **179** agreement and relevant applicable provisions, the issue of whether a duty of confidentiality exists depends on the legitimate expectations of the parties. They presume, however, that '*the parties will usually have the legitimate expectation that any details about the subject-matter of the case and in particular any documents established and produced by them during the proceedings (written submissions, witness statements, documentary evidence, correspondence with the arbitral tribunal etc.) will be kept confidential and will be used only in connection with the arbitration*'.[81]

---

[73]Bucher and Tschanz (1988), para 169.

[74]Bucher and Tschanz (1988), para 169; ATF 111 Ia 259, 2a; ATF 109 Ia 83, 2a; ATF 108 Ia 201.

[75]Rüede and Hadenfeldt (1993), pp. 32–33.

[76]Jolles et al. (2013), p. 134.

[77]Jolles et al. (2013), p. 151.

[78]Bucher (2011), para 3.

[79]Poudret and Besson (2007), para 369.

[80]Stacher (2007), para 413.

[81]Berger and Kellerhals (2015), para 1234.

180   The existence of an implied duty of confidentiality is denied by such authors as Dessemontet, Müller and Ritz. They argue that there is no implied duty of confidentiality flowing from the mere fact of entering into an arbitration agreement. Thus, François Dessemontet argues that there is no presumed confidentiality, but that the party claiming confidentiality needs to prove the existence of such a duty with respect to the specific materials or information.[82] Dessemontet, however, primarily focuses on the specific issue of trade secrets in arbitration proceedings.

181   Christoph Müller argues that there can be no implied duty of confidentiality in international commercial arbitration in the absence of relevant provisions in international treaties and national laws.[83] He does not agree that a general principle of good faith could be a basis for the duty of confidentiality, as the meaning of this principle is too vague—not allowing one to define the scope of the confidentiality obligation.[84]

182   According to Philipp Ritz,[85] there is no implied duty of confidentiality flowing from an arbitration agreement. His conclusion is that '*the mere fact that the parties have agreed to arbitrate disputes does not itself establish a confidentiality obligation*'. In rare circumstances, and provided that Swiss law applies, Ritz has opined that Art. 28 CC against infringement of personality rights can be used for the protection of trade secrets.[86]

183   Thus, Swiss law allows some flexibility with regard to the existence of a confidentiality duty over the arbitration proceedings. There is indeed no specific provision on confidentiality of arbitration proceedings in the Swiss PILA, and the Swiss Federal Court has not yet ruled on this issue. As to the legal scholars, their opinions are still greatly divided.

3.2.3.9   Arbitral Practice and Analysis

184   As we have seen, national courts and legal scholars in several countries disagree about the existence of a duty of confidentiality in arbitration proceedings. Putting aside the rules and court practices at the national level, from an international perspective, is it possible to infer the existence of an implicit confidentiality obligation from generally accepted arbitration practice as customary law?

185   As discussed above (Sect. 2.6.2), the role of 'arbitral precedent' is not clearly defined. Therefore, the effect of a particular decision or a series of similar decisions issued by arbitral tribunals is unclear. The fact that awards are published only

---

[82]Dessemontet (1996), p. 31.

[83]Müller (2005), pp. 217–226.

[84]Müller (2005), p. 225.

[85]Philipp Ritz has extensively studied this topic in his PhD thesis entitled 'Die Geheimhaltung im Schiedsverfahren nach schweizerischem Recht' and his article 'Privacy and Confidentiality Obligation on Parties in Arbitration under Swiss Law'.

[86]Ritz (2010), p. 239.

sporadically, and are therefore not known to the persons not involved in a particular arbitration case, does not help to develop a uniform practice.

One should not completely disregard prior arbitral decisions, however. Even if they do not have a binding effect, prior arbitral decisions can influence subsequent arbitral practices in other ways. Most arbitrators are designated because of their experience. Their decisions will necessarily be influenced by this experience, particularly in areas where neither the applicable law and rules nor the parties' agreement provide clear answers. A good example of such a decision is an ICC case reported by Yves Fortier.[87] In this case, an arbitral tribunal operating under the ICC rules enjoined the parties to respect the confidentiality of the proceedings, even in the absence of applicable rules regulating confidentiality obligations. **186**

The Tribunal was asked to make an order on an alleged breach of confidentiality in an arbitration proceeding conducted in Paris under the ICC Rules. The parties alleged that there were information leaks from the proceeding, apparently coming from both sides.[88] Although there was no contractual or legal basis for a duty of confidentiality, and based on their own experience, the arbitrators called on the parties to respect the confidentiality of the proceedings: **187**

> While the confidentiality of ICC proceedings is not mentioned in the ICC Rules [...] it has been the experience of the members of this Tribunal and their colleagues whom they have consulted who often act as ICC arbitrators that, as a matter of principle, arbitration proceedings have a confidential character which must be respected by everyone who participates in such proceedings... We invite both parties, in the future to respect the confidential character of the proceedings.[89]

This case shows that an arbitral tribunal can dispose of its discretionary powers and order the parties to an arbitration proceeding to respect the confidentiality of the proceeding, even in the absence of applicable rules regulating confidentiality, and apparently even without the express agreement of the parties. This does not mean that in a similar situation, another arbitral tribunal seated in Paris under the ICC Rules would necessarily decide in the same way. However, the reported decision provides guidance. It demonstrates a possible approach in a similar situation. **188**

In line with this decision, Serge Lazareff strongly believes that confidentiality goes to the very nature of arbitration, although conceding that there might be legitimate questions as to the origins of this duty. He states that he is '*utterly convinced that confidentiality is an inherent part of international commercial arbitration, subject to the sole exception of absolute and overriding public interest*'.[90] By contrast, Andreas Furrer thinks that given the '*diverse legal backgrounds of international business arbitrations*', as well as different expectations of those **189**

---

[87]Fortier (1999), pp. 132–133.

[88]Fortier (1999), pp. 132–133.

[89]Fortier (1999), pp. 132–133.

[90]Lazareff (2009), p. 81.

involved in an arbitration, agreement is unlikely on a mandatory principle of confidentiality, based exclusively on customary law.[91]

190   We have seen that many jurisdictions and arbitration institutions introduce rules on confidentiality of arbitration proceedings. Also, it has been demonstrated by the example of Australia, where the regulation of the issue of confidentiality changed several times over the last 25 years to finally rule in favour of the obligation of confidentiality, that the current trend is towards confidentiality rather than non-confidentiality. However, as long as there is no consensus, the parties' obligation of confidentiality cannot be established as a *lex mercatoria* principle. Thus, the issue of the existence of the parties' implied duty of confidentiality needs to be decided by each jurisdiction.

191   We have seen that several jurisdictions, such as Australia, England, Singapore, Sweden and the United States have already taken a position on the issue of confidentiality, while Switzerland and France have not definitively resolved the issue. Notwithstanding these differences, however, we think that a compromise can be found. In our opinion, *de lege ferenda* this compromise could be the recognition of an obligation of confidentiality subject to a certain number of exceptions.[92] We will set out our arguments and a detailed proposal in the section dealing with the possibility of uniform rules on confidentiality (see below Sect. 3.7).

192   In our opinion, the parties' implied obligation of confidentiality should already be recognised in such jurisdictions as France and Switzerland. While we will provide our arguments in favour of confidentiality in further sections,[93] the problem remains in identifying the legal basis of the parties' obligation of confidentiality, in the absence of express rules and agreement. As we will see below, the main difficulties in recognizing an implied duty of confidentiality came from the fact that there was no clear regulation of this issue and, in particular, because exceptions to the obligation of confidentiality were not clearly defined.[94] In our view, these are some of the main reasons why the basis of the duty of confidentiality was questioned.

193   Once the necessity of regulating in favour of confidentiality is recognised, the issue of the basis of a confidentiality duty will become less problematic. We agree that there is no perfect solution between the many proposed options. In our view, the most preferable is the one saying that confidentiality is an implied obligation arising out of the arbitration agreement. Indeed, one can hardly deny the private nature of arbitration and the fact that the parties generally enter into an arbitration agreement with the expectation that their arbitration proceedings would be confidential. Although an implied duty of confidentiality does not allow to determine the scope of the confidentiality obligation, it has the benefit of protecting the parties from bad faith disclosures not justified by any legitimate interest. Depending on the circumstances, the general principle of good faith and the protection of personality rights

---

[91]Furrer (2008), p. 807.

[92]See, in particular, Sect. 3.2.4.

[93]See, in particular, Sects. 3.2.4 and 3.7.

[94]See, in particular, Sects. 3.2.4 and 3.7.

provisions[95] can also be invoked as other sources of the parties' obligation of confidentiality.

3.2.4 Balance of the Interests Involved and Analysis of the Arguments for and Against Confidentiality

3.2.4.1 Introduction

Given the controversy of the subject, it is important to examine the main interests involved and to analyse arguments for and against the parties' obligation of confidentiality. **194**

3.2.4.2 Balance of the Various Interests Involved

3.2.4.2.1 Parties' Interests to Maintain the Privacy of the Dispute

There are many reasons why the parties may not wish the details of their dispute to be publicly known or be disclosed to third parties. Since the reason for initiating an arbitration is a dispute between given parties, each party will try to reveal the most disadvantageous facts about the other party. Thus, all parties would generally be interested in keeping confidential at least some information relating to their arbitration. A party accused of not respecting its contractual obligations would not want its reputation to be damaged in the eyes of its existing and potential customers and counter-parties. The losing party would be particularly interested in keeping confidential details and results of its arbitration proceeding. Also, a party would certainly want to keep certain internal information, including but not limited to trade secrets and know-how, secret from its competitors. **195**

Consequently, the parties have an interest to maintain privacy of their dispute. This is the core problem of confidentiality in international commercial arbitration, its *raison d'être*. **196**

3.2.4.2.2 Interests Requiring Disclosure

The question is what interests requiring disclosure of confidential information can be involved. *First*, the public interest may require disclosure of confidential information. The public interest comes into play if arbitral proceedings affect third parties' interest or involve the functioning of a state.[96] As opposed to investment arbitration, **197**

---

[95] See below Sect. 6.2.2.1 discussing the protection of personality rights under Swiss law.
[96] See, for example, Tweeddale (2005), p. 69; Gu (2004), p. 7; Tjio (2009), p. 13.

there is generally no public interest involved in international commercial arbitration disputes. In some situations, however, the public interest can be invoked in commercial arbitrations as well. As we will see below, in some cases, the parties should be allowed to disclose confidential information when it is required by the public interest (see below Sect. 5.3.4). Therefore, the public interest exception should be admitted, but confidentiality can still be recognised as a general principle.

198   *Second*, in the same section dealing with exceptions to the duty of confidentiality, we will also see that, in certain cases, the interests of a party can justify disclosure of confidential information (see below Sects. 5.3.2 and 5.3.3). It will be the case, for example, if a party needs to disclose certain information relating to an arbitration to enforce an arbitral award. The circumstances allowing a party to disclose information relating to an arbitration will be discussed in detail below, but the existence of exceptions should not prevent confidentiality from being admitted as a general principle.

199   *Third*, we will also see below that the interests of justice can require disclosure of arbitration materials (see below Sect. 5.3.3). Thus, the interests of justice will justify the use of evidence from an arbitration in a court proceeding to avoid the court to be misled. As will be discussed, this should be another exception to the general rule of confidentiality.

200   *Finally*, we will see in the section dealing with confidentiality regarding arbitral awards that systematic publication of arbitral awards can be in the interests of the system as a whole, in particular, for creating a consistent arbitral case law and for enhancing transparency of the arbitration (see below Sect. 4.4.5). We will also see that systematic publication of arbitral awards can be achieved without compromising the parties' interests in the confidentiality of arbitral proceedings.

201   As a general remark, it should be mentioned that public interests are more important in state court proceedings as administration of justice is a state function financed by taxpayers. The principle of openness of court proceedings aims to ensure the equal treatment of the parties, but also to allow citizens to control the independence, the impartiality and the proper administration of justice.[97] Thus, each state is responsible for creating an efficient and transparent system of justice. The situation is fundamentally different in arbitration as it is a private consent-based system receiving normally no public financing and existing because the parties choose to submit the resolution of their dispute to an independent third party and to pay for these services. This obviously gives more weight to the parties' private interest.

---

[97]Würzburger (2014), para 4.

3.2.4.3 Arguments for and Against Confidentiality as an Implied Obligation

3.2.4.3.1 Parties' Expectations of Confidentiality and Attractiveness of Arbitration

Two important and interrelated arguments in favour of confidentiality are (i) parties' **202** expectations on confidentiality of arbitration and (ii) the fact that many parties choose arbitration because they believe it to be confidential.

As we have seen above,[98] arbitration has traditionally been viewed as confiden- **203** tial. The assumption of confidentiality existed at least until 1995, when the High Court of Australia issued a decision in *Esso/BHP etc. v. Plowman*.[99] Due to this long-existing assumption and because arbitration is a private dispute settlement where hearings are held privately and awards are not systematically published, the parties usually have legitimate expectations that the arbitration proceeding will be confidential.

According to a survey conducted by Queen Mary University of London, the **204** second most frequently listed valuable characteristic of international arbitration for the in-house counsel subgroup was "confidentiality and privacy".[100] This shows that many parties expect arbitration proceedings to be confidential and opt for arbitration for the reason of its confidentiality. Thus, rejecting confidentiality could damage the reputation of arbitration and reduce its attractiveness.

3.2.4.3.2 Correlation Between Privacy of Hearings and Confidentiality

As we will see below, privacy of hearings, as opposed to confidentiality of arbitra- **205** tion proceedings, is non-controversial.[101] Although the two notions are different, there is a correlation between them as privacy of hearings primarily serves the goal of maintaining confidentiality of arbitration. Thus, the fact that privacy of hearings is guaranteed in order to maintain confidentiality should be one more argument in favour of confidentiality of arbitration proceedings.

---

[98]See, for example, Sect. 3.2.3.

[99]Esso Australia Resources Ltd. and Others v. Sidney James Plowman and Others, Arbitration International, Volume 11 No. 3, 1995, 235.

[100]Queen Mary University of London in partnership with White & Case 2015 International Arbitration Survey, 6.

[101]See below Sect. 4.5.

3.2.4.3.3 Differences in Regulation of Confidentiality

206   One might argue that confidentiality of arbitration cannot be achieved because there are irreconcilable differences in regulation of this issue in different jurisdictions. However, as we will see below, the existing differences of regulation are not irreconcilable.

207   Thus, in the Australian *Esso/BHP* case, the parties seeking disclosure of information on the price increase were public entities supplying gas and electricity to the general public. They asked for permission to disclose this information to the Minister of Energy, the Government and the public and the disclosure sought was thus responding to the public interest. Therefore, in this case, we think that the judges could have affirmed the existence of an implied duty of confidentiality while recognising a public interest exception.

208   We have also seen that although the Australian common law denies the existence of an implied duty of confidentiality, the regulation provided by the AIAA has significantly changed in the last 20 years, each time to move towards more confidentiality in international commercial arbitration.[102] According to the 2015 amendments of the AIAA, the parties are bound by a duty of confidentiality unless they decide to 'opt-out' from the AIAA confidentiality provisions.[103]

209   In the French *Nafimco* case, the Court of Appeal could have held in favour of the existence of an implied duty of confidentiality while allowing a party to disclose certain arbitration materials to pursue its legitimate rights. In this case, a party was challenging the arbitral award and the appeal was not abusive or frivolous. As we will see below,[104] this case is one of the generally admitted exceptions to the principle of confidentiality.

210   In the Swedish *Bulbank* case, the Stockholm City Court went too far by declaring the arbitration agreement and the final award invalid as a consequence of the confidentiality breach. This decision was overturned by the Svea Court of Appeal which found that the parties could not be bound by a duty of confidentiality, unless they concluded an express agreement on confidentiality. We think that the Svea Court of Appeal could have overturned the Stockholm City Court decision through a different reasoning. It could have admitted the existence of an implied duty of confidentiality, in which case A.I. Trade Finance would be in breach of its confidentiality duty. However, as we will see below, not every breach of confidentiality duty should amount to a fundamental breach.[105] In our opinion, it should be the case only if the parties agreed that confidentiality was a condition to the arbitration agreement or if there are other serious reasons to believe that such a breach results in a substantial deprivation of the benefits of the arbitration agreement to any party.

---

[102]Shirlow (2015), pp. 1–2; see above Sect. 3.2.3.4.

[103]Art, 22(2) AIAA; Nottage (2017), pp. 1–2; Shirlow (2015), p. 2.

[104]See below Sect. 5.3.2.

[105]See below Sect. 6.2.3.

Also, we think that even a fundamental breach of the arbitration agreement should not result in annulment of the arbitral award.[106]

In the US *Panhandle* case, the District Court of Delaware rejected PEPL's application for a protective order against the disclosure of certain arbitration materials. In this case, the Court had to weigh the parties' interest in the confidentiality of the arbitration materials against the interests of justice—coupled with the interests of the Federal Government in its role of litigant requesting disclosure. The Court ruled in favour of the second interest. First, it considered that PEPL failed to establish the basis of the confidentiality obligation. Second, the Court assumed for the purpose of the argument that there was an obligation of confidentiality, but found that PEPL failed to provide specific examples of the hardship that it would suffer as a result of this disclosure. In our opinion, the Court could have reached the same decision by following just the second set of reasoning. **211**

Therefore, the differences in regulation of confidentiality are not irreconcilable. Although in the cases mentioned above state courts denied the existence of an implied duty of confidentiality, they could have reached the same conclusions while admitting an implied duty of confidentiality. Also, the Australian example shows that the general trend should be towards introducing a provision on the parties' obligation of confidentiality into national arbitration laws. **212**

3.2.4.3.4 Legal Uncertainty

The divergence in regulation of confidentiality in different jurisdictions results in legal uncertainty for the parties. Some jurisdictions have already opted for the existence of a confidentiality duty or its absence, but others are still undecided. Both situations, i.e. the absence of uniformity between different jurisdictions and the absence of clear rules within one jurisdiction, can result in legal uncertainty. **213**

On the one hand, since international arbitration is a mixture of different legal cultures, a conflict of laws may arise. It will be the case if the laws of two jurisdictions are potentially applicable and one of them opted for an implied duty of confidentiality while the other opted for its absence.[107] **214**

On the other hand, the applicable law can be silent as to whether the parties are bound by a confidentiality duty. Let's assume there is an arbitration with a seat in Lausanne and applicable ICC Rules; the parties reached no agreement on confidentiality. Given the absence of a specific provision in the ICC Rules and absence of the parties' express agreement, the Swiss *lex arbitri* will regulate this issue. However, as we have seen above, it is not clear whether the parties are bound by a confidentiality obligation under Swiss law. **215**

The only solution for avoiding these situations of legal uncertainty would be to find a uniform approach on regulation of the parties' obligation of confidentiality. **216**

---

[106]See below Sect. 6.2.3.

[107]For more details on the applicable law, see below Sect. 3.2.5.

3.2.4.3.5 Myriad of Exceptions to Confidentiality

217 Some argue that confidentiality of arbitration cannot be admitted as a principle because of the difficulty to determine exceptions to the duty of confidentiality. Thus, in the Australian *Esso/BHP* case, the High Court considered that the existence of an implied duty of confidentiality should be denied, in particular, because complete confidentiality could not be achieved as there could be many circumstances allowing a party to disclose information relating to arbitration.[108] Also, the Singapore High Court reasoned that the absence of a provision on an obligation of confidentiality was due, in particular, to the existence of many exceptions to the duty of confidentiality.[109] In England, the lawmakers did not introduce a provision on confidentiality as a general principle into the English Arbitration Act of 1996 because of the 'the myriad exceptions to these principles [of confidentiality]'.[110]

218   We agree that a complete confidentiality cannot always be achieved, because, as we will see below in the section dealing with exceptions to the duty of confidentiality, there are certain cases where a party should be allowed to disclose confidential information (see below Sect. 3.5). This, however, does not mean that confidentiality as a general principle should not be recognised. This only implies that exceptions to the parties' duty of confidentiality should be clearly identified.

3.2.5 Applicable Law

219 In a given arbitration proceeding, which law shall apply to the parties' obligation of confidentiality? There can be several options. The applicable law will depend, in particular, on the source of the parties' duty of confidentiality. But as we have seen above, there is much controversy about the source of this duty in the absence of express agreement and applicable arbitration rules on confidentiality. In any case, some possible applicable laws include: the law governing the arbitration agreement, *lex arbitri, lex fori* and the law applicable to the underlying contract.[111] Sometimes the applicable law depends on the conflict of laws of the forum, which also contributes to uncertainty regarding the applicable law.

220   *First*, if the source of the confidentiality obligation is the arbitration agreement, whether because the parties included a specific provision on confidentiality in their arbitration agreement, or because confidentiality is considered to be an implied term of the agreement to arbitrate, the law governing the arbitration agreement will most

---

[108]Esso Australia Resources Ltd. and Others v. Sidney James Plowman and Others, Arbitration International, Volume 11 No. 3, 1995, 244. See above Sect. 3.2.3.5.

[109]AAY and others v AAZ AS, High Court, Suit [Y], Case No. [2009] SGHC 142, 15 June 2009, 54. See above Sect. 3.2.3.3.

[110]Report on the Arbitration Bill, paras. 11 to 16, in Merkin and Flannery (2014), pp. 433–444.

[111]Born (2014), pp. 2812–2813; Lew (2011), p. 6; Poudret and Besson (2007), para 369.

likely be applied.[112] Unless the parties designated the law governing the arbitration agreement, the competent authority will have to choose between the law governing the contract and the law of the seat of the arbitration.[113]

Faced with such a choice, we think that the competent authority should opt for the law of the seat of the arbitration. If a confidentiality obligation finds its source in the arbitration agreement, the existence and the scope of such an obligation is mostly connected to procedural issues of the arbitration. When the parties chose their seat, they should have assumed that the law of the seat of the arbitration would govern procedural issues related to the arbitration. Thus, it is the law of the seat that has the closest connection in this situation. **221**

Second, if the confidentiality obligation stems from the law governing the arbitration (*lex arbitri*), relevant provisions of the *lex arbitri* will apply. **222**

Third, if the parties' confidentiality obligation finds its source in one of the contractual obligations contained in the underlying contract and not related to the arbitration agreement, the law of the underlying contract should apply to such an obligation. **223**

Fourth, when a state court is requested to enforce the arbitral award or to grant interim measures, the *lex fori* is applicable. Since the relevant state court decision will in most cases be published, there is a risk that confidential information from the arbitral proceedings will be disclosed. The question of whether and how the relevant court decision will be published is subject exclusively to the *lex fori*. **224**

Fifth, if an alleged breach of confidentiality leads to a tort claim, the law governing tort liability will apply.[114] Other examples of possible applicable laws include the law governing the corporate obligations of a party, and the law of a country where a party is engaged in certain types of activities or transactions.[115] **225**

These are just a few examples of the laws which might apply to different aspects of confidentiality. Even from this short analysis, one can see that there is a certain amount of risk related to confidentiality obligations for the parties searching for legal certainty. In addition to making an express agreement on confidentiality (or non-confidentiality), the parties could reduce the risk of legal uncertainty by agreeing on carefully drafted choice of forum (or arbitration) and choice of law clauses. It would, however, be difficult for these clauses alone to cover all possible situations related to confidentiality. Moreover, it is impossible to exclude mandatory provisions of the law, if any, which will apply to the relevant question of confidentiality. **226**

---

[112]Born (2014), pp. 2812–2813.

[113]Blackaby et al. (2015), para 3.33.

[114]De Ly et al. (2012), p. 368.

[115]De Ly et al. (2012), p. 368.

3.2.6 Intermediary Conclusions

227 The debate over the existence of an implied duty of confidentiality in arbitration is far from over. Legal practice in different countries varies, and legal scholars are greatly divided on the issue. Some courts and scholars have favoured an implied duty of confidentiality. According to this view, the parties should be bound by a confidentiality obligation even if there is no specific source imposing it.

228 But even within this view, there are different opinions as to the origins of the implied duty. The prevailing opinion holds that the parties implicitly agree on a confidentiality duty by the very fact of entering into an arbitration agreement. Another common opinion is that arbitration proceedings are by their very nature confidential. Some authors also consider that the legitimate expectations of the parties regarding confidentiality of the arbitration proceeding serve as a sufficient basis for a duty of confidentiality. Finally, in some common law jurisdictions (England and Singapore), judges have found that the confidentiality duty originates in substantive law.

229 On the other hand, other courts and legal scholars do not favour the existence of an implied duty of confidentiality. In this alternate view, parties to an arbitration do not have a confidentiality obligation unless they have expressly agreed on confidentiality, or if there is a specific provision on confidentiality in the applicable rules or laws.

230 As for regulation in the seven jurisdictions discussed above, we have seen that the existence of an implied duty of confidentiality is undisputed in England and Singapore; rejected (if the parties opt-out from the AIAA confidentiality provisions and in the absence of express agreement on confidentiality) in Australia, Sweden and the U. S.; and still under discussion in France and in Switzerland. This divergence results in a significant risk of legal uncertainty for the parties to an arbitration proceeding. To avoid this risk, the parties can enter into an express agreement on confidentiality or they can adopt arbitration rules containing a provision on confidentiality. However, in the future, we think it would be more judicious to have a uniform approach on the issue of confidentiality in different jurisdictions. As demonstrated by the Australian example, the way to move forward should be towards greater confidentiality and this can be achieved through introducing confidentiality provisions into national arbitration law.

231 In our opinion, this uniform approach should be based on universally recognising the parties' duty of confidentiality. Arbitration exists as a method of dispute resolution only because the parties choose to submit their dispute to an arbitration. One of the reasons the parties make this choice is because they believe arbitration proceedings to be confidential. Denying confidentiality might have a negative impact on the attractiveness of arbitration. As to the differences in regulation of confidentiality by different jurisdictions, they are not irreconcilable. One of the difficulties that some lawmakers and judges saw in introducing confidentiality as a general principle was that there were many circumstances allowing a party to disclose information relating to an arbitration. While we agree that a complete confidentiality cannot be achieved, confidentiality can still be established as a general principle if exceptions to the parties' duty of confidentiality are clearly identified.

The parties have an interest in maintaining privacy of their dispute. Since **232** arbitration is a private consent-based system of dispute resolution, the interests of the parties should prevail. When the public interest comes into play because arbitral proceedings affect third parties' interest or involve the functioning of a state, disclosure of certain information related to an arbitration should be admitted, but as an exception to the principle of confidentiality.

Thus, *de lege ferenda*, we think that parties to arbitration should have an **233** obligation of confidentiality subject to certain exceptions. In our opinion, the parties' implied duty of confidentiality should already be recognised in Switzerland and France, where the regulation of this issue is not clear-cut.

As to the law applicable to the parties' duty of confidentiality, depending on the **234** situation, there can be several options: the law governing the arbitration agreement, *lex arbitri*, *lex fori*, the law applicable to the underlying contract, etc. For the parties searching for legal certainty, it would be advisable to make an express agreement on confidentiality (or non-confidentiality) and to draft a choice of forum and choice of law clauses.

3.3 Arbitrators' Duty of Confidentiality

3.3.1 Introduction

Like judges in the state system of justice, arbitrators are bound by a duty of **235** confidentiality.[116] This may seem surprising, given that the professional activities of arbitrators are generally not supervised by the state and not subject to state regulation. Arbitrators—unlike judges—are not vested with judicial powers by the state. The duty of confidentiality that binds arbitrators arises originally from the contract between the arbitrators and the parties who designate and compensate them. It is the contract that typically confers on arbitrators a quasi-judicial role, turning them into private judges. The arbitrator's duty of confidentiality is therefore normally *contractual*.

In the present section, we will first review the source of the arbitrators' duty of **236** confidentiality. Second, we will analyse its precise scope.

---

[116]See, for example, Girsberger and Voser (2016), para 842; Born (2014), pp. 2002–2005.

3.3.2   Basis for the Duty of Confidentiality

237   As mentioned above, the arbitrator's duty of confidentiality derives, in most cases, from the contract. But it is also interesting to explore whether there are any other sources for the arbitrator's duty of confidentiality. Rules on the status of arbitrators and the scope of their duties can be found in national legislation, arbitration rules, ethical codes and express contractual provisions. We will start by analysing the regulations provided in national legislation and will then turn to arbitration rules and ethical rules of professional bodies and associations, finishing with a brief overview of express contractual provisions.

3.3.2.1   National Legislation

238   First, we must look into national arbitration laws, which can contain provisions on the arbitrator's duty of confidentiality. Other domestic legislation, such as the law on contracts, can be of relevance. This is due to the contractual nature of the relationship between arbitrators and parties.[117]

3.3.2.1.1   National Arbitration Laws

239   Although many national arbitration laws do not address the arbitrator's duty of confidentiality, some contain specific rules. Thus, Art. 24(2) of the Spanish Arbitration Act provides that the arbitrators are bound by a duty of confidentiality regarding the information coming to their knowledge in the course of the arbitral proceedings.

240   Art. 4(5) of the Law of the Republic of Kazakhstan on International Arbitration of 2004 has a similar provision. It prohibits arbitrators from disclosing information *'which became known to them in the course of arbitration proceedings'*. In addition, the arbitrators are immune from being called as witnesses with respect to the information they learned when serving as arbitrators.[118]

241   Rule 26 of Schedule 1 to the Scottish Arbitration Act of 2010 regulates the issue of confidentiality. Rule 26(1) in combination with Rule 26(4) prohibits arbitrators from disclosing any information relating to the dispute, the arbitral proceedings, and the award. In addition, in accordance with Rules 26(2) and 26(3) of Schedule 1 to the Scottish Arbitration Act, the arbitral tribunal must inform the parties of their confidentiality obligations and must take reasonable steps to prevent unauthorised disclosure of confidential information by any third party involved in the conduct of the arbitration.

---

[117]Gaillard and Savage (1999), p. 598.

[118]Art. 4(5) of the Law of the Republic of Kazakhstan on International Arbitration of 2004.

Section 23C(2) AIAA imposes upon the arbitral tribunal, as a general rule, an **242** obligation of confidentiality regarding the arbitral proceedings. The parties can, however, 'opt-out' from these provisions.[119]

3.3.2.1.2 Contract Law Provisions

Most authors admit that notwithstanding the quasi-judicial role of arbitrators, the **243** nature of the relationship between the parties and the arbitrators is contractual.[120] The situation may, however, vary depending on the relevant jurisdiction.

Under Swiss law, for example, a relationship between the parties and the arbi- **244** trator is considered to be a *sui generis* contract, a so-called "receptum arbitri" (*Schiedsrichtervertrag*).[121] The Swiss Supreme Court considers that the nature of the relationship between the arbitrator and the parties is contractual; the contractual relationship arises from procedural law, although private substantive law can be applied by analogy.[122] As explained by Berger and Kellerhals, the mutual rights and obligations of the arbitrator and the parties are determined by private law, unless they *'directly arise from the arbitration agreement or the applicable arbitration law (lex arbitri)'*.[123]

Legal provisions on the agency contract, i.e., Articles 394 ff CO,[124] regulate the **245** main aspects of the relationship between the arbitrator and the parties.[125] The CO does not contain a specific provision on the agent's duty of confidentiality. Art. 398 (2) CO nevertheless imposes an obligation of diligent and faithful performance which includes an obligation of confidentiality, usually called a 'duty of discretion' (*devoir de discrétion*).[126]

Under Swiss law, the agent's responsibility is, in principle, regulated by the same **246** rules as the employee's responsibility (Art. 398(1) CO). Therefore, we should also refer to Art. 321a(4) CO, which normally applies to an employment relationship. Based on this provision, an arbitrator has an obligation not to reveal confidential

---

[119]Art, 22(2) AIAA; Nottage (2017), pp. 1–2; Shirlow (2015), p. 2.

[120]Gaillard and Savage (1999), p. 598; Schöldström (1998), pp. 25–27; Furrer (2008), p. 811; Jolles et al. (2013), pp. 136–137.

[121]ATF 136 III 597, recital 5; TF 4A_490/2013, 28.01.2014, recital 3.2.3.1; Jolles et al. (2013), p. 137; Berger and Kellerhals (2015), para 963.

[122]ATF 111 Ia 72, recital 2C.

[123]Berger and Kellerhals (2015), para 963.

[124]It should be noted, however, that not all provisions regulating the agency contract apply to arbitral contracts (Voser and Fischer 2013, p. 53).

[125]Furrer (2008), p. 811; Meyer-Hauser (2004), p. 71; Hoffet (1991), p. 213; Berger and Kellerhals (2015), para 964.

[126]Bucher and Tschanz (1988), para 116; Furrer (2008), p. 811; Meyer-Hauser (2004), p. 71; Jolles et al. (2013), p. 137; Werro (2012b), Commentary of Art. 398 CO, paras 23–24.

information to any third party. The arbitrator and the parties can, however, derogate from this rule at least to some extent, since it is not mandatory.[127]

247   As for the law applicable to the arbitrator's status and to the arbitrator's relationship with the parties, according to the majority of legal scholars, this should be the *lex arbitri*.[128] Therefore, in our opinion, the *lex arbitri* should also apply to the issue of the arbitrator's duty of confidentiality.

3.3.2.1.3 Other National Law Provisions

248   The arbitrator's duty of confidentiality can also originate from other national law provisions. For example, in France, such a duty finds its source in the Criminal Code which provides in Art. 226-13 that a person having disclosed the confidential information that was entrusted to him because of his profession or temporary mission will be punished by 1-year in prison and a EUR 15,000 fine.[129] Serving as an arbitrator falls under the scope of this provision as the arbitrator is entrusted with a temporary mission.

3.3.2.2 International Arbitration Rules and Ethical Rules of Professional Bodies and Associations

249   More and more institutional rules contain express provisions on the arbitrator's duty of confidentiality. Such provisions can be found, for example, in the Swiss, the DIS, the WIPO, the ICAC, the SIAC, the HKIAC, the JCAA and the AAA Rules.[130] For example, Art. 39(1) of the SIAC Rules provides that '*any arbitrator, including an Emergency Arbitrator… shall at all times treat all materials relating to the proceedings and the Award as confidential*'.

250   If the applicable arbitration rules do not specifically regulate the issue of the arbitrators' duty of confidentiality, this does not mean that arbitrators do not have to maintain the confidentiality of the arbitration proceedings. For example, the ICC Rules do not contain a provision on arbitrator confidentiality, but commentators on the ICC Rules argue that '*due to their quasi judicial role, arbitrators are widely viewed as subject to an obligation of confidentiality.*'[131]

251   The arbitrator's duty of confidentiality can also be regulated by ethical codes of professional bodies and associations. Provisions regulating confidentiality can be

---

[127]Dunand (2013), Commentary of Art. 321a CO, para 3.

[128]See, for example, Born (2014), p. 1966; Poudret and Besson (2007), para 437.

[129]Loquin (2015), para 327.

[130]Swiss Rules, Art. 44(1); DIS Rules, Art. 44(1); WIPO Rules, Art. 78; ICAC Rules, Art. 46.3; SIAC Rules, Art. 39(1); HKIAC Rules, Art. 42(2); JCAA Rules, Art. 38(2); AAA Rules, Art. 37(1).

[131]Webster and Bühler (2014), para 22–46.

found, for example, in the CIArb Code of Ethics[132]; the Code of Professional and Ethical Conduct of the Hong Kong Institute of Arbitrators[133]; and the AAA/ABA Code of Ethics for Arbitrators in Commercial Disputes.[134]

3.3.2.3 Express Contractual Provisions

The relevant arbitration institution can request arbitrators to sign a declaration of confidentiality.[135] Thus, the ICSID Arbitration Rules provide that each arbitrator is to sign a confidentiality declaration before or at the first session of the Tribunal in the following form:

252

> I shall keep confidential all information coming to my knowledge as a result of my participation in this proceeding, as well as the contents of any award made by the Tribunal.[136]

If the relevant institution does not require such a declaration and if there is no provision in the institutional rules on arbitrator confidentiality, the parties can invite the arbitrators to sign an express confidentiality undertaking. The text of this declaration or agreement can be tailored according to the needs of the parties. As mentioned above,[137] the arbitrators' duty of confidentiality can also find its source in the parties' agreement on confidentiality entered into before an arbitration, if it specifically extends to arbitrators. This agreement will apply to arbitrators once they accept to serve as arbitrators.

253

3.3.3 Scope of the Duty of Confidentiality

3.3.3.1 In General

In the course of arbitration proceedings, arbitrators learn of information and documents relating to the parties, to the witnesses, and to the dispute. Subject to a limited number of exceptions, arbitrators are to keep secret all such information and all such documents.[138] Some rules/codes provide quite generally that arbitrators are bound by the duty of confidentiality regarding all information acquired during the

254

---

[132] Art. 8 CIArb Code of Ethics.

[133] Art. 4 Code of Professional and Ethical Conduct of the Hong Kong Institute of Arbitrators.

[134] Canon VI(B) AAA/ABA Code of Ethics for Arbitrators in Commercial Disputes.

[135] Smeureanu (2011), p. 143.

[136] Art. 6(2) of the ICSID Arbitration Rules.

[137] See above Sect. 2.2.

[138] See, for example, Jolles and Canals de Cediel (2004), p. 94.

arbitration proceeding. For instance, Canon VI(B) of the AAA/ABA Code of Ethics for Arbitrators in Commercial Disputes stipulates that the

> '*arbitrator should keep confidential all matters relating to the arbitration proceedings and decisions*'.

255   Other rules set out a list of documents and/or issues covered by the duty of confidentiality. For example, the Swiss Rules extend the arbitrators' confidentiality obligation to

> '*all awards and orders as well as all materials submitted by another party in the framework of the arbitral proceedings not already in the public domain*'.[139]

Further, Art. 44(1) of the DIS Rules provides that arbitrators shall not disclose

> '*any information concerning the arbitration, including in particular the existence of the arbitration, the names of the parties, the nature of the claims, the names of any witnesses or experts, any procedural orders or awards, ad any evidence that is not publicly available*'.

256   If we review, for example, the provisions of Swiss contractual law imposing an obligation of confidentiality on arbitrators, we will see that the scope of the data covered by confidentiality is very extensive as well. As mentioned above, the relationship between a party and an arbitrator is qualified as an agency contract under Arts 394 ff CO.[140] It can be deduced from commentaries to Art. 398 CO that the arbitrator's duty of confidentiality should cover all documents and information that he receives from the parties while serving as an arbitrator.[141]

257   The arbitrator's duty of confidentiality exists not only vis-à-vis the parties, but also vis-à-vis the fact and expert witnesses.[142] Indeed, the witnesses might have their own interest in avoiding outside disclosure of the information they communicate in their testimony. In the jurisdictions, such as Spain and Kazakhstan, where the arbitration laws impose on arbitrators a duty of confidentiality regarding all information coming to their knowledge in the course of the arbitral proceedings, the arbitrator's duty of confidentiality towards witnesses will find its source in the national arbitration law. Other national laws, not related to arbitration, can be of relevance. For example, in Switzerland, such a duty can originate from Art. 28 CC protecting the personality rights.[143] Therefore, where a witness's testimony contains

---

[139]Art. 44(1).

[140]See above Sect. 3.3.2.1.2.

[141]Werro (2012b), Commentary of Art. 398 CO, para 22.

[142]Hoffet (1991), p. 234.

[143]For more details on violation of personality rights, see below Sect. 6.2.2.1. Also see below Sect. 6.3 discussing remedies and sanctions in case of confidentiality breach by arbitrators.

sensitive information, even a waiver of confidentiality by the parties may sometimes not be sufficient to allow an arbitrator to disclose the witness's testimony.

3.3.3.2 Confidentiality of Arbitrators' Deliberations

One of the purposes of the arbitrator's duty of confidentiality is to prevent arbitrators from disseminating information on the arbitration proceedings to any third party outside the case. In addition, however, arbitrators must not disclose certain information to anyone outside their panel. In principle, arbitrators are not permitted to disclose the content of the tribunal's deliberations. The confidentiality of deliberations is an important guarantee of arbitrators' independence intended to ensure the integrity of the arbitral process.[144] Indeed, the primary purpose of the confidentiality of the deliberations is to allow the arbitrators to express their opinions and adjudicate freely and safely without any outside pressure from the parties or from any other interested persons.

258

Very few national arbitration laws regulate the secrecy of deliberations.[145] More commonly, institutional rules provide that arbitrators are bound by a duty of confidentiality regarding the tribunal's deliberations.[146] Ethical and professional rules also impose this duty,[147] which is acknowledged by many legal authors.[148] Given the uniform approach to the secrecy of deliberations, this aspect of confidentiality could, in our opinion, form part of the *lex mercatoria* principles governing arbitration proceedings.

259

The secrecy of deliberations means (i) that arbitrators must prevent any third person from assisting in their deliberations and (ii) that the opinions exchanged between the arbitrators during the deliberations cannot be communicated to the parties or to anyone else outside of the panel.[149] Thus, the arbitrators are to keep the deliberations secret not only from third parties, but also from the parties and from the members/employees of the relevant arbitration institution.[150]

260

---

[144]Born (2014), p. 2810; Smeureanu (2011), p. 51.

[145]See, *e.g.*, Rule 27 of the Scottish Arbitration Rules. Although Art. 1479 of the French Civil Code protects confidentiality of the arbitral deliberations in domestic arbitrations, there is no similar provision in the section dealing with international arbitrations.

[146]See, *e.g.*, Swiss Rules, Art. 44(2); LCIA Rules, Art. 30.2; Abu Dhabi Rules, Art. 33(2); DIAC Rules, Art. 41.2; HKIC Rules, Art. 42.4.

[147]See, *e.g.*, Canon IV.C of the AAA/ABA Code of Ethics for Arbitrators in Commercial Disputes; Art. 26 of the Model Rules on Arbitral Procedure of the International Law Commission.

[148]See, for example, Berger (2013), p. 256; Berger and Kellerhals (2015), para 1470; Born (2014), p. 2004; Clay (2001), paras 776–778; Lew (2011), p. 8 [of the electronic version]; Jolles et al. (2013), p. 138; Berger and Kellerhals (2015), para 1470.

[149]Clay (2001), para 776; Gaillard and Savage (1999), para 1374.

[150]Nesbitt and Darowski (2015), p. 558.

261   The Swiss Supreme Court had to adjudicate a case in which the results of the award were known to one of the parties before notification of the award.[151] The leak came to light when the losing party paid the amount awarded to the prevailing party before the award was officially released.[152] The Swiss Supreme Court explained that confidentiality of deliberations covers '*all opinions expressed in the course of the discussion, that is, ultimately, the way in which the majority was reached*'.[153] It considered that the leak was regrettable, but did not amount to a breach because only the results of the deliberations were revealed, and not the secrecy of the deliberations themselves.[154] In particular, it was not established that a dissenting opinion of an arbitrator was revealed.[155]

262   In a later decision, the Swiss Supreme Court confirmed that revealing the results of the deliberations before the award is notified did not constitute a breach of confidentiality of deliberations.[156] In this case, the President of the arbitral tribunal informed all parties of the decision taken by the arbitral tribunal before a reasoned award was rendered.[157] The claimant argued that this approach violated procedural public policy and asked the Court to annul the arbitral award.[158] It is in this context that the Swiss Supreme Court referred to its earlier decision confirming that revealing the results of deliberations does not amount to a violation of public order.

263   According to the Swiss Supreme Court, not all violations of the procedural rules will constitute a violation of procedural public policy.[159] The latter is found '*only if fundamental and generally recognised principles have been violated, resulting in a decision incompatible with the acknowledged values of the rule of law*'.[160] In its more recent decision, the Swiss Supreme Court has confirmed its practice and stated that violation by an arbitrator of his duty of confidentiality cannot be, as a general rule, a basis for challenging an arbitral award.[161]

264   We agree that revealing the result of deliberations before the award is notified does not meet this standard and therefore does not amount to a violation of

---

[151]TF 4P.61/1991 of 12.11.1991, in: ASA Bull. 264 (1992) as Moser v. BMY.

[152]TF 4P.61/1991 of 12.11.1991, in: ASA Bull. 264 (1992) as Moser v. BMY, recital 1b/bb.

[153]TF 4P.61/1991 of 12.11.1991, in: ASA Bull. 264 (1992) as Moser v. BMY, recital 1b/bb; see also Lalive et al. (1989), p. 414.

[154]TF 4P.61/1991 of 12.11.1991, in: ASA Bull. 264 (1992) as Moser v. BMY, recital 1b/bb.

[155]TF 4P.61/1991 of 12.11.1991, in: ASA Bull. 264 (1992) as Moser v. BMY, recital 1b/bb.

[156]TF 4P.154/2005 of 10.11.2005, in: ASA Bull. 55 (2006) as La République du Liban v. Y. and Z., recital 6.2.

[157]TF 4P.154/2005 of 10.11.2005, in: ASA Bull. 55 (2006) as La République du Liban v. Y. and Z., recital 6.2.

[158]TF 4P.154/2005 of 10.11.2005, in: ASA Bull. 55 (2006) as La République du Liban v. Y. and Z., recital 6.2.

[159]TF 4P.154/2005 of 10.11.2005, in: ASA Bull. 55 (2006) as La République du Liban v. Y. and Z., recital 6.1; ATF 129 III 445, recital 4.2.1.

[160]TF 4P.154/2005 of 10.11.2005, in: ASA Bull. 55 (2006) as La République du Liban v. Y. and Z., recital 6.1; ATF 129 III 445, recital 4.2.1.

[161]TF 4A_510/2015, 8.03.2016, recital 4.2.

procedural public policy. Depending on the circumstances, it can, however, violate the principle of equal treatment of the parties.

Indeed, there is a great risk of violating the principle of equal treatment of the **265** parties when arbitrators disclose information regarding the deliberations and the future award to *one party* before the official release to *all* parties.[162] There are several reasons why arbitrators should refrain from doing this. First, a party informed that it will lose could start a challenge procedure against the arbitrators or take measures to hide its assets.[163]

A party which is informed of the final outcome before the other party will also **266** have a privileged position if there are still ongoing settlement negotiations. For example, if informed by an insider from the tribunal that it will be required to pay damages, a party could try to reach a settlement to pay a lesser amount.[164]

We also consider it inappropriate for arbitrators to disclose the content of **267** deliberations *after* the award is released. However, there can be some exceptions. For example, Gary Born and Pierre Lalive report that arbitrators sometimes discuss the performance of counsel after notification of the award, without revealing details of the arbitrators' deliberations:

> [M]any international arbitrators are prepared to meet with counsel after a final award has been rendered (and the time for any correction, annulment, or other post-award proceeding has expired) and discuss the performance of counsel, without revealing details of the arbitrators' deliberations. Such communications are constructive and should not be considered contrary to the confidentiality of the arbitrators' deliberations.[165]

> I am aware of a few cases where, after an award has been rendered, the arbitrators have organised a meeting with the parties to discuss the performance. It is exceptional and I have never done this, but it seems like a good idea. Of course, there are cases where the hostility between the parties is so great that this would simply be impossible.[166]

The process of deliberations will largely depend on the panel. Deliberations may **268** take different forms,[167] whether oral or in writing (through emails, letters, faxes, draft awards, memoranda or any other work product).[168] Deliberations can also take place during an informal meeting, for example, over lunch or during a cocktail party. Informal discussions are also to be covered by the confidentiality of deliberations:

> A rule of confidentiality of the deliberations must, if it is to be effective, apply generally to the deliberation stage of the tribunal's proceedings and *cannot realistically be confined to what is said in a formal meeting* of all the members in the deliberation room. The form or forms the deliberations take varies greatly from one tribunal to another. Anybody who has had experience of courts and tribunals knows perfectly well that *much of the deliberation*

---

[162]Derains (2005), p. 225.

[163]Berger (2013), p. 257.

[164]Derains (2005), pp. 225–226.

[165]Born (2014), p. 2811.

[166]Q&A with Professor Pierre Lalive, GAR, Volume 3- Issue 5, 1 November 2008.

[167]Bredin (2004), pp. 47–51.

[168]Berger and Kellerhals (2015), para 1345; Berger (2013), pp. 256–257.

work, even in courts like the ICJ [International Court of Justice] which have formal rules governing the deliberation, is done less formally. [. . .] Revelations of such informal discussion and of suggestions made, could be very damaging and seriously threaten the whole deliberations process (italics added).[169]

269 Violation of the secrecy of deliberations cannot give rise *per se* to annulment or non-recognition of the award.[170] However, the arbitrator can be held personally liable for the damages caused by the breach of his confidentiality duty.[171]

270 Finally, arbitrators are not only subject to a confidentiality duty, but are also holders of the right to the confidentiality of the deliberations. It is their obligation, but is also a prerogative,[172] as disclosure of details on the deliberations can be used against the arbitrators to challenge the award—and also to pursue them for liability. Thus, arbitrators owe a duty of confidentiality regarding the content of deliberations vis-à-vis their colleagues.

271 In our opinion, the nature of this duty is contractual. Under Art. 530 of the Swiss Code of Obligation, if two or more persons combine their efforts in order to achieve a common goal and if this partnership does not fulfil the distinctive criteria of any other types of partnerships codified in the Code, such a relationship should be qualified as a simple partnership (*contrat de société simple*). In the relationship between arbitrators-members of the same panel, the arbitrators get together with the common goal of rendering an award and their partnership does not have the distinctive features of any other types of partnership existing under the Swiss law. Thus, such a relationship should be qualified as a simple partnership (*contrat de société simple*).[173] This partnership does not have a legal personality and is in fact a contractual relationship.[174] Parties to this contract have a duty of loyalty[175] and thus, a duty of discretion vis-à-vis each other.

3.3.4 Intermediary Conclusions

272 As discussed above, a number of sources provide for a duty of confidentiality of arbitrators. However, even without written rules imposing an obligation of confidentiality, arbitrators are undoubtedly bound by such a duty given their quasi-judicial role and the fiduciary nature of their relationship with the parties. Also, many authors agree on the necessity of maintaining the confidentiality of the

---

[169]Challenge Decision of the Appointing Authority, Sir Robert Jennings, on the Challenge of Judge Bengt Broms in IUSCT Case of 7 May 2001, 38 Iran-US C.T.R. 386 (2001).

[170]Berger (2013), p. 258; Gaillard and Savage (1999), para 1374; Smeureanu (2011), p. 51.

[171]Berger (2013), p. 258; Gaillard and Savage (1999), para 1345.

[172]Berger (2013), p. 257; Gaillard and Savage (1999), para 1374.

[173]Arts 530–551 CO.

[174]Chaix (2017), para 8.

[175]TF 4A_619/2011, 20.03.2012, recital 3.6; Philippin, 125.

proceedings by arbitrators, including during the deliberations.[176] As emphasized by Catherine A. Rogers, '*the personal integrity and ethical discretion of individual arbitrators remains an important source of protection for confidential informa-tion*.'[177] As to the secrecy of deliberations, which is generally codified by arbitration rules and recognised by most legal scholars, this aspect of confidentiality could, in our opinion, form part of the *lex mercatoria* principles governing arbitration proceedings.

The scope *ratione materiae* of the arbitrators' duty of confidentiality is extensive.   **273** Although requirements can vary depending on the applicable rules, arbitrators are generally required to keep confidential all documents and all information relating to the parties, to the witnesses and to the dispute which have become known to them in the course of the arbitration proceedings, unless the disclosure is required by the applicable law. As to the persons to whom the duty of confidentiality is owed, the arbitrators are required to maintain confidentiality not only vis-à-vis the parties, but also vis-à-vis their colleagues on the panel and witnesses.

3.4 Duty of Confidentiality of Arbitration Institutions

Arbitration institutions, as well as their members and employees, are usually bound   **274** by a duty of confidentiality regarding the matters they treat. In the present section, we will briefly examine the basis and the scope of this duty of confidentiality.

The nature of a relationship between the parties and the relevant arbitration   **275** institution is contractual.[178] Views differ on how the contract between the parties and the arbitration institution is formed, i.e., which actions represent an offer and a corresponding acceptance.[179] According to Smeureanu, arbitration institutions make a public offer by publishing their arbitration rules, and the parties accept this offer when referring to the arbitration rules in their arbitration agreement.[180] Parties' acceptance of the arbitration rules is communicated to the institution when one of the parties submits a request for arbitration.[181] Therefore, the arbitration rules contain binding contractual provisions for the relevant arbitration institution.

The provisions of arbitration rules dealing with confidentiality often impose an   **276** obligation of confidentiality on arbitration institutions. Such provisions can be found in the Swiss Rules (Art. 44(1)), SCC Rules (Art. 3), DIS Rules (Art. 44(1)), ACICA Rules (Art. 22(2)), Milan Rules (Art. 8(1)), Rules of the Russian Federation

---

[176]See, for example, Furrer (2008), p. 811; Gaillard and Savage (1999), p. 612; Rogers (2014), para 2.127.

[177]Rogers (2014), para 2.127.

[178]Born (2014), p. 1983.

[179]Timár (2013), p. 115, with further references.

[180]Smeureanu (2011), p. 143.

[181]Smeureanu (2011), p. 143.

Chamber of Commerce and Industry (Art. 25), WIPO Rules (Art. 78) and ICDR Rules (Art. 30(1)). For example, Art. 44(1) of the Swiss Rules provides:

> Unless the parties expressly agree in writing to the contrary, the parties undertake to keep confidential all awards and orders as well as all materials submitted by another party in the framework of the arbitral proceedings not already in the public domain, except and to the extent that a disclosure may be required of a party by a legal duty, to protect or pursue a legal right, or to enforce or challenge an award in legal proceedings before a judicial authority. *This undertaking also applies to* the arbitrators, the tribunal-appointed experts, the secretary of the arbitral tribunal, *the members of the board of directors of the Swiss Chambers' Arbitration Institution, the members of the Court and the Secretariat, and the staff of the individual Chambers.* (italics added)

277   An obligation of confidentiality can also be imposed on arbitration institutions when the relevant arbitration rules contain a provision dealing specifically with the confidentiality duty of the members and employees of the institutions.[182] For example, Art. 6 of the Statutes of the International Court of Arbitration (Appendix I to the ICC Rules) provides:

> The work of the Court is of a confidential nature which must be respected by *everyone who participates in that work in whatever capacity.* The Court lays down the rules regarding the persons who can attend the meetings of the Court and its Committees and who are entitled to have access to materials related to the work of the Court and its Secretariat. (italics added)

278   The scope of the duty of confidentiality, as regulated by most institutional rules, is rather extensive. The language of the provision can be very general, requiring personnel of the relevant institution to keep confidentiality regarding the conduct of arbitral proceedings or simply stating that the '*work of the Court is of confidential nature*'.[183] It can also be more specific, listing the type of documents and information to be treated as confidential. This is the case, for example, in the Swiss Rules cited above or in the WIPO Rules (Art. 78(a)):

> Unless the parties agree otherwise, the Center and the arbitrator shall maintain *the confidentiality of the arbitration, the award* and, to the extent that they describe information that is not in the public domain, *any documentary or other evidence disclosed during the arbitration* [. . .] [emphasis added].

279   Considering the rather extensive scope of application of these provisions, and the fact that confidentiality is one of the professional duties of members and employees

---

[182] Art. 78 of the WIPO Rules; Art. 6 of the Appendix I to the ICC Rules.

[183] Appendix I to the ICC Rules, Art. 6.

of the arbitration institutions, we think that the obligation of confidentiality of members and employees of arbitration institutions should generally cover all information and documents that they receive while exercising their professional activity.

The arbitration literature suggests that the contract between the parties and an   **280**
arbitral institution is governed, like the arbitrator's contract, by the *lex arbitri*.[184] The qualification of the contract with the arbitral institution will depend on the governing law. Under German law, for example, the institution's contract is regarded as a contract for the management of the affairs of another person (*Geschäftsbesorgungsvertrag*) or as a mixed or *sui generis* type of contract.[185] In France, the contract with an arbitral institution is qualified as a mixed contract having the characteristics of both an agency contract (*mandat*) and a contract for work and services (*contrat d'entreprise*).[186] Under Swiss law, the institution's contract has the characteristics of an agency contract.[187]

In addition to investigating applicable arbitration rules, one must also consider the   **281**
applicable law, which will govern the issues not settled by the parties. The rules of the law applicable to the contract between the parties and an arbitral institution will very likely impose a duty of confidentiality on the arbitral institution regarding the conduct of the arbitral proceedings.[188] For example, under Swiss law, such an obligation will find its source in Art. 398(2) CO imposing on the agent an obligation of diligent and faithful performance.

Therefore, even in the absence of any relevant provision on confidentiality in the   **282**
arbitration rules, members and employees of arbitration institutions must almost certainly respect the confidentiality of all information they learn and all documents they receive in the framework of an arbitration proceeding while exercising their professional duties. One issue that may vary among different institutions, however, is how the publication of arbitral awards is regulated. This matter will be discussed in more detail below (see Sect. 4.4 below).

3.5   Counsel's Duty of Confidentiality

3.5.1   *Introduction*

It is important to make a distinction between the duty of confidentiality owed by the   **283**
parties and the obligation of confidentiality owed by counsel. While representing his client in an arbitration proceeding, counsel acts on behalf of his client. If he breaches the duty of confidentiality while acting on behalf of the client within the scope of

---

[184]Timár (2013), p. 112, with further references.

[185]Timár (2013), p. 113, with further references.

[186]Timár (2013), p. 113, with further references.

[187]Ritz (2007), p. 203. Agency contract (*contrat de mandat*) is regulated by Arts 394–406 CO.

[188]See, for example, Art. 398(2) CO.

instructions provided by the client, such a breach will in principle be attributable to the party and not to his lawyer.

284   Although party's representatives interact directly with other persons involved in the arbitration (arbitrators, the adverse party, witnesses, etc.), they do not have a direct relationship with them as long as they act on behalf of their client. Thus, in the present section, we will mainly discuss the counsel's duty of confidentiality vis-à-vis his client.

285   The counsel's duty of confidentiality is not something specific to arbitration, but is rather a fundamental principle existing in virtually all domestic legal systems. This obligation is based on ethical, contractual and often statutory duties. The lawyer's duty of confidentiality is usually expressed as both an obligation and a right to keep confidential the information received from clients and advice given to them.[189] The Code of Conduct for Lawyers in the European Union explains the rationale behind the counsel's duty of confidentiality:

> 2.3.1 It is of the essence of a lawyer's function that he should be told by his client things which the client would not tell to others, and that he should be the recipient of other information on a basis of confidence. Without the certainty of confidentiality there cannot be trust. Confidentiality is therefore a primary and fundamental right and duty of the lawyer. The lawyer's obligation of confidentiality serves the interest of the administration of justice as well as the interest of the client. It is therefore entitled to special protection by the State.

286   It is, however, not easy to define in general the basis and the scope of this duty because of the lack of sufficiently-developed, substantive international rules on representation of the parties and representatives' professional conduct in international arbitration. This issue is mainly regulated by domestic rules and they cannot always be readily transposed to international arbitration for several reasons.

287   First, it is often not easy to determine the applicable law. This problem is particularly complicated because party representatives in arbitration are often subject to domestic rules of several jurisdictions which may have conflicting norms.[190] Second, domestic rules are designed for domestic settings and are not always adapted for international arbitration proceedings which may combine features of both common and civil law approaches. Finally, the observance of domestic rules on professional conduct is to be supervised by local professional bodies or courts.[191] The arbitral tribunal, in most cases, will not have jurisdiction over the matter, other than deciding whether to give effect to an objection based on the legal privilege.

288   The attorney's duty of confidentiality can be regulated on different levels. First, the lawyer's professional secrecy is considered a cornerstone of the attorney-client relationship in all jurisdictions. This duty is often imposed through statutory rules

---

[189]See IBA International Principles on Conduct for the Legal Profession, Art. 4.2, 21.

[190]IBA Guidelines on Party Representation in International Arbitration, Preamble, 1.

[191]Born (2014), p. 2851.

applicable to the lawyers admitted to the relevant bar or practising in a specific jurisdiction. Second, provisions on the duty of confidentiality may be contained in the contract between the party and its representative as well as in domestic law contractual provisions. Third, an express duty of confidentiality may be imposed on the party representative in the national arbitration laws or applicable institutional rules of arbitration. And finally, professional and ethical rules regulating different aspects of the legal profession, adopted at the national or international level or in a particular area of practice, may also contain provisions on the lawyer's duty of confidentiality.

In the present section, we will start our analysis by clarifying the terminology. **289** The reason is that the counsel's duty of confidentiality is often associated with the legal privilege, although the concepts are very different. Thus, we will first explain the differences between the two concepts (Sect. 3.5.2). Second, we will review how the lawyer's duty of confidentiality is regulated by some international law instruments, which do not relate only to arbitration (Sect. 3.5.3). Although these texts do not typically include detailed regulations, they have the benefit of expressing a general consensus which exists between different jurisdictions. Some of these instruments may have a binding effect.

Third, we will examine the legal basis and the scope for the counsel's duty of **290** confidentiality as regulated in the domestic laws of Switzerland, England and Wales, and the United States (Sect. 3.5.4). We will see that despite the significant differences in the terminology and the regulation of this issue, the same is true for all these jurisdictions: lawyers are bound by an extensive duty of confidentiality regarding all information that they gain as a result of the representation of a client. They owe this duty vis-à-vis their clients.

Finally, we will explore how the rules on the lawyer's duty of confidentiality are **291** transposed in international arbitration (Sect. 3.5.5).

3.5.2 Legal Privilege and Lawyer's Duty of Confidentiality

In civil law countries, an attorney's duty and right to keep confidential the informa- **292** tion regarding his client's affairs is generally called 'lawyer's professional secrecy'.[192] The equivalent concept in common law systems is often designated as 'legal privilege'.[193] The latter refers to the lawyer's right to keep his

---

[192]For example, 'secret professionnel de l'avocat' in Switzerland, 'secret professionnel' in France, 'Berufsverschwiegenheit' in Germany and 'адвокатская тайна' or 'профессиональная тайна адвоката' in Russia.

[193]See, for example, Dal (2011) (full reference in the Bibliography), in which 'legal professional privilege' is used as a translation of 'secret profesionnel de l'avocat'.

communications with the client confidential by withholding testimonial or documentary evidence from legal proceedings.[194]

293   Legal privilege is also known as the attorney-client privilege in the United States, solicitor-client privilege in Canada, client legal privilege in Australia and legal professional privilege in England and Wales. Although the privilege refers to a right (belonging to the client or to the lawyer depending on the jurisdiction), it also implies a duty for a lawyer. In fact, the lawyer has an obligation to assert the legal privilege on behalf of the client unless there is a waiver.[195]

294   It is, however, important to bear in mind that the lawyer's duty of confidentiality (civil law countries) and legal privilege (common law countries) are not the same. Indeed, the lawyer's confidentiality obligations are not limited to the duty of asserting the legal privilege, but also include professional and ethical duties. This is often referred to as the professional duty of confidentiality in common law countries.[196]

295   The main difference between the two is that the legal privilege refers to the right to withhold evidence when the lawyer is compelled by judicial or other public authority, while the duty of confidentiality is an obligation which the lawyer owes to his client in *all* settings and at *all* times. Thus, the very nature of the two legal concepts is fundamentally different. The legal privilege is an evidentiary shield, protecting against compelled disclosures of confidential communications between the client and his attorney.[197] By contrast, the lawyer's duty of confidentiality is not simply an evidentiary shield, but is rather a professional and ethical duty owed by the lawyer in all circumstances.

296   There is also a difference in the scope of the two legal concepts. For example, under the law of England and Wales, the solicitor's duty of confidentiality extends to *all* matters communicated to a solicitor by his client, which is not the case for the legal professional privilege.[198] By contrast, the legal professional privilege protects communications between client and lawyer for purposes of seeking or obtaining legal advice (legal advice privilege)[199] and communications and documents which come into existence after litigation is contemplated or has commenced, for the dominant purpose of obtaining information or advice in connection with such litigation (litigation privilege).[200]

---

[194]Mosk and Ginsburg (2001), p. 346.

[195]Hall (1987), p. 289; Fox et al. (2013), p. 586.

[196]Chapter 4 of the Solicitors Regulation Authority Code of Conduct 2011, Version 14 published on 30 April 2015.

[197]Smith (1999), pp. 326–327.

[198]Taylor (1993), p. 330.

[199]Three Rivers District Council and Others v Governor and Company of the Bank of England [2003] QB 1556; Fox et al. (2013), p. 586.

[200]Three Rivers District Council and Others v Governor and Company of the Bank of England [2003] QB 1556; Fox et al. (2013), p. 587.

Notwithstanding these differences, the legal privilege and the lawyer's duty of **297** confidentiality are two facets of the professional secrecy which protects the confidentiality of communications between a lawyer and his client. If compelled to testify before a court, the lawyer's duty of confidentiality would find its limits, if there was no legal privilege.

Also, the two legal concepts seek to protect the same interests by encouraging full **298** and frank communications between an attorney and his client. On the one hand, the purpose of the legal privilege and of the lawyer's duty of confidentiality is to protect the client's interests. The client should be able to communicate fully and frankly with the lawyer, even with respect to embarrassing or legally damaging matters.[201] It is only in situations where the attorney and client have open communications based on trust that the lawyer will be able to represent the client effectively and, if necessary, to advise the client to refrain from wrongful conduct.[202]

On the other hand, both the legal privilege and the lawyer's duty of confidenti- **299** ality serve a broader public interest, and, in particular, the interests of justice. The public interest requires that all persons have access to effective legal assistance, which is impossible without the relationship of trust between the client and his lawyer. The legal privilege and the lawyer's duty of confidentiality also help to reduce the prevalence of frivolous litigations and to render more effective adversarial proceedings. This is how the English judge Bingham explained the *ratio legis* of the legal privilege in *Ventouris v Mountain*:

> The doctrine of legal professional privilege is rooted in the public interest, which required that hopeless and exaggerated claims and unsound and spurious defences be so far as possible discouraged, and civil disputes as far as possible settled without resort to judicial decision. To this end, it is necessary that actual and potential litigants, be they claimants or respondent, should be free to unburden themselves without reserve to their legal advisers, and their legal advisers be free to give honest and candid advice on a sound factual basis, without fear that these communications may be relied on by an ongoing party if the dispute comes before the court for decision.[203]

These considerations can also apply to the lawyer's duty of confidentiality, as both legal concepts contribute to maintaining the relationship of trust between the lawyer and his client.

In addition, the Swiss Supreme Court considers that the attorney professional **300** secrecy, which includes both the legal privilege and the lawyer's duty of confidentiality, seeks to protect lawyers' interest in exercising their profession.[204] Indeed, lawyers cannot effectively represent their clients' interests without being protected by the legal privilege and without the existence of a relationship of trust with their clients.

---

[201] See, for example, New York Rules of Professional Conduct, Comment 2 on the Rule 1.6.

[202] See, for example, New York Rules of Professional Conduct, Comment 2 on the Rule 1.6.

[203] Ventouris v Mountain [1991] 1 W.L.R. 607.

[204] ATF 117 Ia 341, recital 6a; TF 18.10.1993, in: SJ 1994 106, recital 3b. Also see Corboz (1993), p. 79; Reymond (2007), p. 63.

301 While we focus our analysis on the lawyer's duty of confidentiality, the legal privilege is also relevant for the purpose of our research. Indeed, it is an extension of the lawyer's duty of confidentiality which allows a lawyer to keep confidentiality of his communications with the client even when compelled to disclose them by the court. For example, if a counsel representing a client in an arbitration is compelled to testify on details of this arbitration before a court, there is a risk that the information on the arbitration proceedings will be revealed to the public. If this information is subject to the legal privilege, the lawyer will be able to refuse testifying by invoking the legal privilege and confidentiality of the arbitration will be maintained.

3.5.3 Regulation of the Lawyer's Duty of Confidentiality by International Law Instruments

302 There are a number of international law instruments, not applying only to arbitrations, which regulate certain aspects of the counsel's duty of confidentiality. It should be noted, however, that the issue is primarily regulated at the national level by the rules governing the conduct of legal advisors and legal representatives.[205]

303 There may be international law conventions, codes or other texts which become binding upon their ratification or adoption at the national level. Thus, Art. 17 of the International Covenant on Civil and Political Rights and Arts 6 and 8 of the ECHR protect the secrecy of relations between attorneys and their clients in the provisions dealing with the right to privacy and the procedural guarantees of a fair trial.[206]

304 An express provision containing the attorney's duty of confidentiality is contained in the Code of Conduct for European Lawyers. This Code prepared by the Council of Bars & Law Societies of Europe ('CCBE') was adopted at least to some extent by all EU Member States and some other European countries.[207] The Code's provisions are binding for lawyer-members of the bars in almost 30 European countries. Art. 2.3 of the Code requires that lawyers respect the confidentiality of all information that comes within their knowledge in the course of their professional activity. It also provides that this obligation is not limited in time and extends not only to lawyers, but also to their associates and staff. Although the drafters of the Code did not necessarily have arbitration in mind when preparing the text, it will apply also in an arbitration setting as long as the parties' representatives are admitted to the bar of one of the countries that adopted this Code.

---

[205]Born (2014), p. 2383 and further references mentioned therein.

[206]TF 1P.32/2005, 11.07.2005, recital 3.3; TF 11.04.1996, in: SJ 1996 453; TF 2P.313/1999, 08.03.2000, recital 2a; ATF 117 Ia 341, recital 4; ATF 102 Ia 516, recital 3b; Bohnet and Martenet (2009), para 1790; Fox et al. (2013), p. 586; Pattenden (2003), para 3.03.

[207]See for the status of adoption of the Code www.ccbe.eu/fileadmin/user_upload/NTCdocument/Status_of_the_CCBE_C1_1386165089.pdf.

Most of the other texts adopted at the international level, however, are of a **305** non-binding nature. They provide guidelines or principles which crystallise a generally-accepted framework in certain areas of law and practice. If adopted by the parties, such instruments can become binding and take on a contractual nature. In addition, the arbitral tribunal may apply them as a matter of discretion or national legislators can use them as a source of inspiration for legislative reform.

Some texts discuss only the issue of legal privilege, while others focus on the **306** counsel's duty of confidentiality or regulate both issues. Thus, the UNIDROIT Principles of Transnational Civil Procedure contain provisions on the attorney-client privilege, but not on counsel's obligation of confidentiality. The UNIDROIT Principles are intended to be standards for adjudication of transnational commercial disputes, including international arbitration proceedings.[208] Art. 18 of the UNIDROIT Principles provides that the tribunal should take into account the confidentiality of professional communications and that it should not impose direct or indirect sanctions further to a party's failure to disclose evidence or other information protected by such evidentiary privilege.

Among the texts dealing with counsel's obligation of confidentiality are the IBA **307** International Principles on Conduct for the Legal Profession, IBA International Principles on Social Media Conduct and the Charter of Core Principles of the European Legal Profession.

Although not specifically tailored for the purpose of international arbitration **308** proceedings and having no binding force, the IBA International Principles on Conduct for the Legal Profession are worth mentioning as they '*express the common ground which underlies all the national and international rules which govern the conduct of lawyers, principally in relation to their clients.*' Art. 4 of the Principles imposes on lawyers a duty and grants them a right to keep confidential '*the affairs of present or former client, unless otherwise allowed or required by law and/or applicable rules of professional conduct.*'

The IBA also developed guidelines aimed at alerting bar associations and regu- **309** latory bodies about the challenges posed by online social media in order to promote and encourage professionally-responsible social media usage within the legal profession. Art. 4 of the IBA International Principles on Social Media Conduct provides as follows:

Confidentiality

It is important that lawyers can be trusted with private and confidential information, and that the public perceive this. Bar associations and regulatory bodies should remind lawyers that social media platforms are not appropriate for dealing with client data or other confidential information unless they are fully satisfied that they can protect such data in accordance with their professional, ethical and legal obligations.

---

[208]UNIDROIT Principles of Transnational Civil Procedure, Scope and Implementation and Comment P-E to the Scope and Implementation.

In addition, bar associations and regulatory bodies should encourage lawyers to consider client confidentiality more generally when using social media. For example, information that locates a lawyer geographically and temporally could be used to show professional involvements with a client who does not want to publicise that he or she is seeking legal advice. Even the use of hypothetical questions or anonymous fact patterns may inadvertently reveal confidential information. More specifically, they should call attention to the relevant rules of professional conduct in their jurisdiction.

310   At the European level, the Council of Bars and Law Societies of Europe ('CCBE') adopted in 2006 the Charter of Core Principles of the European Legal Profession aimed at applying to all of Europe, not necessarily only to the member, associate and observer states of the CCBE. This Charter was not conceived as a code of conduct; it is of non-binding nature. The purpose of the Charter is *'to help bar associations that are struggling to establish their independence; and to increase understanding among lawyers of the importance of the lawyer's role in society; it is aimed both at lawyers themselves and at decision makers and the public in general'*.

311   This Charter contains ten core principles common to the national and international rules regulating the legal profession. One of these principles relates to the lawyer's right and duty to keep clients' matters confidential and to respect professional secrecy.[209] Commentary on the Charter stresses the dual nature of this principle, i.e. that observance of confidentiality is the lawyers' right and duty, but also a fundamental right of the client. It also points to the fact that there are differences in how this issue is regulated in different jurisdictions; the Charter covers all related concepts, i.e. legal professional privilege, duty of confidentiality and professional secrecy.

3.5.4   Regulation of the Lawyer's Duty of Confidentiality in Domestic Laws

3.5.4.1   Introduction

312   Although some aspects of the lawyer's duty of confidentiality are regulated at the international level, there is generally little in the way of detailed regulation. Also, as we have seen above, most of the international law instruments are of a non-binding nature. Therefore, we will examine rules on the attorney's duty of confidentiality included in national legal systems.

313   In the present section, we will review and compare the domestic law regulation provided in several jurisdictions: Switzerland, England and Wales, and the United

---

[209]CCBE Charter of Core Principles of the European Legal Profession, Principle (b).

Table 3.1 Lawyer's duty of confidentiality in Switzerland, England and Wales and in the United States

	Switzerland	England and Wales	United States
Lawyer's duty of confidentiality	Professional secrecy[a]	Professional duty of confidentiality	Professional duty of confidentiality
		Legal professional privilege (legal advice privilege and litigation privilege)	Attorney-client privilege
			Work-product doctrine

[a]Le 'secret professionnel' in French and 'das Berufsgeheimnis' in German

States.[210] As we will see, however, the language referring to the lawyer's duty of confidentiality will change depending on the jurisdiction. As demonstrated in Table 3.1, we will discuss the following legal concepts, included in what we call the 'lawyer's duty of confidentiality': (i) professional secrecy in Switzerland, (ii) the professional duty of confidentiality and legal professional privilege in England and Wales, and (iii) the professional duty of confidentiality, attorney-client privilege and the work-product doctrine in the United States.

For each jurisdiction, we will examine the legal basis as well as the *ratione* **314** *materiae* and *ratione personae* scope of the lawyer's duty of confidentiality and the legal privilege. We will then compare their scope in Switzerland, England and Wales, and the United States. We will see that notwithstanding some significant differences, there are also many similarities in the regulation of the lawyer's duty of confidentiality and the legal privilege in these three jurisdictions.

3.5.4.2 Switzerland

3.5.4.2.1 Legal Basis of the Lawyer's Professional Secrecy

Under Swiss law, lawyers' professional secrecy is an obligation, but also an eviden- **315** tiary privilege.[211] As a rule, Swiss legal scholars do not distinguish between the lawyer's professional duty of confidentiality and the legal privilege; both legal notions are encompassed in the lawyer's professional secrecy. As we will see below, however, the scope of information covered by the lawyer's professional duty of confidentiality is broader than the scope of information protected by the legal privilege.[212]

---

[210]For the United States, we will discuss the general situation in the U.S. and will take as an example the regulation in the State of New York.

[211]Bohnet and Martenet (2009), para 1789.

[212]See below Sect. 3.5.2.

316 First, the lawyer's professional secrecy is a fundamental right protected by the Federal Constitution in Art. 13(1) on the protection of privacy and in Arts 29 and 32 (2) on procedural guarantees.[213]

317 Second, the lawyer's professional duty of confidentiality is expressed in both public and private law provisions: Art. 321 of the Criminal Code, Art. 13 LLCA, Arts 398(2) and 41 CO and Arts 27-28 CC.[214] The issue of professional secrecy is regulated exclusively at the federal level and cantons do not have the competence to legislate.[215] Therefore, the cantons which have provisions on professional secrecy in their legislation—either restricting or extending the scope of the federal law provisions—are not in conformity with federal law.[216]

318 Prior to the LLCA's entry into force on 1 June 1992, the lawyer's professional secrecy was regulated at the federal level only by Art. 321 of the Criminal Code.[217] Thus, violations of professional secrecy were subject to criminal sanctions. The LLCA introduced a positive obligation on lawyers to respect the duty of professional secrecy.[218] Art. 13 LLCA provides that lawyers are bound by the professional secrecy regarding all information that was entrusted to them by their clients as a result of their professional activity. This duty is unlimited in time and implies that lawyers cannot disclose the information covered by professional secrecy to any third persons.

319 In addition, Arts 394 ff CO on the agency contract apply to the contractual relationship between the lawyer and his client. These articles do not contain a specific provision on the agent's duty of confidentiality. Nevertheless, Art. 398 (2) CO imposes on the agent an obligation of diligent and faithful performance which includes an obligation of confidentiality (*devoir de discretion*).[219]

320 The confidential nature of the relationship between the lawyer and his client is also protected by Arts 27-28 CC safeguarding personality rights.[220] In addition, if there is no contractual relationship with the lawyer, a tort claim can be available to a person having suffered damages as a result of the lawyer's breach of confidentiality under Arts 41 ff CO.[221]

321 The legal privilege finds its source in the criminal, administrative and civil procedure rules releasing the lawyer from the duty to testify and to produce documents covered by professional secrecy: Arts 163(1)(b) et 166 (1)(b) of the Code of

---

[213]Bohnet and Martenet (2009), para 1790.

[214]ATF 91 I 200, recital 3.

[215]Chappuis (2016), p. 162.

[216]Chappuis (2016), pp. 162–163; Bohnet and Martenet (2009), para 1810.

[217]Reymond (2007), p. 63.

[218]Reymond (2007), p. 63.

[219]Werro (2012b), Commentary of Art. 398 CO, paras 23–24.

[220]ATF 91 I 200, recital 3. Also Sect. 6.2.2.1 for more details on regulation of personality rights violation.

[221]Bohnet and Martenet (2009), para 1799. Also see below Sect. 6.5 discussing remedies and sanctions in case of confidentiality breach by counsel.

Civil Procedure, Arts 171 and 248 of the Code of Criminal Procedure, Arts 41(2) and 50(2) of the Federal Law on the Criminal Administrative Law, Arts 16(2) and 17 of the Federal Law on the Administrative Procedure.[222]

Professional and ethical rules of the Swiss Bar Association[223] and of the lawyers' **322** cantonal bar associations[224] also contain provisions on the lawyers' duty of professional secrecy. According to Art. 15 of the Professional and Ethical Rules of the Swiss Bar Association, professional secrecy implies that lawyers cannot disclose any information that was entrusted to them as a result of their professional activity to any third person and for an unlimited period of time.

3.5.4.2.2 Ratione Materiae Scope of the Lawyer's Professional Secrecy

Under Swiss law, a lawyer is bound by a professional secrecy regarding any **323** information that was entrusted to him by his clients as a result of his professional activity.[225] The duty of professional secrecy covers the information (i) that is not publicly known, (ii) that is not accessible to every person, (iii) with respect to which the client has an interest in its non-disclosure, and (iv) which the client actually wants to be kept confidential.[226] For example, the mere fact that the lawyer is representing a particular client is already subject to professional secrecy.[227]

The scope of activities protected by the legal privilege is more restricted as it **324** covers only the information and documents communicated to the lawyer in the course of 'typical' advocates' activities, i.e. legal representation and the provision of legal advice.[228] In our opinion, activities such as representation of clients' interests before an arbitral tribunal and providing legal advice in relation to arbitration proceedings should undoubtedly fall within the scope of 'typical advocates' activities.[229] As we will see, this is not very different from the English law regulation which protects these two 'typical' lawyers' activities by the legal advice privilege and the litigation privilege. By contrast, activities such as serving as a board member, an arbitrator or a mediator, even if carried out by a lawyer, are not protected by legal privilege as they fall outside of the scope of 'typical' advocates' activities.[230]

---

[222]Bohnet and Martenet (2009), para 1801.

[223]Art. 15 of the Code suisse de déontologie de la Fédération suisse des avocats.

[224]In the canton of Vaud, for example, all provisions of the *Code suisse de déontologie* are an integral part of the ethical rules of the Vaud Bar Association, called *Usages du barreau vaudois* (Art. 1 of the *Usages du barreau vaudois*).

[225]Art. 13(1) LLCA; Arts 398(1) and 321 CO; TF 2C_42/2010, 28.04.2010, recital 3.1.

[226]Corboz (1993), p. 83.

[227]TF 2C_42/2010, 28.04.2010, recital 3.1.

[228]TF 8G.9/2004, 23.03.2004, recital 9.6.4; Bohnet and Martenet (2009), para 1818.

[229]See, for example, Reiser and Valticos (2015), p. 197.

[230]Bohnet and Martenet (2009), paras 1820–1832.

325   For example, a lawyer serving as an arbitrator is bound by the obligation of confidentiality regarding all matters entrusted to him as a result of the arbitrator's activity. By contrast, this lawyer will not be entitled to invoke legal privilege regarding his arbitrator activities because they are not considered 'typical' lawyers' activities protected by legal privilege.

3.5.4.2.3   Lawyers Bound by the Lawyer's Professional Secrecy

326   Under Swiss law, a distinction needs to be made, in particular, between the following types of lawyers: (i) lawyers practising in the framework of a monopoly (*l'avocat exerçant dans le cadre d'un monopole*), (ii) in-house lawyers, and (iii) legal counsel (*l'avocat-conseil*).[231]

327   Lawyers practising in the framework of a monopoly are lawyers registered within the Cantonal Lawyers' Registry (*Registre cantonal des avocats*) and are thus allowed to represent individuals and legal entities before judicial authorities in Switzerland.[232] These are mainly Swiss qualified lawyers, but, under certain conditions, lawyers admitted to practice in EEA countries can also be registered within the Cantonal Lawyers' Registry.[233] There is a monopoly for party representation before certain judicial authorities.[234] Lawyers practising in the framework of a monopoly are subject to the confidentiality duty as set out in Art. 321 of the Criminal Code and Art. 13 LLCA and may invoke legal privilege before public authorities in civil, criminal and administrative proceedings.[235]

328   In-house lawyers owe a duty of loyalty to their employer under Art. 321a CO. There is, however, much debate as to whether they have a duty of professional secrecy and whether they are entitled to withhold documents and refuse to testify on the basis of legal privilege. The prevailing view is that in-house lawyers are not bound by professional secrecy under Art. 321 of the Criminal Code and Art. 13 LLCA.[236] When faced with this question, the Swiss Supreme Court decided to leave it open.[237] However, it specified that an in-house lawyer is entitled to invoke legal privileges under certain circumstances: when the information is communicated

---

[231]Bohnet and Martenet (2009), para 1808.

[232]See, e.g., Arts 2(2), 4-11 LLCA.

[233]Arts 27–28, 30–32 LLCA.

[234]See, e.g., Art. 68 of the Code of Civil Procedure, Art. 40 of the Law on the Federal Supreme Court, Art. 127 of the Code of Criminal Procedure.

[235]Arts 163(1)(b) et 166 (1)(b) of the Code of Civil Procedure, Arts 171 and 248 of the Code of Criminal Procedure, Arts 41(2) and 50(2) of the Federal Law on the Criminal Administrative Law; Arts 16(2) and 17 of the Federal Law on the Administrative Procedure; Bohnet and Martenet (2009), para 1809.

[236]Bohnet and Martenet (2009), para 1812; Burckhardt (2012), p. 285.

[237]TF 1B_101/2008, 28.10.2008, recital 4.3 (translated in Bohnet, Grands arrêts, 241).

exclusively to the in-house lawyer and he is the only one having control over this information.[238]

Thus, in-house lawyers are not bound by professional secrecy under Art. 321 of the Criminal Code and Art. 13 LLCA, but there is still debate on whether in-house lawyers should be granted the right to invoke privileges. To resolve this issue and grant to in-house lawyers the right to invoke privileges, the Swiss Federal Council elaborated in 2008 a draft law on in-house lawyers,[239] but this draft law was abandoned in 2010 as a result of the consultation procedure.[240] A parliamentary initiative on '*Protection du secret professionnel des jurists d'entreprise*' proposing to introduce a new Art. 160a CPC to grant the right to invoke privilege to in-house lawyers was launched in 2015.[241] The outcome of this initiative will not become clear before the fall of 2020.[242] **329**

Legal counsel (*avocats-conseil*) are lawyers who are qualified to practise law and provide legal advice as independent lawyers, but are not registered within the Cantonal Lawyers' Registry and thus not allowed to practise in the framework of a monopoly.[243] Some cantons, like Vaud, have a specific registry for legal counsel (*Registre cantonal des avocats-conseils*).[244] Legal counsel can be subject to criminal liability under Art. 321 of the Criminal Code.[245] The LLCA, however, does not apply to them,[246] which means that the LLCA disciplinary sanctions are not applicable to the legal counsel having breached professional secrecy as defined in Art. 13 LLCA. Since legal counsel are subject to Art. 321 of the Criminal Code, they are entitled to the legal privileges provided by the laws on civil, criminal and administrative procedure.[247] **330**

The question is whether, under Swiss law, lawyers representing parties in international arbitration proceedings are subject to the duty of professional secrecy and are thus entitled to invoke legal privileges. As described above, lawyers registered with the Cantonal Lawyers' Registry, as well as those who are not members of this Registry but provide legal advice as independent lawyers (*avocat-conseils*) are subject to the duty of professional secrecy under Art. 321 of the Criminal Code. **331**

---

[238]TF 1B_101/2008, 28.10.2008, recital 4.4.1 (translated in Bohnet, Grands arrêts, 241).

[239]FF 2009 2755.

[240]Report of May 2010 of the Federal Office of Justice on the results of the consultation procedure on the Federal Law on in-house lawyers.

[241]https://www.parlament.ch/fr/ratsbetrieb/suche-curia-vista/geschaeft?AffairId=20150409 (last visited on 13 September 2018).

[242]https://www.parlament.ch/fr/ratsbetrieb/suche-curia-vista/geschaeft?AffairId=20150409 (last visited on 13 September 2018).

[243]Bohnet and Martenet (2009), para 1810.

[244]Arts 37–39 of the Vaud Law on the Law Profession.

[245]Bohnet and Martenet (2009), para 1811; Chappuis (2016), p. 176.

[246]Bohnet and Martenet (2009), para 1810; Chappuis (2016), p. 176.

[247]Arts 163(1)(b) et 166 (1)(b) of the Code of Civil Procedure; Arts 171 and 248 of the Code of Criminal Procedure; Arts 41(2) and 50(2) of the Federal Law on the Criminal Administrative Law; Arts 16(2) and 17 of the Federal Law on the Administrative Procedure.

They are entitled to invoke legal privileges provided by the laws on civil, criminal and administrative procedure.[248]

332   Most authors agree that Art. 321 of the Criminal Code is also applicable to foreign lawyers licensed to provide legal advice and represent clients in courts of their home jurisdiction and practising in a professional and independent manner in Switzerland.[249] Therefore, foreign lawyers are entitled to invoke legal privileges provided by the Swiss laws on civil, criminal and administrative procedure.[250] As a consequence, it is our view that foreign lawyers representing clients in international arbitration proceedings are bound by professional secrecy duties when Swiss law applies as the *lex arbitri*.

3.5.4.3 England and Wales

3.5.4.3.1 Legal Basis and Scope

333   There is no statutory basis for legal professional privilege in England and Wales.[251] It was originally considered as a rule of evidence, but the concept has evolved and it is generally admitted now that legal professional privilege is a substantive legal right.[252] Further to a decision of the House of Lords, it is a fundamental human right protected by Arts 6 and 8 ECHR.[253] Indeed, the privilege can be asserted not only in adversarial proceedings, but also in investigative proceedings and in other cases where no proceedings exist or are only in contemplation.[254]

334   There are two categories of legal professional privilege in England and Wales: the legal advice privilege and the litigation privilege.[255] The legal advice privilege protects communications between client and lawyer for the purposes of seeking or obtaining legal advice.[256] Litigation privilege protects communications and documents which come into existence after litigation is contemplated or has commenced,

---

[248]Arts 163(1)(b) et 166 (1)(b) of the Code of Civil Procedure; Arts 171 and 248 of the Code of Criminal Procedure; Arts 41(2) and 50(2) of the Federal Law on the Criminal Administrative Law; Arts 16(2) and 17 of the Federal Law on the Administrative Procedure.

[249]See, for example, Corboz (1993), p. 82; Maurer and Gross (2010), p. 155; Moreillon and Parein-Reymond (2016), p. 561. For developments on the difference of treatment between EU/EFTA lawyers and other foreign lawyers, see Chappuis and Steiner (2017), p. 12.

[250]Arts 163(1)(b) et 166 (1)(b) of the Code of Civil Procedure; Arts 171 and 248 of the Code of Criminal Procedure; Arts 41(2) and 50(2) of the Federal Law on the Criminal Administrative Law; Arts 16(2) and 17 of the Federal Law on the Administrative Procedure.

[251]Fox et al. (2013), p. 586.

[252]Fox et al. (2013), p. 586; Malek (2018), para 23-01.

[253]Fox et al. (2013), p. 586; Pattenden (2003), para 3.03.

[254]Malek (2018), para 23-01.

[255]Fox et al. (2013), pp. 586–587.

[256]Three Rivers District Council and Others v Governor and Company of the Bank of England [2003] QB 1556; Fox et al. (2013), p. 586.

for the primary purpose of obtaining information or advice in connection with such litigation.[257]

The Solicitors Regulation Authority Code of Conduct contains conduct require- **335**
ments, including the solicitor's duty to keep clients' affairs confidential unless disclosure is required or permitted by law or the client consents to disclosure.[258] Chapter 4 provides in particular:

> Protection of confidential information is a fundamental feature of your relation-ship with clients. It exists as a concept both as a matter of law and as a matter of conduct. This duty continues despite the end of the retainer and even after the death of the client.[259]

The scope of information protected by the solicitor's duty of confidentiality is broader than what is covered by legal professional privilege. Indeed, the solicitor's duty of confidentiality extends to all matters communicated to a solicitor by his client.[260]

3.5.4.3.2 Lawyers Bound by the Confidentiality Duty and Entitled to Legal Privilege

In England and Wales, solicitors and barristers are bound to respect the duty of **336**
confidentiality by the rules of professional conduct. For barristers, the duty of protecting the confidentiality of each client's affairs is contained in the Code of Conduct of the Bar Standards Board Handbook, section C3 rC15.5.

It is chapter 4 of the Solicitors Regulation Authority Code of Conduct that applies **337**
to solicitors practising in England and Wales. These provisions apply, in particular, to solicitors and their employees, registered European lawyers and their employees, and registered foreign lawyers practising in England and Wales.[261] For solicitors practising outside of England and Wales, the rules of professional conduct are contained in the Solicitors Regulation Authority Overseas Rules. The guidance note to Rule 1.6 provides that solicitors should follow the local legal or regulatory requirements of the jurisdiction in which they practise in relation to confidentiality. If

---

[257]Three Rivers District Council and Others v Governor and Company of the Bank of England [2003] QB 1556; Fox et al. (2013), p. 587.

[258]Chapter 4 of the Solicitors Regulation Authority Code of Conduct 2011, Version 14 published on 30 April 2015.

[259]Chapter 4 of the Solicitors Regulation Authority Code of Conduct 2011, Version 14 published on 30 April 2015.

[260]Taylor (1993), p. 330.

[261]Chapter 13 of the Solicitors Regulation Authority Code of Conduct 2011, version 14 published on 30 April 2015.

no such requirements exist, solicitors should be guided by what they consider to be the best interests of each client in the circumstances.[262]

338   The legal professional privilege applies to communications with a solicitor and barrister holding a current practising certificate.[263] If the lawyer does not have a current practising certificate, but the client did not know this and acted in good faith, the legal professional privilege will still apply.[264]

339   The legal advice privilege also extends to communications with foreign lawyers if the requisite lawyer-client relationship exists. The English Courts stated in *Re Duncan, Garfield v Fay [1968] P 306*:

> There is nothing [in the previous case law on the privilege] to suggest that [the judges] intended to limit the rule to legal advisers whose names appear on the roll of Solicitors of the Supreme Court or who are members of the English Bar. The basis of the privilege is just as apt to cover foreign legal advisers as English lawyers.

340   The legal advice privilege extends as well to in-house lawyers employed by government departments or commercial companies. As stated in *Alfred Crompton Amusement Machines Ltd v Customs and Excise Comrs* [1972] 2 QB 102:

> They are, no doubt, servants or agents of the employer. For that reason [the first-instance judge] thought they were in a different position from other legal advisers who are in private practice. I do not think this is correct. They are regarded by the law as in every respect in the same position as those practice on their own account. The only difference is that they act for one client only, and not for several clients. They must uphold the same standards of honour and etiquette. They are subject to the same duties to their client and to the court. They must respect the same confidences. They and their clients have the same privileges. . . I speak, of course of their communications in the capacity of legal advisers.

341   Communications with non-lawyers providing legal advice are not protected by the legal professional privilege unless there are statutory exceptions. Such exceptions exist regarding patent and trade mark agents,[265] licensed conveyancers,[266] authorized advocates and litigators.[267]

---

[262]Guidance note to Rule 1.6, Part 1 of the Solicitors Regulation Authority Overseas Rules 2013, version 14 published on 30 April 2015.

[263]Fox et al. (2013), p. 588.

[264]Fox et al. (2013), p. 588.

[265]Copyright, Designs and Patents Act 1988, ss 280 and 284.

[266]Administration of Justice Act 1985, s 33.

[267]Courts and Legal Services Act 1990, s 63.

3.5.4.4 United States

3.5.4.4.1 Legal Basis and Scope

In the United States, the principle of client-lawyer confidentiality is given effect in **342** three legal notions: the professional duty of confidentiality, the attorney-client privilege and the work-product doctrine.[268]

The professional duty of confidentiality is established in the legal ethics code of **343** the relevant state. At the federal level, the ABA Model Rules of Professional Conduct are considered an important guide. Art. 1.6 of the ABA Model Rules imposes on lawyers a duty to keep confidential information relating to the representation of a client. In the state of New York, the confidentiality duty is codified in Rule 1.6 of the New York Rules of Professional Conduct. This provision prohibits a lawyer from knowingly revealing confidential information or from using such information to the disadvantage of a client or for the advantage of the lawyer or a third person.

Under the New York Rules of Professional Conduct, the attorney's duty of **344** confidentiality covers all information gained during or relating to the representation of a client, whatever its source.[269] It includes (a) information that is protected by the attorney-client privilege, (b) likely to be embarrassing or detrimental to the client if disclosed, or (c) information that the client has requested be kept confidential.[270] The duty of confidentiality does not extend to (i) a lawyer's legal knowledge or legal research, or (ii) information that is generally known in the local community or in the trade, field or profession to which the information relates.[271]

The attorney-client privilege originated from common law case development, but **345** it has now been statutorily codified in some jurisdictions.[272] In the jurisdictions where the privilege has not been codified, it remains a common law principle.[273] In the state of New York, the attorney-client privilege protection is granted if the following conditions are met: (i) a client, (ii) seeks legal advice, (iii) from a lawyer, (iv) in circumstances indicating that the communications between lawyer and client for that purpose are made in confidence.[274]

The work-product doctrine provides protection to the materials prepared in **346** anticipation of litigation.[275] As opposed to the attorney-client privilege, its primary

---

[268]ABA Model Rules of Professional Conduct, Comment 3 on Rule 1.6 (https://www.nysba.org/WorkArea/DownloadAsset.aspx?id=50671; last visited on 13 September 2018).

[269]New York Rules of Professional Conduct, Rule 1.6.

[270]New York Rules of Professional Conduct, Rule 1.6.

[271]New York Rules of Professional Conduct, Rule 1.6.

[272]32 AMJUR POF 3d 189; New York Civil Practice Law and Rules, § 4503.

[273]32 AMJUR POF 3d 189.

[274]32 AMJUR POF 3d 189.

[275]Hickman v Taylor, 329 U.S. 495; Rule 26(b)(3) of the Federal Rules of Civil Procedure; Bondi (2010), pp. 153–154.

goal is to protect the attorney in his advocacy role.[276] The work-product doctrine does not protect the communications of the client, but rather materials created by counsel in anticipation of litigation.[277] It has a broader scope of application than the attorney-client privilege as it protects materials that are not even seen or reviewed by the client[278]; litigation needs only be contemplated, not necessarily imminent at the time the work is performed[279]; and 'litigation' is construed broadly to include administrative and federal investigations.[280]

347   As shown above, the scope of the information protected by the lawyer's duty of confidentiality is broader than that covered by the attorney-client privilege and the work-product doctrine. Another significant difference is that the professional duty of lawyer-client confidentiality applies in all settings and at all times, while the attorney-client privilege and the work-product doctrine apply when a lawyer is compelled by a judicial or other governmental body to testify or produce information or evidence concerning the client.[281]

3.5.4.4.2   Lawyers Entitled to the Attorney-Client Privilege and Bound by the Confidentiality Duty

348   In the United States, any lawyer competent to render legal advice and permitted by law to do so in any jurisdiction is entitled to invoke the attorney-client privilege.[282] As opposed to most civil law jurisdictions, 'non-bar in-house attorneys' are entitled to invoke attorney-client privilege.[283] As to a foreign lawyer, he will be eligible for the protection of the attorney-client privilege if he performs functions similar to U.S. lawyers.[284] Thus, a foreign lawyer practicing arbitration and permitted by law to render legal advice is entitled to invoke the attorney-client privilege.

349   As to the lawyer's professional duty of confidentiality, only lawyers admitted to practise law in one of the U.S. jurisdictions will be subject to such duty. For example, the confidentiality duty imposed on lawyers by Rule 1.6 of the New York Rules of Professional Conduct applies to individuals who are admitted to practise law in the state of New York.

---

[276]Bondi (2010), p. 153.

[277]Bondi (2010), pp. 153–154.

[278]Grand Jury Proceedings, 601 F.2nd 162, 171 (5th Cir. 1979); Bondi (2010), p. 152.

[279]Holland v. Island Creek Corp., 885 F. Supp. 4, 7 (D.D.C. 1995).

[280]Grand Jury Proceedings, 867 F.2nd 539 (9th Cir. 1989); Sealed Case, 676 F.2nd 793 (D.C. Cir. 1982).

[281]ABA Model Rules of Professional Conduct, Comment 3 on Rule 1.6.

[282]Marin (1997), p. 1589; Renfield Corp. v. E. Remy Martin & Co., 98 F.R.D., 444.

[283]Marin (1997), p. 1588; Renfield Corp. v. E. Remy Martin & Co., 98 F.R.D., 444.

[284]Marin (1997), p. 1589; Renfield Corp. v. E. Remy Martin & Co., 98 F.R.D., 444.

3.5.4.5   Comparative Law Analysis

There are many similarities in the regulation of the duty of confidentiality and the   **350**
legal privilege between different jurisdictions. As we have seen, in all the above-
mentioned jurisdictions, lawyers are bound by a duty of confidentiality regarding all
information that they gain during or relating to the representation of a client. Also,
the scope of the information covered by the professional duty of confidentiality is
generally broader than the scope of information protected by the legal privilege.
Another common feature is the fact that in many jurisdictions, the scope *ratione
temporis* of the duty of confidentiality is unlimited and survives the death of the
client.[285]

Quite similarly, the lawyer's duty of confidentiality extends to all information that   **351**
he gains during the representation of a client, *whatever its source*. Thus, under Swiss
law, some commentators consider that the lawyer is bound by the confidentiality
duty independently of the source of the information, even if it comes from the
adverse party.[286] Likewise, Rule 1.6 of the New York Rules of Professional Conduct
imposes on the lawyer a duty not to knowingly reveal the information gained during
or relating to the representation of a client, whatever its source.[287]

Despite these similarities, there are also some significant differences relating, in   **352**
particular, to the qualification and regulation of legal privilege. These include, for
example, qualification of the legal privilege as a substantive or procedural matter,
availability of the legal privilege to in-house counsel, whether and how the right to
the privilege can be lost, and whether the legal privilege belongs to the attorney or to
the client.

With respect to the last issue, under Swiss law, although the lawyer has an   **353**
obligation of confidentiality vis-à-vis the client, he is still the owner of the secret
when it comes to the legal privilege. Indeed, even if the client releases the lawyer
from his duty, the lawyer is free to decide whether he will disclose the information
covered by the legal privilege.[288] In England and Wales, the legal professional

---

[285]For example, in England (Derby Magistrates' Court, ex parte B [1996] AC 487; Taylor 1993, p. 586) and in Switzerland (Art. 13(1) LLCA).

[286]Maurer and Gross (2010), p. 180; Corboz (1993), p. 86; Bohnet and Martenet (2009), p. 758. The opposite view is supported by Jolles et al. (2013), p. 135.

[287]It is, however, important to distinguish between disclosure to a third party and such a disclosure to the client. Let's assume that A has a lawsuit against B and that B sends by mistake a document relevant to the lawsuit to A's lawyer. Since A's lawyer has a duty to act in the best interests of his client, the lawyer would be in breach of his duties if he decided to conceal this piece of information from his client, A. The fact that a lawyer owes a duty of confidentiality to his client, but not to the adverse party. A different issue is the disclosure of the information received from the adverse party to third persons, i.e. persons not involved in the litigation. In this respect, the lawyer is undoubtedly bound by the duty of confidentiality.

[288]ATF 136 III 296, 3.3; Bohnet and Martenet (2009), para 1853.

privilege belongs to the client.[289] Only the client can waive the privilege, and absent such waiver, the lawyer cannot waive the privilege.[290]

354   As for the availability of the legal privilege to in-house counsel, the issue has been much debated. While in common law jurisdictions such as England, New Zealand and the United States, legal privileges extend to in-house lawyers, this is not the case in civil law jurisdictions like Switzerland, France and Sweden.[291] These differences are confirmed by the worldwide survey Lex Mundi, which presents a country-by-country overview of the availability of protection from disclosure of communications between in-house counsel and the officers, directors or employees of the companies they serve.[292] The Lex Mundi survey reveals that there are substantial differences in the application and the scope of this privilege.[293]

355   In-house counsel are not bound by a lawyer's duty of confidentiality because they are employed by the company and are not in a lawyer-client relationship. However, they owe a duty of confidentiality based on the contractual relationship with the employer. As to the *ratione materiae* scope of the lawyer's duty of confidentiality, there seems to be no major differences in regulation of the jurisdictions discussed above. In general terms, the duty of confidentiality covers all information gained by the lawyer during his representation of a client and related to this representation. Quite obviously, publicly-known matters and facts generally known in the relevant field or profession are not subject to confidentiality.

3.5.5   Regulation of the Lawyer's Duty of Confidentiality in International Arbitration

3.5.5.1   Introduction

356   As mentioned above, there is a lack of sufficiently-developed, substantive international rules on representatives' professional conduct in international arbitration. The lawyer's duty of confidentiality is mainly regulated at the national level. Some texts specifically designed for international arbitration proceedings, however, contain rules on the counsel's duty of confidentiality and/or the legal privilege.

357   In the present section, we will first examine what are the requirements to the parties' representatives in international arbitration proceedings. Second, we will review the regulation provided by international arbitration law instruments. Third,

---

[289]Fox et al. (2013), p. 586.

[290]Fox et al. (2013), p. 586.

[291]http://www.lexmundi.com/lexmundi/InHouseCounsel_AttorneyClientPrivilege_Guide.asp (last visited on 13 September 2018).

[292]http://www.lexmundi.com/lexmundi/InHouseCounsel_AttorneyClientPrivilege_Guide.asp (last visited on 13 September 2018).

[293]http://www.lexmundi.com/lexmundi/InHouseCounsel_AttorneyClientPrivilege_Guide.asp (last visited on 13 September 2018).

we will briefly examine the scope of the duty of confidentiality. Finally, we will explore the problem of the applicable law and will see that there is a multitude of existing options.

3.5.5.2 Parties' Representatives in International Arbitration

In arbitration proceedings, there are generally no mandatory requirements for parties' representatives regarding education, training, experience, or bar admission.[294] Indeed, parties are free to exercise their autonomy and to select their representatives based on the criteria relevant to them, including, for example, specific professional experience, legal background, language skills and reputation. The parties' right to be represented or assisted by a person of their choice is stipulated, for instance, in Art. 5 of the 2010 UNCITRAL Rules and in Art. 13 (6) of the HKIC Rules.   **358**

Representation by non-lawyers is generally possible, and sometimes even expressly provided for by certain arbitration rules and laws.[295] Thus, the IBA Guidelines on Party Representation in International Arbitration provide the following definition for party representatives: **359**

> '*Party Representative*' or '*Representative*' means any person, including a Party's employee, who appears in an arbitration on behalf of a Party and makes submissions, arguments or representations to the Arbitral Tribunal on behalf of such Party, other than in the capacity as a Witness or Expert, and whether or not legally qualified or admitted to a Domestic Bar.[296]

As a rule, there are no restrictions related to counsel's nationality, or their country of residence or practice. There have been, however, a few examples when foreign counsel was prohibited from representing parties in international arbitration.[297] Thus, David W. Rivkin reported in a 1991 article the instances where countries such as Singapore, Japan, Portugal and Turkey imposed restrictions on representation by foreign counsel in international arbitration.[298] There can also be indirect barriers that effectively restrict the parties' right to freely choose their representative by imposing, for example, certain tax regulations or visa requirements on foreign lawyers.[299] These are, however, marginal cases deviating from the international   **360**

---

[294]For more details on legal representation in international arbitration, see Born (2014), pp. 2832–2849; Rivkin (1991), pp. 402–412.

[295]Art. 36 of the English Arbitration Act; Art. 5 of the 2010 UNCITRAL Rules; Art. 13(a) of the WIPO Rules; Born (2014), pp. 2847–2848.

[296]IBA Guidelines on Party Representation in International Arbitration, Definitions, 4.

[297]Rivkin (1991), pp. 402–406; Born (2014), pp. 2837–2840.

[298]Rivkin (1991), pp. 402–406.

[299]Born (2014), p. 2840.

norm.[300] As observed by Gary Born, '*the decisive trend over the past several decades has been towards recognition of the parties' right to legal (or other) representatives of their choice in international arbitration.*'[301]

361   For the purpose of the present section dealing with the counsel's duty of confidentiality, we have focused on the *lawyer*'s duty of confidentiality. However, it needs to be kept in mind that depending on the jurisdiction, the terms used to designate lawyers, and the requirements for obtaining such qualification, can vary substantially. Likewise, rules on the existence of legal privilege and its scope regarding lawyers admitted to foreign bars and in-house lawyers are different. As discussed above, while some countries admit that the legal privilege should apply to in-house lawyers, other domestic legislations provide the contrary.

362   There is however no doubt that in-house lawyers should be bound by the duty of confidentiality in arbitration proceedings. We did not address the issue of the in-house lawyers' duty of confidentiality in a separate section, as they do not generally have a specific status in arbitration proceedings. In most cases, in-house lawyers provide instructions to the outside counsel on behalf of the party. Thus, in-house lawyers are associated with the party on behalf of which they provide instructions. Like any other employee, in-house lawyers are bound by the duty of confidentiality regarding the matters they treat for their employers. Under Swiss employment law, for example, the employee must not exploit or reveal confidential information obtained while in the employer's service.[302] In addition, depending on the relevant jurisdiction, in-house lawyers can also be bound by a professional duty of confidentiality imposed by domestic rules on lawyers working in-house.

3.5.5.3   International Arbitration Law Instruments

363   Although it is rather uncommon, some texts specifically designed for international arbitration proceedings contain specific rules on the counsel's duty of confidentiality and/or the legal privilege. On the one hand, there are non-binding guidelines, which can be given binding force by agreement of the parties. For example, the IBA Rules on Evidence contain provisions on the attorney-client privilege, but not on counsel's obligation of confidentiality. As already mentioned above, the IBA Rules can be used as procedural guidelines, leaving a wide flexibility and discretion to the arbitrators, or can be given a binding force by agreement of the parties.[303] According to Art. 9(2)(b) of the IBA Rules on Evidence, the arbitral tribunal must exclude from evidence or production any document, statement, oral testimony or inspection to which legal privilege applies.

---

[300]Born (2014), p. 2840.

[301]Born (2014), p. 2845.

[302]Art. 321a (4) CO.

[303]Lew et al. (2003), p. 553; Forword to the IBA Rules on Evidence.

In addition, the IBA Guidelines on Party Representation in International Arbitra-   **364**
tion refer to both privilege and confidentiality. These Guidelines can be adopted by
the parties entirely or partially by agreement.[304] If the arbitral tribunal establishes
that it has the authority to rule on the relevant issue, it can also apply the Guidelines
on its own initiative, subject to any applicable mandatory provisions.[305] It is clear
from the text of the Guidelines that relevant considerations of privilege and confidentiality are to be taken into account in the course of the arbitral proceedings,[306] but
the Guidelines do not contain any definition of the confidentiality and privilege or
the scope of their protection.

On the other hand, there are rules of arbitration institutions which become binding   **365**
once the parties agree to adopt them for the conduct of their ongoing or future arbitral
proceedings. Most of the institutional rules do not address in any detail the lawyer's
duty of confidentiality. Only some rules have a specific provision on the confidentiality obligations of parties' representatives.[307] Thus, Art. 44.1 of the DIS Rules
imposes a duty of confidentiality on the *parties and their outside counsel*.

3.5.5.4 Scope of the Counsel's Duty of Confidentiality

In international arbitration, the counsel's duty of confidentiality is often examined in   **366**
the context of legal privilege. There are indeed important practical implications as
the privilege is often invoked as a basis to withhold evidence during document
production. The lawyer's duty of confidentiality is generally ignored in arbitration
literature. Indeed, if counsel breaches his duty of confidentiality, the client will more
likely bring his complaint before the competent domestic court rather than to the
arbitral tribunal.

Neither the international arbitration guidelines, nor the arbitration rules we have   **367**
examined above define the scope of the legal privilege and the scope of the lawyer's
professional duty of confidentiality. Regarding the scope of application of the legal
privilege, one needs to look into the applicable domestic law rules as the privilege
reflects the public policy of a particular legal system. In addition, the rules on
privilege vary substantially depending on the jurisdiction. We will examine the
problem of applicable law below.

As for the scope of the lawyer's professional duty of confidentiality, we have seen   **368**
in the previous sections that there is common ground between the regulations

---

[304]IBA Guidelines on Party Representation in International Arbitration, Preamble, 2.

[305]IBA Guidelines on Party Representation in International Arbitration, Preamble, 2.

[306]See, for example, Arts 10, 11, 15 and 27(e) of the IBA Guidelines on Party Representation in International Arbitration.

[307]See, for example, Section 44.1 of the DIS Rules; Art. 24(2) of the Beijing Arbitration Commission Arbitration Rules, Art. 36(2) of the China International Economic and Trade Arbitration
Commission (CIETAC) Arbitration Rules, Art. 38(2) of the Japan Commercial Arbitration Associations Commercial Arbitration Rules, Art. 21(3) of the Rules of Arbitration of Tokyo Maritime
Arbitration Commission (TOMAC) of the Japan Shipping Exchange.

provided by national legal systems and by international law instruments.[308] This common ground is reflected in the principle that the counsel's duty of confidentiality should cover all information obtained during the counsel's representation of a client and related to this representation. We think that a similar approach should be adopted in international arbitration. Therefore, in our opinion, party representatives in international arbitration must keep confidential all matters that become known to them as a result of the party's representation and related to this representation.

3.5.5.5 Applicable Law

369 As discussed earlier,[309] depending on the jurisdiction, the lawyers' duty of confidentiality may be associated with such legal concepts as professional secrecy, the professional duty of confidentiality, legal privilege and the work-product doctrine. Although the terms may vary, most jurisdictions are familiar with the following two legal concepts: the professional duty of confidentiality and the legal privilege. We will examine the problem of applicable law regarding these two principles.

370 In international arbitration, the professional duty of confidentiality is not often examined since, in most cases, it is outside the arbitral tribunal's competence. Indeed, if there is an alleged breach of a lawyer's duty of confidentiality, the client will most likely make a complaint to the lawyer's bar association and/or will bring an action before the competent state court. The lawyer's bar will generally apply rules of the local bar and its domestic law provisions. The competent court will determine the applicable law based on the conflict of laws of the *lex fori*.

371 The most obvious solution would be to subject the lawyer to the rules of professional conduct of the country where he is admitted to practise law. Other options would be the place of qualification and the place of practice. Thus, for a lawyer having qualified in Russia, admitted to the New York state bar and practicing arbitration in Switzerland, we have three options of applicable law. Thus, there is a risk of 'double' or 'triple' deontology when a lawyer is subject to ethical rules of several jurisdictions. If there are differences in the scope of confidentiality duty between the relevant jurisdictions, it may be more cautious for a lawyer to comply with the most stringent rules.

372 As for legal privilege, this rule and principle has its practical importance in international arbitration as it is often used as an argument for objecting to the production of documents. There is, however, much uncertainty regarding the law applicable to privilege claims in international arbitration.[310] Arbitral tribunals, faced with the problem of deciding on the law to be applied to privilege claims, have very little guidance given the multitude of choices they have. In many cases, counsel claim privilege and arbitrators make their decisions in relation to these claims

---

[308]See above Sect. 3.5.4.5.

[309]See above Sect. 3.5.4.5.

[310]Kuitkowski (2015), p. 64.

without referring to the applicable law. In fact, arbitrators and counsel often make decisions based on their own experience as well as rules of their country of origin, practice, bar admission or legal studies.

The laws applicable to the legal privilege may be the *lex arbitri*, the law governing the parties' arbitration agreement or the law with which the allegedly privileged communication has the closest connection.[311] The law of the closest connection is probably the preferable option.[312] Indeed, what is considered privileged reflects the public policy of a particular legal system.[313] Therefore, it would not be justified to undercut this legal system in favour of the law of the seat or in favour of the law governing the arbitration agreement with which the allegedly privileged communication has no connection.[314] On the other hand, application of the law with which the allegedly privileged communication has the closest connection has the disadvantage of not applying the same law in the same situation to different parties, which might be contrary to the principle of equal treatment. **373**

The question of which law has the closest connection with the privilege is not, however, clear-cut. When a specific communication between an attorney and his client is questioned, one could argue that the law of the place where the communication is made should apply. The problem is that the place of communication is sometimes fortuitous (e.g., email containing legal advice sent from an airport) and thus does not serve the intended goal.[315] **374**

Other possible options for the applicable law include the country of the client's domicile, or the place of the lawyer's qualification or practice. This can, however, result in complex situations since the client is not necessarily domiciled in the country where his lawyer was qualified, the lawyer may be qualified in several countries and may practise outside of the country of his qualification. Also, a client may be represented by a team of lawyers practising from different offices situated in multiple jurisdictions. Gary Born suggests that the tribunal should apply the privilege law of the state in which the senior external lawyer involved in the communications is qualified.[316] This appears to be a sound solution to the problem, but it cannot apply in all situations. There can indeed be a situation where two senior external lawyers qualified in different jurisdictions work as a team representing the same client. If both lawyers are involved in the allegedly privileged communication, we will have two possible applicable laws. In addition, there is a potential problem of the parties' unequal treatment, as there is a risk that different laws will apply in the same situation to different parties. **375**

---

[311]Born (2014), p. 2383.

[312]See more developments on this issue in Born (2014), p. 2383; Furrer (2008), p. 811.

[313]Born (2014), p. 2384; Mosk and Ginsburg (2001), p. 346.

[314]Born (2014), p. 2384.

[315]Born (2014), p. 2384.

[316]Born (2014), p. 2386.

376   It is also suggested in the arbitration literature to apply cumulatively competing substantive rules or opt for the application of alternative choice of law rules.[317] Under the cumulative approach, privileges under all laws applicable to the client and its representative should be respected.[318] This means, however, again that different laws may apply in the same situation to different parties. To avoid this problem, another option is to apply alternative choice of law rules, which requires application of the most protective privilege rules to all parties.[319] This solution was adopted, for example, by Art. 22 of the ICDR Rules regulating the issue of privilege:

> When the parties, their counsel, or their documents would be subject under applicable law to different rules, the tribunal should, to the extent possible, apply the same rule to all parties, giving preference to the rule that provides the highest level of protection.

377   Although this option seems to resolve the problem of the parties' equal treatment, it is not supported by a satisfactory analytical basis. As commented by Born, '[*i*]*t is very difficult to justify granting one party legal rights that it does not otherwise possess, merely because its counter-party enjoys them.*'[320]

378   According to certain authors, adopting 'a most protective privilege' approach would not be an obstacle to searching for the truth, but would be an acknowledgement that the parties are to be treated equally and that legal privileges are to be respected.[321] We agree with this opinion. In our view, the application of the most protective privilege rules to all parties is the most preferable option as it guarantees equal treatment of the parties and it has therefore the practical benefit that the parties would hardly have reasons to complain about being unequally treated.

3.5.6   Intermediary Conclusions

379   As highlighted above, depending on the jurisdiction, different legal concepts can be encompassed in what we generally referred to as "lawyer's duty of confidentiality". Yet, it is important to understand that, at least in common law jurisdictions, legal privilege and lawyer's duty of confidentiality are different legal concepts.

380   While the legal privilege refers to the right and obligation to withhold evidence when the lawyer is compelled by judicial or other public authority, the duty of confidentiality is an obligation which the lawyer owes to his client in all settings and at all times. Also, the scope of application of the legal privilege is generally more

---

[317]Furrer (2008), p. 811.

[318]Furrer (2008), p. 811.

[319]Born (2014), p. 2386; Grégoire (2016), pp. 150–151.

[320]Born (2014), p. 2385.

[321]Von Schlabrendorff and Sheppard (2005), p. 774.

limited as compared to the duty of confidentiality. In civil law countries, these two legal concepts are generally encompassed in the obligation of professional secrecy. In common law countries, a distinction is often made between legal privilege and lawyers' ethical and professional duties of confidentiality.

International arbitration rules and national arbitration laws tend to ignore the issue **381** of the counsel's duty of confidentiality, but a significant effort has been made at the international level to create uniform rules. While most of these rules are not binding, the Code of Conduct for European Lawyers stands out as its provisions are binding for lawyer-members of the bars in almost 30 European countries. Thus, the notion of the lawyers' duty of confidentiality contained in this text expresses a general consensus at the European level. Its scope of application is quite large since it requires lawyers to respect the confidentiality of all information that becomes known to them in the course of their professional activity.[322]

However, most issues related to the counsel's duty of confidentiality are resolved **382** by domestic rules. Even though there are some differences in the qualification and regulation of the lawyer's duty of confidentiality, the essence of this duty is rather similar in many jurisdictions. In general terms, it covers practically all information obtained by the lawyer during the representation of a client and related to this representation.

In international arbitration, there are generally no mandatory requirements for **383** parties' representatives regarding education, training, experience, bar admission or any other qualifications. Most party representatives, however, have sophisticated legal training and are bound by the lawyers' professional conduct rules at least in one jurisdiction. These rules will almost inevitably impose a duty of confidentiality on the lawyers. In our opinion, even in the absence of such rules and express agreement imposing the confidentiality duty, any counsel representing a party in international arbitration has an ethical obligation to keep confidential all matters that he obtains during the representation of a party and related to this representation.

As to the law applicable to the lawyer's professional duty of confidentiality, it **384** will most likely be governed by the rules of professional conduct of the country where the lawyer is admitted to practice law. However, the risk of 'double' deontology when a lawyer is subject to ethical rules of several jurisdictions cannot be excluded. Regarding the law applicable to the legal privilege, among several possible options, we think that the most preferable solution is to apply alternative choice of law rules, which requires application of the most protective privilege rules to all parties.

---

[322] Art. 2.3 of the Code of Conduct for European Lawyers.

3.6 Third Persons' Duty of Confidentiality

3.6.1 Introduction

385   In addition to the parties, arbitrators, counsel and the arbitration institution, there are a number of third persons who will have access to information and documents relating to the arbitration proceedings. These include the secretary to the arbitral tribunal, fact witnesses, expert witnesses appointed by the parties or by the tribunal, translators and interpreters, court reporters, etc. The question is whether these individuals are bound by a duty of confidentiality and how to ensure that confidentiality is respected if it is desired, but is not provided for by the applicable arbitration rules.

386   First, we will review the basis of the duty of confidentiality with regard to third persons. We will see that sources for third parties' duty of confidentiality can be found in national arbitration laws, national contract law provisions and the rules of professional conduct. We will also discuss whether institutional arbitration rules have a direct binding effect on third persons.

387   Second, we will examine the basis of the duty of confidentiality as applied specifically to (i) fact witnesses, (ii) expert witnesses, (iii) tribunal secretaries and other tribunal auxiliaries, (iv) counsel auxiliaries, and (v) other third persons. We will see that the nature of the relationship with most third persons is contractual. As to a party-witness relationship, we will opine that the existence of a contract cannot be excluded.

3.6.2 Basis of the Duty of Confidentiality

388   *First*, the third person's duty of confidentiality can find its source in national arbitration laws. As already mentioned, however, most national arbitration laws do not contain provisions on confidentiality. If a provision on confidentiality mentioning a particular group of individuals (witnesses, interpreters or other) nevertheless exists, it will have a binding effect.

389   *Second*, there can be other national law provisions imposing the duty of confidentiality. For example, contractual law provisions applying to the employment relationship between the secretary to the arbitral tribunal and an arbitrator, or between paralegals or other staff members of the counsel's team and the law firm. If there is no employment relationship, there can also be a contract for the provision of services, as in the case for a party-expert relationship. It needs to be noted, however, that these contracts create a confidentiality obligation only vis-à-vis a contractual counterparty, but not towards other persons involved in the arbitration proceedings.

390   *Third*, there are a number of arbitration rules which impose a duty of confidentiality on third parties, including expert witnesses, fact witnesses, interpreters,

reporters, and the secretary(ies) to the arbitral tribunal.[323] Third parties can also be designated in more general terms. For example, the Arbitration Rules of the Japan Commercial Arbitration Association mention

> '[t]he arbitrators, the JCAA (including its directors, officers, employees, and other staff), the Parties, their counsel and assistants, *and other persons involved in the arbitral proceedings*' (italics added).

The binding nature of institutional arbitration rules upon third persons is, how-   **391**
ever, questionable. Arbitration rules are binding upon the parties because the parties agreed to such rules in their arbitration agreement or otherwise adopted them. Since third persons are not parties to the arbitration agreement and if they do not otherwise adopt the relevant arbitration rules, provisions of the arbitration rules do not have a direct binding effect on them.

It could be argued, however, that by agreeing to participate in the arbitration   **392**
proceedings, third persons implicitly agree that the rules governing these arbitration proceedings apply to them. While we think this is true for expert witnesses because they participate in the arbitration proceedings as professionals, the situation is different regarding fact witnesses. Indeed, the witnesses participate in the arbitration proceedings not because of the professional experience and knowledge, but because they have witnessed specific facts relevant for the outcome of the dispute. Since they have no professional and personal interest in participating in the arbitration proceedings, the arbitration rules should not directly apply to them.

Nevertheless, even when the arbitration rules do not have a binding effect, the   **393**
relevant provision on confidentiality should be used as a guide indicating that a particular arbitration institution expects that third persons participating in the arbitration will respect the confidentiality of the arbitration proceedings.

Finally, there exist rules of professional conduct or ethical obligations applicable   **394**
to witnesses from certain professions, including doctors, accountants, and priests. Although these rules are not specifically designated for arbitration proceedings, they impose confidentiality duties and thus can be of relevance.

---

[323] Art. 8(1) of the Milan Rules, Art. 25 of the International Arbitration Court of the Chamber of Commerce and Industry of the Russian Federation, Art. 44(1) of the Swiss Rules, Art. 24(2) of the Beijing Arbitration Commission Arbitration Rules, Art. 36(2) of the China International Economic and Trade Arbitration Commission (CIETAC) Arbitration Rules, Arts 42.2 and 42.1 of the HKIAC Rules, Art. 15.1 of the Kuala Lumpur Regional Centre for Arbitration Rules, Art. 40(1) of the Cairo Regional Centre for International Commercial Arbitration Rules.

3.6.3   Fact Witnesses' Duty of Confidentiality

3.6.3.1   Introduction

395   The problem of the fact witness's duty of confidentiality has not been much discussed in the arbitration literature.[324] While it is rather common to see the parties enter into a confidentiality agreement with their expert witness, this is usually not the case regarding fact witnesses. In the absence of an express agreement on confidentiality, are fact witnesses bound by a duty of confidentiality and if so, what are the potential sources of such duty? We will examine these questions in the present section.

396   We will first provide a legal qualification of the party-witness relationship. As will be shown below, the existence of a contractual relationship can be admitted when a party and a witness expressly agree to enter into a contract on the provision of 'witness services'. We will then review whether the witness' duty of confidentiality may find its origins in other sources, such as the employment relationship with a party, or in the applicable arbitration rules.

3.6.3.2   Legal Qualification of the Party-Witness Relationship

397   A potential source for the witness's duty of confidentiality could be his contract with the party, if such contract exists. The question of the legal nature of a relationship between a witness and the party calling him is very important, but has not been much studied in the legal literature. Several authors argue that a contractual relationship exists between the party and the witness 'called' by the party.[325] We will examine further whether this is the case and will refer primarily to the regulation provided on this issue by Swiss law.

398   Under Swiss law, a contract can be defined as a legal act formed by an exchange of at least two mutual and concordant expressions of intent directed to produce legal effect.[326] Thus, we will need to analyse (i) whether an agreement can exist between a party and a witness and (ii) whether a party and a witness intend that this agreement produce legal effect.

399   In civil law court proceedings, there cannot be a question of the existence of a contractual relationship with a witness in state court proceedings as witnesses are generally called by the court.[327] The court can compel a witness if he does not appear before the court voluntarily.[328] Under Swiss law, parties can call a witness only if the

---

[324]See, however, Ritz (2007), pp. 157–160.

[325]Ritz (2007), p. 157; Rüede and Hadenfeldt (1993), p. 267; Schlosser (2005), p. 792.

[326]Engel (1997), p. 158; Morin (2012), para 2.

[327]See, for example, Art. 170(1) of the Swiss Code of Civil Procedure.

[328]See, for example, Art. 167(1)(c) of the Swiss Code of Civil Procedure.

court permits the witness to be heard.[329] The proximity of a witness to one of the parties will nevertheless affect his credibility.

In international arbitration proceedings, the situation is different because wit-   **400** nesses are ordinarily 'called' by the parties and not by arbitrators.[330] Each party has the opportunity to present testimony of witnesses as evidence of the facts it seeks to prove. The right to call witnesses in arbitration is considered a procedural right stemming from the party's right to present its case and 'be heard'. It is not an obligation to call fact witnesses, but parties often exercise this right when it serves their interests, for example, if the facts are complicated and cannot be proved only by documentary evidence, or if testimony of a witness can clarify or explain the facts contained in documents.

According to generally admitted practice, it is not improper for a witness to be   **401** related to the party as its employee, officer or other representative.[331] The parties are also permitted to have contacts with their witnesses or potential witnesses, to interview them and to have discussions about their prospective testimony.[332]

In many cases, a fact witness is called because he worked for one of the parties to   **402** the arbitration when the facts subject to the dispute took place. In other cases, a fact witness is related to the party 'presenting' him in another way (having worked, for example, as an external advisor to the company). It is often the case that a fact witness is still employed by the party calling him at the time the arbitration is taking place. If, however, there is no, or no longer, such employment contract, is it possible to admit the existence of a party-witness contractual relationship based solely on the provision of 'witness' services'?

The party-witness relationship is usually established in arbitration proceedings   **403** when a party becomes aware that there is a person who can assist it in proving alleged facts necessary to its claims or defences. The party approaches this person to ask whether he is willing to cooperate by providing witness testimony. There is generally no obligation for a witness to provide testimony in international arbitration proceedings, although in some cases there may be a possibility to compel a witness by applying to the relevant local court for judicial support. There can be a number of reasons other than altruistic motives why a person accepts to serve as a witness: employment relationship with the party, the witness is a contractual partner of the party, etc.

If the person accepts to be a witness, he will typically provide at least some of the   **404** following 'services': reviewing and commenting on documentary evidence (contracts, emails, etc.) relating to the facts on which the witness will testify, preparation of a witness statement (and rebuttal witness statement(s), in some cases),

---

[329]Art. 170(2) of the Swiss Code of Civil Procedure; Schweizer (2011), CPC commenté, Art. 170 para 3.

[330]See, for example, Art. 4(1) of the IBA Rules on Evidence.

[331]Art. 4(2) of the IBA Rules on Evidence.

[332]Art. 4(3) of the IBA Rules on Evidence.

participation in preparatory sessions prior to the hearing, and provision of testimony at the hearing.

405   Witnesses in international arbitrations are usually not paid for their testimony, but may be indemnified for their costs and expenses, such as travel expenses. In our opinion, a witness can also be compensated for the time he spends preparing his testimony. There is, however, a risk that such an agreement could be considered *contra bonos mores* in some jurisdictions. We understand that lawyers from jurisdictions where witnesses are called by a judge and parties are not allowed to have direct contact with them can find the idea of a witness's compensation worrying. There is indeed a risk that a party 'buys' the content of a testimony rather than merely indemnifying the witness for his expenses and the time he spends on preparing his witness statement and his hearing testimony.[333] To avoid this risk, any indemnification or compensation of a witness should be reasonable.

406   Thus, in the framework of a party-witness relationship, a witness promises to a party to provide a number of 'services' relating to his testimony and this party usually undertakes to indemnify the witness and, in some cases, to compensate him. If a party and a witness succeed in reaching an agreement on the provision of these services, the first condition is met.

407   As to the second condition of the parties' intent that their agreement produce legal effect, it will be met in a situation where a party and a witness expressly agree to enter into a binding contract. They can also specifically agree on the legal consequences of any violations of the obligations under the contract. In this case, a contractual relationship will be admitted unless the terms of such a contract violate mandatory provisions of the applicable law. This can be the case, for example, if the purpose of the contract is to influence a witness or is to advance another illegal or immoral purpose.[334] We will examine further how Swiss law would qualify such a contract.

3.6.3.2.1 Qualification Under Swiss Law

408   In situations where a party reaches an agreement with the witness on compensation, a relationship with reciprocal obligations exists. By providing his testimony, a witness performs services from which at least one of the parties to the arbitration benefits. The party pays compensation to the witness which is the counter-performance for rendering the witness 'services'. Thus, this can be qualified as an ordinary synallagmatic contract (*contrat synallagmatique*) where both parties are to carry out reciprocal obligations.[335]

409   Under Swiss law, a contract for the provision of services without an obligation to achieve a specific result is usually qualified as an agency agreement (*contrat de*

---

[333]Schlosser (2005), p. 779.

[334]For example, Art. 20(1) CO and Art. 169 of the Russian Civil Code.

[335]Tercier and Pichonnaz (2012), para 244.

mandat).[336] It is regulated by Arts 394 ff CO. Under the agency contract, the agent undertakes to provide services. These services should consist in an obligation to do something as opposed to an obligation to refrain from an activity or to tolerate it.[337] Thus, the obligation that a witness undertakes to provide testimony in an arbitration can be considered as a service within the meaning of Art. 394 CO.

Under the principle of freedom of contract recognised by most legal systems,[338] **410** the parties are free to determine the terms of their agreement, but their liberty will be restricted by the rules of public policy. Thus, if the agreed compensation is unreasonably high, it may lead to the conclusion that the purpose of the agreement is to influence the witness. In most legal systems, such an agreement will be declared void as having an illegal content.[339]

If there is no compensation provided in exchange of serving as a witness, the **411** situation is different as the parties do not obtain equivalent benefits from their relationship. Such contracts, however, exist. In Swiss law, they are qualified as '*contrats bilatéraux imparfaits*' or '*unvollkommen zweiseitige Verträge*'. This term refers to a contract under which only one party has to perform the main obligation while the other party does not have to perform any corresponding obligation in exchange, but can have accessory obligations.[340] An example of this type of contract is the non-compensated agency contract called '*mandat gratuit*'. Although it is non-compensated, it is the same agency contract mentioned above and regulated by Arts 394 ff CO. Indeed, under Art. 394(3) CO, compensation of the agent is not mandatory for the relationship to be qualified as an agency contract, but can take place where agreed or customary.[341]

However, it is sometimes difficult to distinguish between a non-compensated **412** agency agreement and a non-contractual relationship called '*acte de complaisance*' or '*Gefälligkeit*'.[342] The existence of a contractual relationship will be decided on a case-by-case basis depending on the particular circumstances of each situation. As explained by the Swiss Supreme Court:

> To decide whether it is a contractual or a non-contractual relationship, one should examine the circumstances of a particular case and, in particular, the type of services, their basis, their purpose, their legal and economic significance, how this service was provided, as well as interests of each party. Whether the person performing the services has his own legal or

---

[336]Werro (2012b), Commentary of Art. 394 CO, paras 3, 5.

[337]An obligation to refrain from an activity or to tolerate it can be subject to the agency contract only in addition to the main obligation to do something (positive obligation) (Werro 2012b, Commentary of Art. 394 CO, para 4).

[338]See, for example, Art. 19 CO or Art. 1(1) of the Russian Civil Code.

[339]For example, Art. 20(1) CO and Art. 169 of the Russian Civil Code.

[340]Tercier and Pichonnaz (2012), para 246. If the other party does not have to perform any obligation, such a contract would be qualified as a 'contrat unilatéral' or 'einseitigen Verträge' (Tercier et al. 2016, para 341).

[341]Tercier et al. (2016), paras 4306–4307, 4559; Werro (2012b), Commentary of Art. 394 CO, para 41.

[342]Werro (2012b), Commentary of Art. 394 CO, paras 41–42; Werro (1993), paras 699–710.

economic interest to provide assistance or whether the beneficiary of the services has an identifiable interest to be advised and assisted in a qualified manner is an indicator that there is an intent to be contractually bound. In this regard, it is up to the person which relies on a contractual relationship to prove the circumstances which made him believe, according to the principle of confidence, the legal intent of the other party (Art. 8 CC).[343]

413   In our opinion, it would generally be difficult to prove the witness's intent to be contractually bound if his services are not compensated. In the assumption we used, however, the parties expressly agreed to enter into a binding contract. As a result, there should be no hesitation between a non-compensated agency agreement and the non-contractual '*acte de complaisance*' relationship. Therefore, if there is a contractual relationship between a party and a witness, such a relationship will be qualified under Swiss law as an agency contract under Arts 394 ff CO.

3.6.3.3 Basis of the Witnesses' Duty of Confidentiality

3.6.3.3.1 Party-Witness Contract

414   When a party and a witness enter into a contract, they can expressly agree on the witness's duty of confidentiality. Absent such an agreement, the question is whether the witness's duty of confidentiality can be implied from the provisions dealing with the agency contract under Swiss law. If Arts 394 ff CO apply to the party-witness relationship, a witness should be bound by a duty of confidentiality in accordance with Art. 398(2) CO. Indeed, as mentioned above, Art. 398(2) CO imposes an obligation of diligent and faithful performance which should include, according to Swiss commentators, an obligation of confidentiality.[344]

415   Philipp Ritz thinks, however, that the confidentiality obligation of Art. 398(2) CO is not applicable to a witness.[345] He bases his analysis mainly on the comparison of a regulation regarding a witness in arbitration proceedings and a witness in court proceedings.[346] He explains, for example, that because the witnesses in both situations bear the same responsibility in case of false testimony, a witness in arbitration proceedings cannot be treated less favourably as compared to a witness in court proceedings, who is not bound by a duty of confidentiality.[347] Also, Ritz argues that a witness does not have an obligation of cooperation with the arbitral tribunal and can decide to instead provide his testimony to a state court if he does not want to be bound by confidentiality.[348]

---

[343]Loose translation of ATF 116 II 695, recital 2(b), JdT 1991 I 625.

[344]Bucher and Tschanz (1988), para 116; Furrer (2008), p. 811; Meyer-Hauser (2004), p. 71; Jolles et al. (2013), p. 137.

[345]Ritz (2007), pp. 157–158.

[346]To see his analysis in more detail, see Ritz (2007), pp. 157–158.

[347]Criminal sanctions are identical in both cases in accordance with Arts 306–309 of the Swiss Criminal Code.

[348]Ritz (2007), p. 158.

Contrary to Ritz's opinion, we think that Art. 398(2) CO should apply to a **416** witness if the party-witness relationship is governed by the agency contract provisions. Indeed, the situation of a witness who contractually undertook to provide his testimony in arbitration proceedings is fundamentally different from the situation of a witness called to testify by the state court. As mentioned before, there is no contractual relationship with a witness in state court proceedings as witnesses are generally called by the court[349] and the parties can call a witness only if the court permits the witness to be heard.[350]

Also, a possibility that a fact witness actually demands to be heard in a public **417** court instead of in arbitration seems very unrealistic. In our opinion, the contractual nature of the relationship between a party and a witness justifies the application of Art. 398(2) CO. Consequently, we think that a witness should be bound by the confidentiality obligation imposed by Art. 398(2) CO. He will owe this duty, however, only vis-à-vis his contractual counterparty, but not towards other persons involved in the arbitration proceedings.

3.6.3.3.2 Employment Relationship

If there is an employment relationship between the party and its witness, witness's **418** duty of confidentiality towards his employer may result from the employment contract. Even if the employment contract does not contain such a duty, some national laws impose on the employee an obligation of confidentiality towards his employer. Under Swiss employment law, for example, the employee must not exploit or reveal confidential information obtained while in the employer's service.[351] Thus in Switzerland, unless the employment contract provides otherwise, there is a confidentiality duty owed by the employee to his employer. This duty is, however, not specific to arbitration proceedings. The notion of confidential information is broad and will cover all information that is not publicly known and that cannot be easily accessed.[352]

3.6.3.3.3 Institutional Arbitration Rules

As mentioned above, a number of institutional arbitration rules impose on witnesses **419** an obligation of confidentiality,[353] but they have no direct binding effect.

---

[349] Art. 170(1) of the Swiss Code of Civil Procedure.

[350] Art. 170(2) of the Swiss Code of Civil Procedure; Schweizer (2011), CPC commenté, Art. 170 para 3.

[351] Art. 321a(4) CO.

[352] Dunand (2013), Commentary of Art. 321a CO, para 39.

[353] Art. 8(1) of the Milan Rules, Art. 25 of the International Arbitration Court of the Chamber of Commerce and Industry of the Russian Federation, Art. 44(1) of the Swiss Rules, Art. 24(2) of the

Theoretically, it can be argued that by accepting to testify, a witness agrees to be bound by the rules governing the proceedings, including the arbitration rules. In our opinion, however, given a witness's limited role and likely lack of knowledge of arbitration proceedings, the witness's willingness to participate in the proceedings cannot be considered as implied consent to the arbitration rules. One solution could be for the arbitral tribunal to alert the witness to the confidentiality duty contained in the arbitration rules, if any such duty exists, and to confirm his willingness to abide by it. In this case, a witness would be directly bound by a confidentiality duty.

420   The WIPO and the ACICA Rules found another solution to the lack of binding effect of arbitration rules with regard to witnesses. They put responsibility for maintenance of the confidentiality by the witness on the party calling this witness. Art. 22.4 of the ACICA Rules, which is almost identical to the text of Art. 76(b) of the WIPO Rules, stipulates:

> To the extent that a witness is given access to evidence or other information obtained in the arbitration, the party calling such witness is responsible for the maintenance by the witness of the same degree of confidentiality as that required of the party.

421   According to this provision, the parties are responsible for any breaches of confidentiality by the witnesses they call. This means, in particular, that a party can be sued for the damages caused by its witnesses' disclosure of confidential information. One should, however, be aware that such a liability exists in most jurisdictions even in the absence of a specific regulation in the applicable arbitration rules. Under Swiss law, for example, there is a similar mechanism in Art. 101(1) CO establishing liability of a party for the acts of his associates who caused any loss or damage in carrying out the tasks delegated to them by that party. It is the so-called '*responsabilité pour le fait d'autrui*'.

422   Under Art. 22.4 of the ACICA Rules and Art. 76(b) of the WIPO Rules, the mechanism of '*responsabilité pour le fait d'autrui*' finds its origins in the contract that the parties enter into by adopting these Rules. If Swiss law applied to an arbitration under the ACICA or the WIPO Rules, we think that this clause would be recognised as valid as there are no mandatory law restrictions to contractually agree on the strict liability regime ('*responsabilité objective*') for third persons' acts. Art. 27 CC could be an obstacle as it protects persons from excessive restrictions of their liberties and undertakings, but it is unlikely that Art. 22.4 of the ACICA Rules and Art. 76(b) of the WIPO Rules would fall under the scope of this provision.

423   The logic of this mechanism is clear: a party calling a witness should take all measures necessary to ensure that its witnesses respect the confidentiality of the proceedings. The *ratio legis* of this provision is thus to encourage parties to require

---

Beijing Arbitration Commission Arbitration Rules, Art. 36(2) of the China International Economic and Trade Arbitration Commission (CIETAC) Arbitration Rules, Arts 42.2 and 42.1 of the HKIAC Rules, Art. 15.1 of the Kuala Lumpur Regional Centre for Arbitration Rules.

that witnesses who testify on their behalf maintain the confidentiality of the information they receive because of their participation in the proceedings. Whether there is an employment relationship or another reason for the witness to cooperate, it is likely that in most cases a third party willing to help a party by testifying as a witness on its behalf in an arbitration proceeding will also be willing to keep any information learned in the proceeding confidential. Where this is not the case, there may be ways to shield certain confidential information from a witness, or a party can even decide not to call such a witness.[354] In any event, confidentiality is a subject that needs to be addressed right away by a party with the witness, even before any confidential information is shared with the witness.

3.6.3.4 Intermediary Conclusions

In the absence of an express provision on confidentiality, there are not many other sources which can impose a duty of confidentiality on witnesses in an arbitration. *First*, if a party and a witness expressly agree to enter into a contract for the provision of 'witness services', the witness's duty of confidentiality can find its source in the applicable contractual law provisions governing this contractual relationship. Under Swiss law, such a contract will be qualified as an agency contract (*contrat de mandat*) and a witness will be bound by the confidentiality duty imposed on the agent by Art. 398(2) CO. However, a witness will owe his confidentiality duty only to his contractual counterparty.   **424**

Second, if there is an employment relationship between a party and a witness, the witness's duty of confidentiality can be based on the applicable contractual law provisions dealing with the employment contract. Under Swiss law, for example, the employee must not exploit or reveal confidential information obtained while in the employer's service.[355] Here again, a witness will owe his confidentiality obligations only vis-à-vis his employer.   **425**

Third, some institutional arbitration rules contain provisions on the witness's obligation of confidentiality, but they are not in principle binding on witnesses. Finally, other arbitration rules, such as the WIPO and the ACICA Rules, place responsibility for the witness's respect of confidentiality obligations on the party calling this witness. Even in the absence of such provisions in the applicable arbitration rules, parties should be alerted about their potential liability for any confidentiality breaches by the witnesses they call.   **426**

Therefore, the best way to ensure that the witness respects the confidentiality of the information he obtains as a result of his participation in the arbitral proceedings is for the party and witness to enter into an express agreement on confidentiality.   **427**

---

[354]Smeureanu (2011), p. 152.
[355]Art. 324a(4) CO.

3.6.4   Expert Witnesses' Duty of Confidentiality

428 Expert witnesses can be appointed by a party or by the arbitral tribunal. While experts' independence is considered an essential condition for the credibility of their testimony, it is worth noting that expert witnesses are retained by the parties and are paid for their services.

429 With respect to tribunal-appointed experts, some legal authors argue that they have a contractual relationship with the tribunal and not with the parties.[356] We think, however, in line with many other authors,[357] that even if experts are appointed by the tribunal, they still have a contractual relationship with the parties. Indeed, they are paid their fees by the parties and they serve the parties' common interest of an equitable resolution of the dispute. The tribunal does not have any personal interest in the performance of the expert's contract and cannot be sued for payment of the experts' fees. If the expert is appointed by one of the parties, the contractual relationship will exist between the expert and the party having appointed him.

430 Under Swiss law, the contractual relationship existing between a party (or the parties) and an expert can be qualified as an agency contract[358] or as a contract for works.[359] According to the Swiss Supreme Court, the contract with an expert will be qualified as a contract for works if the result of the expert report can be promised and guaranteed. This will be the case if the result can be verified on the basis of objective criteria and be evaluated as accurate or false.[360] If the result of the expert report cannot be verified on the basis of objective criteria, such a contract will be qualified as an agency contract.[361]

431 In both cases, however, the expert is bound by the duty of confidentiality. In the case of an agency contract, Art. 398(2) CO imposes an obligation of diligent and faithful performance. The obligation of diligent performance includes, in particular, a duty of discretion which exists even if it is not provided for expressly in the contract.[362] The scope of the agent's duty of discretion is to be examined depending on the circumstances of the case and the applicable regulations, for example, regarding specific professions.[363] The general rule, however, is that all documents and information that the agent receives from the principal while performing the contract should be covered by the duty of confidentiality.[364] The parties can, however, derogate from the rule of Art. 398(2) CO since it is non mandatory.

---

[356]See, for example, Weber (1993), p. 195.

[357]Jolles et al. (2013), p. 142, with further references.

[358]Arts 394 ff CO.

[359]Arts 363 ff CO; ATF III 328, JdT 2001 I 254, recital 2; Jolles et al. (2013), p. 142.

[360]ATF III 328, JdT 2001 I 254, recital 2.

[361]ATF III 328, JdT 2001 I 254, recital 2.

[362]Werro (2012b), Commentary of Art. 398 CO, paras 23–24.

[363]Werro (2012b), Commentary of Art. 398 CO, para 22.

[364]Werro (2012b), Commentary of Art. 398 CO, para 22.

If the contract with the expert is qualified under Swiss law as a contract for works,   **432**
the obligation of confidentiality finds its source in Art. 321a(4) CO[365] applied by
analogy as it is referred to in Art. 364(1) CO.[366] The parties can, however, derogate
from this rule at least to some extent since it is not mandatory.[367] The scope of the
data covered by confidentiality is very broad as it covers all information that is not
publicly known and that cannot be easily accessed.[368]

As explained above, a number of arbitration rules impose on experts an obligation   **433**
of confidentiality.[369] Some of these rules expressly mention tribunal-appointed
experts, but not party-appointed experts.[370] As we explained above, however, even
when the expert is appointed by the tribunal, the expert still has a contractual
relationship with the parties. Therefore, we do not think that there is any particular
reason to treat differently tribunal-appointed and party-appointed experts.

While the arbitration rules bind the parties because they expressly agree to their   **434**
application, why would the arbitration rules have a binding effect on the experts? In
our opinion, by accepting to be an expert in arbitration proceedings, the expert
agrees to be bound by the rules governing the proceedings, including the arbitration
rules. While we think that this argument can hardly apply to fact witnesses, the
situation is different with experts as they participate in the arbitration proceedings as
professionals. As such, they are expected to comply with the rules governing the
arbitration proceedings. Their implicit consent with the relevant arbitration rules can
thus be admitted. Therefore, we think that if there is a provision on expert's
confidentiality duty contained in arbitration rules, it should apply directly to experts.

Finally, to be on the safe side, parties can require from experts a contractual   **435**
undertaking on non-disclosure of confidential information at the time when they
enter into a contractual relationship.

---

[365]Applicable to employment contracts.

[366]Chaix (2017), para 5.

[367]Dunand (2013), Commentary of Art. 321a CO, para 3.

[368]Dunand (2013), Commentary of Art. 321a CO, para 39.

[369]Art. 8(1) of the Milan Rules, Art. 25 of the International Arbitration Court of the Chamber of
Commerce and Industry of the Russian Federation, Art. 44(1) of the Swiss Rules, Art. 24(2) of the
Beijing Arbitration Commission Arbitration Rules, Art. 36(2) of the China International Economic
and Trade Arbitration Commission (CIETAC) Arbitration Rules, Arts 42.2 and 42.1 of the HKIAC
Rules, Art. 15.1 of the Kuala Lumpur Regional Centre for Arbitration Rules, Art. 40(1) of the Cairo
Regional Centre for International Commercial Arbitration Rules.

[370]Art. 25 of the International Arbitration Court of the Chamber of Commerce and Industry of the
Russian Federation, Art. 44(1) of the Swiss Rules, Art. 24(2) of the Beijing Arbitration Commission
Arbitration Rules, Art. 36(2) of the China International Economic and Trade Arbitration Commis-
sion (CIETAC) Arbitration Rules, Art. 40(1) of the Cairo Regional Centre for International
Commercial Arbitration Rules.

3.6.5 Duty of Confidentiality of Tribunal Secretaries and Other Tribunal Auxiliaries

436   Arbitrators often work with the assistance of staff for secretarial and organisational support or to undertake research and provide assistance on substantive issues. The extent of the functions that an arbitrator can delegate to a secretary of the arbitral tribunal (sometimes also called law clerk), is much debated. This is nevertheless not the topic of our research, so we will limit our review to the question of whether a confidentiality obligation is owed by a tribunal secretary and by other tribunal auxiliaries.

437   As mentioned above, an employment relationship often exists between an arbitrator and individuals who provide assistance with respect to the arbitration. Thus, a confidentiality obligation owed by such persons can be provided for expressly in the employment contract. If this is not the case, some laws contain rules providing for a duty of confidentiality even in the absence of express contractual terms. Thus, Art. 321a(4) CO stipulates that the employee must not exploit or reveal confidential information obtained while in the employer's service. The parties can, however, derogate from this rule at least to some extent as it is not mandatory.[371] As already mentioned, the scope of the data covered by the confidentiality is very broad as it covers all information that is not publicly known and that cannot be easily accessed.[372]

438   Some arbitration rules have provisions imposing a confidentiality obligation on tribunal secretaries.[373] They do not have a direct binding effect on the persons assisting the tribunal unless they specifically adopted these rules. It can be argued, however, that tribunal secretaries implicitly adopt the arbitration rules when accepting to work on a specific arbitration case. Indeed, tribunal secretaries are generally well-informed about the regulation of arbitration proceedings and can be expected to be knowledgeable about the applicable arbitration rules.

439   Another indirect source of a confidentiality duty for tribunal secretaries are professional and ethical rules imposing confidentiality obligations on arbitrators. For example, Canon VI(B) of the Code of Ethics for Arbitrators in Commercial Disputes of the American Arbitration Association/American Bar Association provides that an arbitrator may obtain assistance from an associate, a research assistant or other persons if the arbitrator informs the parties of the use of such help and such persons agree to be bound, in particular, by confidentiality obligations.

440   These rules have the benefit of indicating the desirable regulatory regime, but do not have a binding effect *per se*. It is therefore advisable to require from the person assisting the tribunal to sign an express confidentiality undertaking. Another reason for this is that the parties or persons having suffered damages from the tribunal's

---

[371] Dunand (2013), Commentary of Art. 321a CO, para 3.

[372] Dunand (2013), Commentary of Art. 321a CO, para 39.

[373] Art. 44(1) of the Swiss Rules, Arts 42.2 and 42.1 of the HKIAC Rules, Art. 40(1) of the Cairo Regional Centre for International Commercial Arbitration Rules.

auxiliary are allowed, under certain laws, to pursue the arbitral tribunal. This possibility exists in Swiss law under Art. 101(1) CO. Under this provision, a person who uses a third party's services to perform his own obligations is responsible for the third party's behaviour in the same way as for his own acts, provided that the third party's conduct related to the performance of the contract.[374]

3.6.6 Duty of Confidentiality of Counsel Auxiliaries

Regarding counsel auxiliaries, the situation is very similar to the one presented for   **441**
arbitral tribunal auxiliaries. In most cases, counsel auxiliaries will be bound by a confidentiality obligation contained in the employment contract with the law firm. If this is not the case, such an obligation can arise from the applicable law complementing the contract. Thus, Art. 321a(4) CO prohibits the employee from revealing or exploiting confidential information obtained while in the employer's service. The parties can, however, agree that this provision will not apply to their relationship, since it is not mandatory.[375]

Similarly to the situation with tribunal auxiliaries, counsel can also be pursued for   **442**
an employee's failure to respect a confidentiality obligation.

3.6.7 Duty of Confidentiality of Other Third Persons

A number of other persons will inevitably have access to information from the   **443**
arbitration proceedings. These can be third party funders, translators/interpreters, court reporters, as well as other persons assisting over the course of the arbitration proceedings. While it cannot be excluded that there are applicable national rules imposing a duty of confidentiality on persons belonging, for example, to a specific professional group, the existence of such an obligation cannot be guaranteed. Thus, it is strongly advisable to require a contractual confidentiality undertaking from any third person having access to information relating to the arbitration proceedings.

Particular confidentiality issues may arise with respect to third party funding   **444**
arrangements. First, a party may have to disclose information and documents related to an imminent arbitration to several potential third party funders in the course of a case assessment phase.[376] Second, if a third party accepts to provide at least part of the funds necessary to pursue the dispute, it will be entitled to regular updates on the developments of the case during the monitoring phase.[377] These regular updates will

---

[374]ATF 92 II 15, recital 3, JdT 1966 I 526; Thévenoz (2012), Commentary of Art. 101 CO, para 1.

[375]Dunand (2013), Commentary of Art. 321a CO, para 3.

[376]Von Goeler (2016), p. 298.

[377]Von Goeler (2016), p. 298.

normally include both parties' written submissions, documentary evidence, witness and expert evidence, procedural orders and awards issued by the arbitral tribunal.[378] Indeed, since the third-party funder is remunerated by a percentage of a success fee in the event of a settlement or favourable award, it will need to have access to all information allowing to assess and having the influence on the chances of success of the funded party to prevail.

445   If we assume that the parties to the dispute are bound by a confidentiality obligation, such disclosures to a third party funder can be seen as problematic. In our opinion, confidentiality obligations of the parties should not be an obstacle to the funding of the dispute by a third party. On the one hand, the funder will in most cases be bound by an express contractual obligation regarding the information on the funded arbitration. On the other hand, given in particular the confidentiality obligation that the funder will owe to the funded party, it would make no sense to require from the funded party a very strict observation of the confidentiality duty restricting it from any disclosures. Indeed, we think that disclosure should be generally permitted when necessary to seek for professional services, such as need of funding, legal advice or accounting services.

446   Another problem is that the funder can be required to disclose the fact that it is funding an arbitration as part of its statutory obligations. However, as we will discuss further, this should not be considered as a confidentiality breach, since one of the exceptions to confidentiality obligation is when disclosure is required by the law.

3.7   Intermediary Conclusions

447   Having examined the duty of confidentiality of the different groups of persons depending on their role in the arbitration proceedings, it becomes clear that the core issue of our research is the parties' duty of confidentiality. Indeed, as we have seen, the most controversial issue is whether the parties are bound by a duty of confidentiality in the absence of an express undertaking and specific regulation. There is no consensus on this issue between different legal systems and within the arbitration community. *De lege ferenda*, we think that the parties should have an obligation of confidentiality subject to certain exceptions. In such jurisdictions as France and Switzerland, where the existence of the parties' duty of confidentiality in the absence of express provisions on confidentiality is not clear-cut, the parties' implied duty of confidentiality should, in our view, be recognised.

448   There is much less controversy regarding the duty of obligation owed by the arbitrators, arbitration institutions and their staff as well as the parties' counsel. Their duty of confidentiality will in most cases exist because of the duty of discretion owed to the parties due to the existence of a contractual relationship.

---

[378]Roney and von der Weid (2013), p. 193.

Since the lawyers' activity is supervised and regulated in most jurisdictions, the **449** problem of the lawyer's breach of confidentiality relates mainly to the problem of professional misconduct. If a lawyer discloses information upon instructions of his client, this can be regarded as a breach of the party's and not of the lawyer's duty of confidentiality.

Maintaining confidentiality of the arbitral proceedings by third parties cannot be **450** guaranteed without an express contractual undertaking. Although some arbitration rules contain provisions on third parties' duty of confidentiality, this can in fact be misleading as these provisions will not necessarily have a direct binding force upon third persons. In order to be binding, a provision on confidentiality needs to be imposed either contractually or by the applicable national law. Thus, to avoid a situation of legal uncertainty and the risks related to the disclosure of confidential information by third parties, it is advisable to require an express confidentiality undertaking from any third person having access to the information relating to the arbitration.

Chapter 4
Content of the Duty of Confidentiality

4.1 Introduction

Defining the content of the duty of confidentiality is no easy task. There is so much   **451**
that can be included in the content of the duty of confidentiality. Some examples are:
the mere existence of the arbitration, the nature of the dispute, the amount in dispute,
the status of the case, the names of the parties, the names of counsel, the names of
arbitrators, parties' submissions, fact exhibits, documents produced in response to a
request for production of documents, witness statements, expert reports, pleadings,
transcripts of hearings, tribunal's deliberations, the award itself, any details revealing
the content of the award, etc.[1]

As we have seen in the previous section dealing with the persons subject to the   **452**
duty of confidentiality, the scope of the duty of confidentiality for most participants
of the arbitration proceedings is very broad. It is especially true for persons obtaining
information on the arbitration as a result of their professional activity (such as
arbitrators, parties' representatives, members and employees of arbitration
institutions).

It is mostly the scope of *the parties'* duty of confidentiality that is controversial.   **453**
For example, legal practitioners and scholars do not agree on whether a party is
bound by a confidentiality duty in relation to the disclosure of the existence of an
arbitration. Another controversial topic is whether a party should be restricted from
using a document that it submitted as an exhibit in the arbitration outside of the
arbitration proceedings. We will examine this and other questions in the present
section.

First, we will examine the type of information and, in particular, the specific   **454**
matters and issues which can be subject to the duty of confidentiality (Sect. 4.2).
Second, we will analyse which categories of documents exchanged in the course of

---

[1]See, for example, Lew (2011), pp. 106–107.

© Springer Nature Switzerland AG 2019
E. Reymond-Eniaeva, *Towards a Uniform Approach to Confidentiality of
International Commercial Arbitration*, European Yearbook of International
Economic Law 7, https://doi.org/10.1007/978-3-030-19003-3_4

arbitral proceedings can be subject to the parties' duty of confidentiality (Sect. 4.3). Third, we will examine the issue of confidentiality regarding arbitral awards and orders (Sect. 4.4). We will mainly focus on the regulation and practices regarding publication of arbitral awards. Finally, we will turn to the issue of the confidentiality in respect of hearings (Sect. 4.5).

4.2 Information Subject to the Duty of Confidentiality

4.2.1 Introduction

455   The problem regarding disclosure of information, as opposed to disclosure of documents, is that each case is unique. While the categories of potentially confidential documents which can be part of the arbitration record are relatively limited, the number of potentially confidential issues in an arbitration is endless. As we will see, virtually any issue relating to the arbitration proceeding, including the mere fact of the existence of the arbitration proceedings, can be subject to confidentiality. We will therefore examine only some of the issues which can potentially become confidential.

456   In the present section, we will focus on the kind of information which should not be disclosed as being potentially subject to the duty of confidentiality. We will first examine the issue of confidentiality surrounding the existence of the arbitral proceedings (Sect. 4.2.2). We will then review other potentially confidential matters (Sect. 4.2.3).

4.2.2 Confidentiality of the Existence of the Arbitral Proceedings

457   In most cases, not many persons know about the start of an arbitration proceeding. This inner circle is usually limited to the parties and their counsel, the relevant arbitration institution, and the arbitrators. May the mere existence of an arbitration proceeding be disclosed to persons not involved in the relevant arbitration proceeding, or even be publicly disclosed? This is a critical issue since the parties quite often would not like the existence of the arbitration to be known by any third party, let alone the general public.

458   There can be no simple answer to this question, as each case needs to be addressed in context. The answer will depend on the circumstances of each case, but also on the applicable rules and law and on the competent authority which is to rule on the issue. First, we will see that national arbitration laws generally do not regulate the confidentiality of the very existence of arbitration proceedings. Second, we will see that some arbitration rules expressly provide for a confidentiality duty regarding the very existence of arbitration proceedings. Third, we will analyse a few court decisions. These lead to the conclusion that the mere existence of an arbitration can be subject to a duty of confidentiality. Finally, we will see that many legal scholars consider it difficult to impose a strict duty of confidentiality of the existence of arbitration proceedings, given the significant risk of leaks. We think, however, that such a duty should exist as a general rule in order to protect the parties against disclosures that are not justified by any legitimate reasons.

4.2.2.1   National Arbitration Laws

There appear to be virtually no arbitration laws containing express regulations of the confidentiality surrounding the existence of arbitral proceedings. The national reports provided for the Wolters Kluwer Law Chart on Privacy and Confidentiality in Arbitration confirm this.[2]   **459**

There are, however, some arbitration laws which regulate this issue implicitly. For example, Art. 26 of Schedule 1 to the Scottish Arbitration Act provides that confidential information, in relation to an arbitration, means, in particular, any information relating to the dispute and the arbitral proceedings. Depending on how this provision is interpreted, information on the existence of arbitral proceedings can be protected from disclosure by Art. 26.   **460**

The fact that there are no statutory provisions on this issue does not mean, however, that the information on the existence of arbitration is not protected by confidentiality. As we will see below, state courts in France and England established, as a general principle, that the very existence of an arbitration is to be kept confidential. In other countries, where state courts have not had a chance to rule on this issue, the absence of relevant case law does not necessarily mean that a duty of confidentiality does not extend to the mere fact that an arbitration is taking place.   **461**

4.2.2.2   Arbitration Rules

As compared to national arbitration laws, arbitration rules tend to provide more specific regulation on the issue of confidentiality with regard to the very existence of arbitration proceedings. The provisions of several institutional arbitration rules include specific language on this issue. For example, Art. 22.2 of the ACICA Arbitration Rules provides the following: **462**

---

[2]'Privacy and Confidentiality in Arbitration Smart Charts' (www.smartcharts.wolterskluwer.com, last visited on 13 September 2018) includes reports on such countries as Argentina, Australia, Bulgaria, Canada, China, Croatia, Cyprus, England and Wales, Finland, France, Germany, Ghana, Hong Kong, Hungary, India, Italy, Japan, Kazakhstan, Mexico, Netherlands, Nigeria, Pakistan, Philippines, Portugal, Romania, the Russian Federation, Serbia, Singapore, Slovakia, South Africa, South Korea, Sweden, Switzerland, Turkey, Ukraine, and the United States.

The Parties, the Arbitration Tribunal and ACICA shall treat as confidential and shall not disclose to a third party without prior written consent from the parties *all matters relating to the arbitration (including the existence of the arbitration)*, the award, materials created for the purpose of the arbitration and documents produced by another party in the proceedings and not in the public domain except [. . .] (italics added).

463   SIAC Rules have a similar provision. Thus, Arts 39(1) and 39(3) SIAC Rules provide the following:

39.1 Unless otherwise agreed by the parties, a party and any arbitrator, including any Emergency Arbitrator, and any persons appointed by the Tribunal, including any administrative secretary and any expert, shall at all times treat all *matters relating to the proceedings* and the Award as confidential.

[. . .]

39.3 In Rule 39.1, *"matters relating to the proceedings" includes the existence of the proceedings*, and the pleadings, evidence and other materials in the arbitral proceedings and all other documents produced by another party in the proceedings or the Award arising from the proceedings, but excludes any matter that is otherwise in the public domain. (italics added)

464   The WIPO Rules go even further by dedicating a specific provision to this issue:

Confidentiality of the Existence of the Arbitration

Article 75

(a) Except to the extent necessary in connection with a court challenge to the arbitration or an action for enforcement of an award, *no information concerning the existence of an arbitration* may be unilaterally disclosed by a party to any third party unless it is required so by law or by a competent regulatory body, and then only:

(i) by disclosing no more than what is legally required; and

(ii) by furnishing to the Tribunal and to the other party, if the disclosure takes place during the arbitration or to the other party alone, if the disclosure takes place after the termination of the arbitration, details of the disclosure and an explanation of the reason for it.

Notwithstanding paragraph (a), a party may disclose to a third party the names of the parties to the arbitration and the relief requested for the purpose of satisfying any obligation of good faith or candor owed to that third party. (italics added)

In many cases, however, arbitration rules do not regulate confidentiality regarding   **465**
the mere existence of the arbitration. Thus, the Swiss Rules do not contain such a
provision. Based on a literal interpretation of Art. 44 of the Swiss Rules, some
commentators consider that the duty of confidentiality does not, in principle, cover
the existence of the arbitration. They argue that Art. 44 focuses on the protection of
confidentiality of the materials and the outcome of the arbitration, but not of
confidentiality of the existence of the proceedings.[3]

Art. 8 of the Milan Rules imposes a duty of confidentiality regarding the pro-   **466**
ceedings and the arbitral award. Although this provision does not regulate the
specific issue of confidentiality of the existence of arbitral proceedings, a commen-
tator of the Milan Rules opined that the existence of the proceedings should be
covered by the scope of Art. 8.[4]

Another example of a provision allowing such an interpretation is Art. 3 of the   **467**
SCC Rules. It provides that the SCC, the Arbitral Tribunal and any administrative
secretary of the Arbitral Tribunal should maintain the confidentiality of the arbitration and the award. One can claim that *the confidentiality of the arbitration* should
cover the existence of the proceedings, but the opposite claim can arguably be made
as well.

4.2.2.3   State Court Decisions

English and French state courts have consistently held that the parties are bound by a   **468**
duty of confidentiality regarding the existence of the arbitration, unless they have a
legitimate reason to disclose this information. For example, in the case *Department
of Economic Policy and Development of the City of Moscow v. Banker Trust Co.* the
Court of Appeal pointed out in its judgment of 5 June 2003 that the fact of the
commencement of an arbitration is subject to the duty of confidentiality unless there
is a legitimate reason to disclose this fact.[5]

In 1999, a French state court, the Paris Commercial Court, reached a similar   **469**
conclusion in the case *Bleustein et autres v. Société True North et Société FCB
International.*[6] The French Court held that any information related to the existence
(and to the content and the subject matter) of the arbitration proceedings is subject to
the duty of confidentiality, unless a disclosure of this information is required by
the law.

In the proceedings before the Paris Commercial Court, True North issued two   **470**
official press releases through a news agency, announcing its dispute with Publicis

---

[3]Rohner and La Spada (2013), para 11; Hollander (2014), p. 86.
[4]Coppo (2013), p. 142.
[5]Department of Economic Policy and Development of the City of Moscow v. Bankers Trust Co.,
[2003] EWHC 1377 (Comm), para 51; see below Sect. 5.3.2.3.3 for more details on the case.
[6]Bleustein et autres v. Société True North et Société FCB International, Tribunal de commerce de
Paris (Ord. réf.), 22 February 1999, in: Rev. Arb. 2003, Issue 1, 189–194.

and the fact that this dispute was subject to an arbitration proceeding.[7] True North also publicly disclosed that, in the arbitration, it was claiming USD 60 million in damages from Publicis. During the proceedings, Publicis's shareholders, Mr. Bleustein and others, demonstrated before the Paris Commercial Court that (i) the first press release entailed a drop in the value of Publicis' shares of 6.5%; (ii) the second press release provoked a drop of 2.9%; and (iii) this decline continued over the following days.[8] True North did not contest this.

471   The Paris Commercial Court held for the Publicis shareholders and concluded that True North disclosed information in breach of its confidentiality obligations. The Court issued an injunction banning True North from disclosing any information in relation to the existence, the content and the subject matter of its arbitration with Publicis, subject to disclosure required by mandatory legal provisions.[9] It stated that since arbitration is a private proceeding of a confidential nature, and since arbitration has been accepted by the parties, they must avoid any publicity relating to the dispute and the outcome of the dispute. (The Paris Court of Appeal later overruled the decision of the Paris Commercial Court, but on procedural grounds, and without examining the substantive issues relating to confidentiality.[10])

472   In an earlier decision of 18 February 1986, *G. Aïta v. A. Ojjeh*,[11] the Paris Court of Appeal found that Mr Aïta had disclosed confidential facts by filing an appeal to a manifestly incompetent authority.[12] It also held that the defendant suffered damages as a result of this public disclosure of confidential information and enjoined Mr. Aïta to pay damages and the costs of the court proceedings.[13]

---

[7]Bleustein et autres v. Société True North et Société FCB International, Tribunal de commerce de Paris (Ord. réf.), 22 February 1999, in: Rev. Arb. 2003, Issue 1, 190.

[8]Bleustein et autres v. Société True North et Société FCB International, Tribunal de commerce de Paris (Ord. réf.), 22 February 1999, in: Rev. Arb. 2003, Issue 1, 191.

[9]Bleustein et autres v. Société True North et Société FCB International, Tribunal de commerce de Paris (Ord. réf.), 22 February 1999, in: Rev. Arb. 2003, Issue 1, 192.

[10]Société True North et Société FCB International v. Bleustein et autres, Cour d'appel de Paris (14e Ch. B), 17 September 1999, in: Rev. Arb. 2003, Issue 1, 194–197.

[11]G. Aïta v. A. Ojjeh, Cour d'appel de Paris (1ère Chambre suppl.), 18 February 1986, in: Rev. Arb. 1986, 583–584.

[12]See above Sect. 3.2.3.7 for more details on this case.

[13]G. Aïta v. A. Ojjeh, Cour d'appel de Paris (1ère Chambre suppl.), 18 February 1986, in: Rev. Arb. 1986, 583–584. This decision will also be addressed in the section dealing with the remedies against the parties in the case of a confidentiality breach (Sect. 6.2.2.1).

4.2.2.4   Legal Scholars' Views

Although there is some divergence of opinion, most legal scholars agree that it is **473** difficult to impose a duty of confidentiality over the mere existence of an arbitration proceeding.[14] The primary reason is the considerable risk of leaks.

Christoph Müller argues, for example, that it might be unrealistic to think that the **474** fact of the existence of an arbitration will be kept secret. This is because it can be disclosed, for example, as a result of an *exequatur* or appeal of the arbitral award, or if one of the parties has to disclose the fact of the arbitration to comply with its statutory obligations.[15] Weixia Gu agrees, arguing that '*it seems unrealistic and undesirable to establish an absolute prohibition against unilateral publication of the mere existence of the arbitration*'.[16] Finally, Bernhard Berger and Franz Kellerhals maintain that the existence of the arbitration is in principle not to be kept confidential in the absence of an express agreement and relevant applicable provisions.[17]

Andreas Furrer also agrees, arguing that it does not make sense to impose a strict **475** obligation of confidentiality on the parties regarding the mere existence of an arbitration '*when this information spreads from other sources*'.[18] On the other hand, he rightly observes that the parties should not disclose the existence of an arbitration '*solely for the purpose of damaging the other side or causing harm to its business*'.[19]

4.2.3   Other Potentially Confidential Matters

Importantly, some arbitration rules[20] and national arbitration laws[21] provide that *all* **476** *matters* relating to an arbitration proceeding are to be treated as confidential. Art. 22.2 of the ACICA Arbitration Rules for example, provides that

> '[t]*he Parties, the Arbitration Tribunal and ACICA shall treat as confidential and shall not disclose to a third party without a prior written consent from the parties all matters relating to the arbitration*'.

---

[14]*See,* for example, Brown (2001), pp. 1001–1004; Müller (2005), p. 226; Gu (2004), p. 618; Berger and Kellerhals (2015), p. 1234.

[15]Müller (2005), p. 226.

[16]Gu (2004), p. 618.

[17]Berger and Kellerhals (2015), para 1234.

[18]Furrer (2008), p. 813.

[19]Furrer (2008), p. 813.

[20]*See, e.g.,* Art. 22.2 of the ACICA Arbitration Rules; Art. 39 of the SIAC Rules.

[21]*See, e.g.,* Art. 26 of Schedule 1 to the Scottish Arbitration Act.

477   But what could be included in '*all matters relating to the arbitration*'? One
cannot possibly provide an exhaustive list of all the matters (and issues) which may
be subject to confidentiality—because each case is unique. However, we can list
some items of information common to almost any arbitration proceeding: the names
of the parties, the names of the arbitrators, the nature of the dispute, the status of the
case, the amount in dispute, the names of the witnesses and experts, the content of
the witness testimony, the content of the exhibits, etc.

478   Even seemingly harmless and insignificant information, such as the name of the
court reporter, the name of the interpreter, or the time and the venue of the hearing
should be subject to confidentiality.[22] For example, if the time and the venue of the
hearing are disclosed, there is a risk that journalists will come to the site.[23] If
journalists know the name of the court reporter or the name of the interpreter, they
may try to obtain information from these individuals regarding what was said at the
hearing.

479   Assuming that the confidentiality obligation covers the mere fact of the existence
of the arbitration, all other matters related to this arbitration are also to be kept
confidential, unless they are disclosed in such a way that it is impossible to identify
the involved parties. If, however, we assume the opposite, i.e. that the mere existence
of the arbitration is not confidential, then the confidentiality of other issues becomes
more difficult to analyse. The same is true if we assume that the existence of an
arbitration is to be kept confidential, but that, for some reason, it has been made
public.

480   Under the second assumption, if the existence of an arbitration is not covered by
the confidentiality obligation, or when it is already known to the public anyway, the
question is whether the disclosure of additional information on the dispute, such as
the nature of the dispute or the amount in dispute, would be considered as a violation
of a confidentiality obligation. Such a possibility cannot be excluded if such a
disclosure is detrimental to the interests of at least one of the parties. Possibly,
other interests could also be at stake. For example, in the arbitration, a witness could
disclose some facts from his personal background that he would not like to be
disclosed outside of the arbitration proceedings.

481   For illustrative purposes, we can consider a hypothetical situation similar to the
dispute of *Bleustein et autres v. Société True North et Société FCB International.*[24]
Let us assume that there is an arbitration between companies A and B. For some
reason, the fact that there is an arbitration proceeding between the two companies has
already become publicly known. A now reveals to the press that it is claiming USD
100 million from B in the arbitration for a breach of contract. A discloses this
information with the purpose of damaging B's reputation, as B is A's competitor.

---

[22]Hollander (2014), p. 87.

[23]Hollander (2014), p. 87.

[24]Bleustein et autres v. Société True North et Société FCB International, Tribunal de commerce de
Paris (Ord. Réf.), 22 February 1999, in : Rev. Arb. 2003. Issue 1, 189–194. For more details on this
case, see above Sect. 4.2.2.3).

The press release that follows this disclosure provokes a drop in value of the shares of B. In this case, disclosure by A would likely be considered as a breach of its confidentiality obligations even though the existence of the arbitration was already known to the public.

4.2.4   Intermediary Conclusions

Although it is important to identify matters and categories of information that might   **482**
be subject to confidentiality, one cannot provide a definite response on whether each particular category of information will be treated as confidential. The answer will depend on the particular circumstances of the case, such as the reasons for and consequences of the disclosure, rather than on which exact piece of information was disclosed.

In a particular case, it would especially be crucial to understand whether there was   **483**
a legitimate reason for disclosure or whether there was another reason justifying an exception to the duty of confidentiality. In our opinion, a breach of the duty of confidentiality should be admitted if the reason for disclosure does not fall under the scope covered by the exceptions to the duty of confidentiality, which we will discuss below (see Sect. 4.5). In particular, the breach of the duty of confidentiality should be admitted if the disclosure was made in bad faith with the purpose of damaging the other party's interest.

4.3   Confidentiality Regarding Documents Exchanged in the Course of Arbitral Proceedings

4.3.1   Introduction

The documents' use is an important issue with respect to the confidentiality duty.   **484**
Arbitration proceedings generate a significant number of documents: pleadings, exhibits, witness statements, expert opinions, requests for production of documents and related documents, documents produced voluntarily and involuntarily, correspondence between all involved, etc. In this section, we will discuss only the documents which are confidential due to the fact that they became available because of arbitration proceedings. Therefore, we will not examine documents which are already confidential by their very nature, such as documents protected by state or commercial secret.

We will see that the main controversy relates to the use of documents *by the*   **485**
parties to an arbitration. Other persons also have access to the documents exchanged in arbitration proceedings, of course, and the scope of their duty of confidentiality is very broad. For them, virtually all documents from the arbitration proceedings

should be included. The issue is more nuanced regarding the content of the duty of confidentiality of the parties.

486   To examine the issue of documents subject to confidentiality, we will proceed as follows. First, we will start with an analysis of the regulation provided by national arbitration laws. We will see that the AIAA and the NZAA contain a very detailed regulation regarding the categories of documents subject to a duty of confidentiality. Second, we will compare the regulation provided by various arbitration rules. Third, we will review several decisions of the English High Court dealing with the issue. Finally, we will see that legal scholars disagree on which categories of documents should be subject to a duty of confidentiality.

4.3.2 National Arbitration Laws

487   As discussed above, not many national arbitration laws have provisions on confidentiality; even fewer specify which particular documents are to be protected by confidentiality obligations. The AIAA and the NZAA are exceptions in this regard because they contain elaborate provisions regulating confidentiality obligations. In both jurisdiction, the confidentiality provisions will apply unless the parties decide to 'opt-out'.[25]

488   Art. 15 of the AIAA and Art. 2 of the NZAA provide almost identical definitions of 'confidential information'. In both laws, 'confidential information' means information relating to the arbitral proceedings or to an award made in those proceedings. It includes:

(i) the statement of claim, statement of defence, and all other pleadings, submissions, statements, or other information supplied to the arbitral tribunal by a party to the proceedings;

(ii) any evidence (whether documentary or other) supplied to the arbitral tribunal;

(iii) any notes made by the arbitral tribunal of oral evidence or submissions given before the arbitral tribunal;

(iv) any transcript of oral evidence or submissions given before the arbitral tribunal;

(v) any ruling of the arbitral tribunal;

(vi) any award of the arbitral tribunal.[26]

489   In further sections, we will examine the confidentiality of arbitral awards and the privacy of hearings (points c), d), e) and f)). As for confidentiality of the documents exchanged in the course of arbitration, the scope of the documents covered by the

---

[25]Sam Luttrell, Isuru Devendra in their report on Australian regulation in 'Privacy and Confidentiality in Arbitration Smart Charts' (www.smartcharts.wolterskluwer.com, last updated in November 2016); Arts 14, 14A to 14I NZAA.

[26]Art. 15 AIAA and Art. 2 NZAA.

AIAA and the NZAA is rather extensive: it covers all parties' submissions, including all pleadings, witness statements, expert reports, and documentary evidence.

Both laws, however, do not expressly extend the duty of confidentiality to the documents that one party may produce in response to another party's document production request, and which are not submitted as evidence during the arbitration proceedings. We think that this could simply be an oversight and that the duty of confidentiality should apply to these documents. One of the reasons is that the parties should not be discouraged from making full and candid disclosure for fear that the produced documents can be disclosed outside of the arbitration. In our opinion, both the documents submitted as exhibits and the documents produced in response to another party's request should enjoy the same degree of confidentiality.   **490**

4.3.3   Arbitration Rules

Many international arbitration rules deal with the issue of confidentiality of documents, although the level of detail varies considerably. Among the guidelines, the IBA Rules on Evidence are worth mentioning. Art. 3.13 of the IBA Rules imposes a duty of confidentiality regarding   **491**

'[a]*ny documents submitted or produced by a Party or non-Party in the arbitration*'

The scope of application of this provision is very broad; it covers

'*all documents produced or submitted in the arbitral proceedings regardless of why or how they were produced and/or submitted, by parties or by non-parties*'.[27]

Thus, the IBA Rules on Evidence extend confidentiality not only to the parties' submissions, including various pleadings, witness statements and expert reports, but also to fact exhibits and documents produced in response to another party's request for production of documents.

The LCIA Rules have a more restricted definition of the *documents subject to confidentiality*.[28] According to Art. 30 of the LCIA Rules, confidentiality covers   **492**

'*all materials in the proceedings created for the purpose of the arbitration and all other documents produced by another party in the proceedings*'.

Similarly, Art. 22.2 of the ACICA Rules extends confidentiality to

---

[27]Zuberbühler/Hofmann/Oetiker/Rohner, para 257.

[28]In both 2008 and 2014 versions.

'materials created for the purpose of the arbitration and documents produced by another party in the proceedings'

Thus, the two provisions treat as confidential:

(i) documents created for the purpose of the arbitration by all the parties to the arbitration (pleadings, witness statements and expert reports); and
(ii) documents produced by another party in the arbitration, e.g., fact exhibits and documents produced in response to a request for production of documents. For a given party to the arbitration, the confidentiality obligation extends only to the documents produced by another party in the arbitration, not to documents the party produces itself. The rationale for this distinction is that a party should not be restricted from the use of its own documents outside of the arbitration only because the document was submitted in the arbitration.

493 Art. 44(1) of the Swiss Rules treats as confidential

'all materials submitted by another party in the framework of the arbitral proceedings'.

Commentators on the Swiss Rules explain that *'all materials'* covers, in particular, written submissions, exhibits, expert reports and correspondence. They specify that this provision applies not only to documents, but also to other materials such as software, audio or video tapes, CDs and DVDs.[29]

494 According to a literal interpretation of Art. 44(1) of the Swiss Rules, a party must keep confidential only the materials submitted by another party, but not the materials this party submitted itself. Regarding the latter, Art. 44(1) does not make a distinction between the documents a party created for the arbitration (pleadings, witness statements, expert reports) and other documents submitted by a party (exhibits, documents produced as part of the document production process).

495 So which approach in existing arbitration rules provides the best solution to the problem of the confidentiality of documents? We hesitate between the approach adopted in the IBA Rules on Evidence and the approach adopted in the LCIA Rules and the ACICA Rules. The main difference relates to the confidentiality of the documents that the party submitted or produced itself in the arbitration. To illustrate this, we will use two specific scenarios.

496 First, let us assume that there is an arbitration between A and B. A submits, as an exhibit, its contract on the supply of goods with C. It appears obvious that B cannot use the exhibit submitted by A for any other purpose than the arbitration. But should A be restricted from using its contract with C for a purpose not related to the arbitration merely because A has submitted it as evidence in the arbitration? Such a disclosure does not affect the interests of B, as it concerns only A and C. Arguably, while there can be other reasons to maintain confidentiality of this document, the

---

[29]Rohner and La Spada (2013), para 10.

mere fact that A submits the contract in the arbitration should not justify restricting its use by A. A's use of the document should not be restricted in this case. From this point of view, Art. 30 of the LCIA Rules and Art. 22.2 of the ACICA Rules make perfect sense: they impose a duty of confidentiality regarding the documents produced by another party, but not regarding the documents that the party submits itself.

In a second example, A submits an exchange of emails between B and C as an **497** exhibit in an arbitration proceeding. A obtained this email exchange in response to its request for production of documents in the arbitration with B. The difference from the previous example is that this document involves B and a third party, but not A. B would very likely not want this document to be disclosed outside of the arbitration. Does the fact that this exchange of emails was submitted as evidence in the arbitration result in a specific privilege for this document? In this case, the answer should be 'yes' because (i) A had access to this document only because of the arbitration; (ii) the document is sensitive for B, but not for A; and (iii) there is a risk that A will disclose this document outside of the arbitration. This second example illustrates that there can be situations when it would be judicious to impose a duty of confidentiality on a party regarding a document that the party submits itself in an arbitration.

Actually, we think that all documents produced by the parties, which became **498** available because of the arbitration, regardless of whether a given document is submitted by a party itself or by another party, should be subject to confidentiality. The parties need to be certain that the documents they disclose will not be used without their consent outside of the arbitration. This will encourage full and frank disclosure, which is necessary for ensuring an effective administration of justice in arbitration proceedings. For this reason, we prefer the solution proposed by the IBA Rules on Evidence, which protects *all documents submitted or produced by a party* as confidential.

As opposed to most institutional arbitration rules, the IBA Rules on Evidence also **499** include documents submitted by a *non-party* to the arbitration in the duty of confidentiality.[30] We agree with this approach. In our opinion, it encourages candour on the part of the persons participating in arbitration proceedings and reinforces the principle of confidentiality of arbitration. If confidentiality of the documents submitted by a non-party is not protected, it would mean, for example, that the documents submitted by an expert in support of his arguments could be freely disclosed outside of the arbitration. We do not believe that such a disclosure would be desirable and thus favour the broad approach on confidentiality adopted in the IBA Rules on Evidence.

Thus, we prefer the language contained in Art. 3.13 of the IBA Rules on **500** Evidence, which stipulates that

---

[30] Art. 3.13 of the IBA Rules on Evidence.

'[a]*ny documents submitted or produced by a Party or non-Party in the arbitra-*
tion ... shall be kept confidential ... and shall be used only in connection with the
arbitration'.

As will be set out below, we propose however to specify that this confidentiality
duty applies only to the documents to which the person wishing to disclose them had
access only because of the arbitration.[31]

4.3.4 English State Court Decisions

501 English case law is generally consistent regarding the broad principle of confidentiality over the documents originating from arbitration proceedings. For the English
High Court, the duty of confidentiality extends to practically all documents
exchanged in the course of arbitration proceedings, including the arbitral award,
pleadings, written submissions, witness statements, documentary evidence, transcripts, and notes of the evidence given in the arbitration.

502 On several occasions, the English High Court has ruled on which documents
should be subject to a duty of confidentiality. In *Dolling-Baker v. Merrett,*[32] the
English Court of Appeal reaffirmed a long-standing principle of English law,
according to which the parties to an arbitration are under an implied duty of
confidentiality. As to the documents covered by the duty of confidentiality, the
Court provided an extensive list, including virtually every document exchanged in
the course of arbitration proceedings. The Court of Appeal held that confidentiality
should extend to '*any documents prepared for and used in the arbitration, or*
disclosed or produced in the arbitration or transcripts or notes of the evidence in
the arbitration or award'.[33]

503 In *Hassneh Insurance v Mew,*[34] the English High Court (Queen's Bench) had to
rule on whether a party could disclose the award and other documents from the
arbitration in a subsequent court proceeding. In the case, the Court held that
disclosure of the award was necessary to protect the interests of the party seeking
the disclosure, but it refused to permit disclosure of other documents. Thus, the
Court judged that the principle of confidentiality was less strict regarding the award
than regarding other documents from the arbitration proceedings.

504 In *Ali Shipping v Shipyard Trogir,*[35] the English Court of Appeal essentially
reversed this decision, rejecting the distinction between the arbitral award and other
documents for the purposes of applying the duty of confidentiality. Here, the Court

---

[31] See Sect. 7.4 proposing a text of the rules on confidentiality.

[32] Dolling-Baker v. Merrett [1990] 1 WLR 1205.

[33] Dolling-Baker v. Merrett [1990] 1 WLR 1205.

[34] Hassneh Insurance Co v Mew [1993] 2 Lloyd's Rep 243.

[35] Ali Shipping v. Shipyard Trogir [1997] EWCA Civ 3054.

held that the principle of confidentiality should apply equally to the award and to other documents from the arbitration. When discussing exceptions to the rule of confidentiality and, in particular, an exception allowing disclosure when it is reasonably necessary to protect the legitimate interest of an arbitrating party, the Court held:

> Although to date this exception has been held applicable only to disclosure of an Award, it is clear (and indeed the parties do not dispute) that the principle covers also pleadings, written submissions, and the proofs of witnesses as well as transcripts and notes of the evidence given in the arbitration.

4.3.5 Legal Scholars' Views

Many legal scholars agree that documents prepared for or resulting from arbitration proceedings, such as pleadings or transcripts of hearings, should be covered by a duty of confidentiality.[36] Their opinions are more nuanced regarding documents submitted as fact exhibits or produced in response to another party's document production request.

505

Sébastien Besson and Jean-François Poudret believe that documents not prepared for arbitration proceedings and submitted as evidence should not be treated as confidential only because they were submitted to the arbitral tribunal.[37] According to these authors, confidentiality should only cover:

506

(i) parties' pleadings (statement of claim, statement of defence, opening statements, etc.);
(ii) documents resulting from the arbitral proceedings (such as transcripts of the hearing); and
(iii) documents produced further to a production order of the arbitral tribunal.[38]

Regarding point (c), it appears that the authors meant to exclude documents produced *voluntarily* by a party in response to a document production request of the adverse party, i.e. produced without being ordered to do so by the arbitral tribunal. At first view, this exclusion seems reasonable. It makes sense to provide more protection to the documents produced as a result of an arbitral tribunal's order. These documents may be particularly sensitive: if the arbitral tribunal had to issue an order, it means that a party initially objected to the production of the documents. However, documents produced voluntarily can also contain sensitive information that a party would not wish to disclose, but must disclose in order to be responsive to

507

---

[36]Brown (2001), p. 1004; Furrer (2008), p. 813; Müller (2005), p. 227; Poudret and Besson (2007), para 374.

[37]Poudret and Besson (2007), para 373.

[38]Poudret and Besson (2007), para 373.

the other party's document production request—if there is no valid reason to make an objection.

508 Andreas Furrer considers that the documents submitted by another party are subject to confidentiality, but not the documents that a party itself submits.[39] According to this author, for example, if a party itself submits an expert report in the arbitration proceedings, it should not be restricted from using it outside of the arbitration.[40] We agree that a party should not be restricted from the use of its own document only because this document was produced in an arbitration. This restriction should, however, be imposed if confidential information regarding the other parties can become available as a result of this disclosure.

509 Christoph Müller argues in favour of the approach adopted in the IBA Rules on Evidence: imposing a duty of confidentiality regarding all documents submitted or produced by a party or a non-party in the arbitration.[41] On the one hand, Christoph Müller admits that the mere fact that a document was submitted in arbitration should not result in a particular privilege for this document.[42] On the other hand, he considers that the parties should not be discouraged from submitting documents as evidence because there is a risk that the other party will use these documents outside of the arbitral proceedings.[43] For this reason, he thinks that all documents submitted as exhibits in an arbitration, to which the party had access only because of its participation in the arbitration, should be treated as confidential unless disclosure outside of the arbitration proceedings is allowed by the parties' consent or by a tribunal's order.[44]

510 As discussed in Sect. 4.3.6, we agree with the broad approach to the confidentiality of documents adopted by the IBA Rules on Evidence. The reason for adopting a broad approach to confidentiality is to avoid discouraging the parties from submitting documents as evidence for fear that the other party will use these documents for purposes not connected to the arbitration. This rule should, however, be nuanced to extend only to the documents to which a person wishing to disclose the documents gained access only because of the arbitration.[45]

4.3.6 Intermediary Conclusions

511 The AIAA and the NZAA are among the few national arbitration laws that contain detailed provisions listing the specific categories of documents subject to

---

[39]Furrer (2008), pp. 815–816.

[40]Furrer (2008), pp. 815–816.

[41]Müller (2005), p. 228.

[42]Müller (2005), p. 228.

[43]Müller (2005), p. 228.

[44]Müller (2005), p. 228.

[45]See Sect. 7.4 proposing a text of the rules on confidentiality.

confidentiality. However, they do not include the documents produced by a party in response to another party's document request, if these documents are not submitted as evidence during the arbitration proceedings. We think that these documents, like the documents submitted as evidence, should be treated as confidential. Imposing a confidentiality duty over the documents produced in response to the other party's document request would encourage the parties to participate in the document production process with openness and candour.

The English Court of Appeal had to rule on the issue of confidentiality in *Ali*   **512** *Shipping v Shipyard Trogir* case. It held that the principle of confidentiality should apply equally to the award and to virtually all documents originating from arbitration, such as '*pleadings, written submission, and the proofs of witnesses as well as transcripts and notes of the evidence given in the arbitration*'.

As for the regulation provided in arbitration rules and the opinions expressed by   **513** legal scholars, there is generally a consensus that the duty of confidentiality should cover all documents created for the purpose of an arbitration and resulting from the arbitration proceedings. This includes such documents as parties' pleadings, witness statements, expert reports, and transcripts of hearings. Opinions differ, however, regarding documents submitted as evidence and documents produced in response to another party's request.

Regarding documents submitted as evidence, some arbitration rules distinguish   **514** between the documents that a party submits itself and the documents submitted by another party. These arbitration rules provide that a party has a duty of confidentiality regarding the documents submitted by another party, but not regarding the documents that the party produced itself. Several legal authors support this approach. We agree that this approach could apply in situations when a document produced by a party does not concern the other party or parties to an arbitration proceeding. In this case, the mere fact that a party submits the document in arbitration should not be a reason to restrict its use by this party.

This solution is, however, not perfect. In some situations, a party should be   **515** restricted from using outside of arbitration the documents that it submitted itself. In our opinion, if a party gained access to the document it submitted only because of the arbitration, and if this document can be sensitive for the other party or parties, the duty of confidentiality should apply as well.

As for documents produced in response to another party's request, some arbitration rules and legal scholars distinguish between the documents that a party produces   **516** voluntarily and the documents that it produces in order to comply with a tribunal's order. According to some authors, only the documents produced further to a production order of an arbitral tribunal should be treated as confidential. In our view, however, both categories of produced documents should be treated as confidential.

Other commentators distinguish between the documents that a party produces   **517** itself and the documents produced by another party in the course of the document production stage. Here, we also think that both categories of documents should be covered by confidentiality.

518   In conclusion, we prefer the solution proposed by the IBA Rules on Evidence: protecting the confidentiality of *all documents submitted or produced by a party*. We also agree with the provision in the IBA Rules on Evidence that generally extends the duty of confidentiality to the documents submitted by a *non-party* in the arbitration.[46] We think that this extensive interpretation of the confidentiality of documents is the best way to deal with the issue. It encourages the candour of the persons participating in arbitration proceedings and reinforces the principle of confidentiality of arbitration. In our view, all documents exchanged in the course of arbitration proceedings should be in principle subject to a duty of confidentiality. This confidentiality duty should, however, be limited to the documents to which a person wishing to disclose the document had access only because of the arbitration.[47]

4.4   Confidentiality Regarding Arbitral Awards and Orders

4.4.1   Introduction

519   Turning from the more general issue of the confidentiality of documents, we now examine whether arbitral awards and orders are protected by confidentiality, or whether they can be disclosed. First, however, we must explain what we mean when using the term 'arbitral award(s)'. In this section, we will use this term to mean both arbitral award(s) and order(s) issued by arbitral tribunals. This generally means all decisions of an arbitral tribunal, including the final award, interim and partial awards, order for interim relief, procedural orders and orders for suspension or termination of the proceedings.

520   We also need to explain what confidentiality means in relation to arbitral awards and orders. Confidentiality is the opposite of publicity. This implies that any form of publicity regarding the arbitral awards could be relevant for the present section. However, we will mainly focus on the problem of publication of arbitral awards. By publication, we mean the act of making information available to people in a printed or electronic form.[48] As to other cases of disclosure, such as the use of arbitral award in parallel state court or arbitration proceedings or filing of the arbitral award to recognise, enforce or challenge an arbitral award, we will examine them in the section dealing with exceptions to the duty of confidentiality (Sect. 4.5).

521   Legal practitioners and scholars have extensively discussed the specific issue of the publication of arbitral awards and orders. Nevertheless, they do not agree on a solution. This is not surprising, because one needs to balance two important interests: securing a predictable legal environment on the one hand, and protecting the

---

[46]Art. 3.13 of the IBA Rules on Evidence.

[47]See Sect. 7.4 proposing a text of the rules on confidentiality.

[48]Cambridge online dictionary.

parties' individual interests to maintain privacy of their dispute on the other. From the perspective of a predictable legal environment, publication of arbitral awards in specialized journals and reviews will be beneficial (and is indeed essential for creating 'arbitral jurisprudence', see below Sect. 4.4.5). From the perspective of parties' individual interests, however, publication of an arbitral award will be detrimental if the parties do not want the details of their dispute to become publicly available.

One may ask why state court decisions may (obviously) be published, without **522** violating any duty of confidentiality, whereas arbitral awards may not be published. There is, however, a major conceptual difference. State court proceedings are organised by the state, which must guarantee a fair and accessible administration of justice.[49] Public hearings and the publication of court decisions are important elements of the public system of justice financed by taxpayers. In other words, publication of court decisions ensures a transparent and predictable legal environment and preserves essential public confidence in the administration of justice. By contrast, arbitration is a private proceeding which is generally funded by the parties. It is the parties' choice to have their dispute resolved by arbitration, and confidentiality is often an important element in this choice.[50]

The issue of publication of arbitral award raises the question on the existence of **523** 'arbitral jurisprudence'. Indeed, 'arbitral jurisprudence' cannot exist without publication of awards. Most legal scholars agree that arbitral awards do not have the binding authority of precedent.[51] For most scholars, the exact role and influence of past arbitral decisions is nuanced. However, none doubts that past arbitral decisions cannot be ignored and should at least be taken into account to some extent.[52] If past arbitral decisions are to play a bigger role, more consistent publication of arbitral awards is needed.

In this section, we will first examine provisions on the confidentiality of arbitral **524** awards contained in arbitration rules. As we will see, many arbitration rules expressly impose a duty of confidentiality regarding arbitral awards and allow publication of awards only with the parties' consent. Second, we will see that fewer national arbitration laws regulate the confidentiality of arbitral awards. Third, we will briefly review how state courts have typically dealt with the issue of confidentiality of arbitral awards. Finally, we will explain why confidentiality of arbitral awards is actually not an obstacle to the systematic publication of arbitral awards.

---

[49] *See, e.g.,* Art. 6 on Right to a fair trial in the ECHR.

[50] *See, e.g.,* 2010 International Arbitration Survey: Choices in International Arbitration, Queen Mary University, 29. Also see above Sect. 3.2.4 discussing balance of the interests involved and analysis of the arguments for and against confidentiality.

[51] *See, e.g.,* Kaufmann-Kohler (2007), p. 374; Born (2014), p. 3827; Perret (2007), p. 33.

[52] See, e.g., Kaufmann-Kohler (2007), p. 374; Born (2014), p. 3827; Perret (2007), p. 33; also see Sect. 2.6.2.

4.4.2 International Arbitration Rules

525 Most arbitration rules contain provisions imposing a duty of confidentiality regarding arbitral awards.[53] However, some arbitration rules do not contain such provisions, e.g., the ICC, AAA or ICAC Rules. And in sharp contrast, the Oslo Rules provide that arbitral awards are not subject to confidentiality unless otherwise agreed by the arbitral award, but in the absence of an express agreement on confidentiality, the award is not regarded as confidential.[54] In general, however, confidentiality is the rule, although it is subject to some exceptions (see Sect. 4.5 below).

526   Many rules, such as LCIA, DIS, WIPO, ACICA and UNCITRAL, require consent of the parties for publication of the arbitral awards. Thus, Art. 30.3 of the LCIA Rules provides that

> '[t]*he LCIA does not publish any award or any part of an award without the prior written consent of all parties and the Arbitral Tribunal*'.

Thus, the LCIA cannot publish the award without the consent of all parties and the assent of the arbitral tribunal. In practice, however, the LCIA does not publish awards on its own initiative.[55]

527   The DIS Rules allow publication only with the prior written consent of all the parties.[56] The DIS Rules also expressly allow the institution to use the information from arbitral awards to compile statistical data, provided that the disclosed information will not allow identification of the persons involved.[57]

528   Here is what Art. 44(3) of the Swiss Rules provides regarding publication of arbitral awards:

> An award or order may be published, whether in its entirety or in the form of excerpts or a summary, only under the following conditions:
>
> a) A request for publication is addressed to the Secretariat;
> b) All references to the parties' names are deleted; and
> c) No party objects to such publication within the time-limit fixed for that purpose by the Secretariat.

Thus, first, Art. 44(3) of the Swiss Rules provides a procedural framework for addressing a request for publication. Such a request needs to be addressed to the Secretariat. Second, this article expressly provides that references to the parties'

---

[53]See, for example, Arts 44(1) and 44(3) Swiss Rules; Arts 30(1) and 30(3) LCIA Rules; Art. 22 (2) ACICA Rules; Art. 33 Abu Dhabi Rules; Art. 3 SCC Rules; Art. 34(5) UNCITRAL Rules; Art. 77 WIPO Rules.

[54]Arts 12 and 13 Oslo Rules.

[55]Nesbitt and Darowski (2015), p. 558.

[56]Art. 44.3 DIS Rules.

[57]Art. 44.3 DIS Rules.

names be deleted. Third, the parties need not give their consent to the publication, but they can object to it within a time-limit fixed by the Secretariat. The time limit will be fixed depending on the particular circumstances of each case, and it can be extended by the Secretariat if justified by the circumstances.[58] If the party (or the parties) do not make such an objection, the award can be published.[59]

More and more institutional rules allow the relevant arbitration institution to publish arbitral awards in anonymous format even without an express consent of the parties. The Milan, SIAC, VIAC and ICDR Rules similarly allow the Secretariat of the relevant institution to publish the awards, provided that the parties' identity remains confidential. Thus, Art. 8.2 of the Milan Rules stipulates that the arbitral award should be published in anonymous format. The main purpose of the publication, is to provide materials for research. Art. 32.12 of the SIAC Rules requires that the names of the parties—and other information allowing identification of the parties—be redacted. Art. 41 of the VIAC Rules allows the Board and the Secretary General to publish '*anonymized summaries or extracts of awards*' in legal journals or in VIAC's own publications. Art. 30(3) of the ICDR Rules permits publishing of **529**

> '*selected awards, orders, decisions, and rulings that have been edited to conceal the names of the parties and other identifying details*'.

The Milan Rules impose an additional requirement on the publication of an award: similarly to the Swiss Rules, no objection to such publication should be made by the parties during the proceedings.[60] Art. 41 of the VIAC Rules has a similar rule, but the objection would have to be made not during the proceedings, but within 30 days of service of the award. Art. 30(3) of the ICDR Rules allows publication unless otherwise agreed by the parties. **530**

4.4.3 National Arbitration Laws

As compared to arbitration rules, fewer national arbitration laws regulate confidentiality regarding arbitral awards. Also, as opposed to arbitration rules, national arbitration laws typically do not regulate the issue of publication of arbitral awards. The very few national laws regulating the confidentiality of arbitral awards can be classified into two categories. On the one hand, we have those which provide for confidentiality of arbitral awards unless the parties agree otherwise. These are, for example, the AIAA, the NZAA and the Scottish Arbitration Act. On the other hand, some national laws provide that arbitral awards are non-confidential unless the **531**

---

[58]Rohner and La Spada (2013), para 27.

[59]Rohner and La Spada (2013), para 28.

[60]Art. 8.2 Milan Rules.

parties agree otherwise. These include the Norwegian Arbitration Act and the International Commercial Arbitration Law of Costa Rica.

532   The NZAA provides that the parties and the arbitration tribunal must not disclose confidential information, which includes *inter alia* the award of the arbitral tribunal.[61] In some cases, however, there are exceptions to this confidentiality rule for arbitral awards.[62] These confidentiality provisions apply to every arbitration with its seat in New Zealand, unless the parties agree otherwise in writing.[63] Notwithstanding the explicit text, however, some authors question whether the parties can 'opt out' of all confidentiality provisions.[64] The AIAA has very similar provisions imposing a duty of confidentiality regarding arbitral awards.[65]

533   Similarly, the Scottish Arbitration Act 2010 prohibits disclosure of confidential information, which includes *inter alia* any information relating to the award.[66] There are, however, some exceptions to this general principle, e.g. express or implied authorisation by the parties.

534   As stated above, the Norwegian Arbitration Act and the International Commercial Arbitration Law of Costa Rica provide that arbitral awards are *not* confidential unless the parties agree otherwise. The Norwegian Arbitration Act provides that the decisions reached by the arbitral tribunal are not subject to confidentiality.[67] The International Commercial Arbitration Law of Costa Rica goes even further as it provides that all final awards are public.[68] Under both acts, however, the parties are allowed to opt out of these provisions and agree on a duty of confidentiality for their proceedings and the award.[69]

4.4.4 State Court Decisions

535   As we have seen above,[70] confidentiality of arbitration is not the rule in every jurisdiction. For example, Swedish law does not recognise confidentiality of arbitration proceedings in the absence of a parties' express agreement on

---

[61] Arts 14B, 2.1(b)(v) and (vi) NZAA.

[62] See below Sect. 4.5.

[63] Art. 14 of the NZAA.

[64] Kawharu (2008), p. 406.

[65] Arts 15(1) and 23C AIAA.

[66] Art. 26 of the Scottish Arbitration Act.

[67] Art. 5 of the Norwegian Arbitration Act of 14 May 2004.

[68] Art. 38(1) of the International Commercial Arbitration Law of Cost Rica.

[69] Art. 5 of the Norwegian Arbitration Act of 14 May 2004 and Art. 38(1) of the International Commercial Arbitration Law of Cost Rica.

[70] See above Sect. 3.2.3 on the implied duty of confidentiality.

confidentiality.[71] This regulation obviously extends to arbitral awards, which are not regarded as confidential further to the discussed above Swedish court decision in *Bulgarian Foreign Trade Bank Ltd. v. A.I. Trade Finance Inc.*[72]

English law, on the other hand, recognises a broad principle of confidentiality over the documents originating from arbitration proceedings, including arbitral awards.[73] As discussed above, the English High Court judged in *Hassneh Insurance v Mew* that the principle of confidentiality was less strict regarding the award than regarding other documents from arbitration proceedings,[74] but the English Court of Appeal rejected this difference in treatment in *Ali Shipping v Shipyard Trogir.*[75]

536

The confidentiality duty regarding arbitral awards is, however, subject to exceptions under English law. The English High Court and the Privy Council[76] have dealt with disclosure of arbitral awards on several occasions. They consistently decided that confidentiality of arbitration should not be an obstacle to the use of arbitral awards in another proceeding if such disclosure is justified by a legitimate reason. We will discuss these decisions in the section dealing with the exceptions to the duty of confidentiality (see below Sect. 4.5).

537

4.4.5 Tensions Between Confidentiality and Publication of Arbitral Awards

4.4.5.1 Current Publication Practices

One might argue that publication of an arbitral award is not compatible with the confidentiality of the corresponding arbitration proceedings. If we assume that the arbitral award and the information contained therein are confidential, there is indeed some tension, because publication of the arbitral award is a form of disclosure. As we have seen above, many arbitration rules and national arbitration laws recognise the confidential nature of arbitral awards. Despite this, many arbitration rules allow publication of arbitral awards provided certain requirements are met. And some institutions have the practice of publishing a selection of their awards in a redacted form.

538

---

[71]Brocker and Löf (2013), p. 201; Heuman (2003), p. 14; Shaughnessy (2006), pp. 316–317; Madsen (2007), p. 194.

[72]Judgment of the Supreme Court of Sweden rendered in 2000 in Case N T 1881-99: The Bulbank Case, in: Stockholm Arbitration Report, Volume 2, 2000, 137–160.

[73]See Sect. 4.3.4.

[74]Hassneh Insurance Co v Mew [1993] 2 Lloyd's Rep 243.

[75]Ali Shipping v. Shipyard Trogir [1997] EWCA Civ 3054.

[76]The Judicial Committee of the Privy Council is the court of final appeal for the UK overseas territories and Crown dependencies, and for those Commonwealth countries that have retained the appeal to Her Majesty in Council or, in the case of Republics, to the Judicial Committee (http://jcpc.uk/).

539   Selected ICC awards are published, for example, in the ICC Court Bulletin, the Collection of ICC Arbitral Awards, the Yearbook Commercial Arbitration, the *Journal du Droit International* (Clunet), *Les Cahiers de l'Arbitrage*. The SCC awards were published between 1999 and 2009 in the Law Journal of the Stockholm Chamber of Commerce.[77]

540   The Yearbook Commercial Arbitration is an important source of institutional and *ad hoc* arbitral awards. Each month, the ITA (Institute for Transnational Arbitration) Arbitration Report publishes various arbitration materials online, including reports on the arbitral awards.[78]

541   The Kluwer arbitration website contains an important collection of arbitral awards selected by authors and editors of Kluwer Law International publications, the Editorial Staff at ICCA, and the ITA Board of Reports.[79] This collection includes all arbitral awards included in print publications published and licensed by Kluwer Law International.[80] CLOUT, a legal database of worldwide court decisions and arbitral awards related to UNCITRAL texts, is another comprehensive online tool for searching arbitral awards. CLOUT allows searching of arbitral awards dealing only with the UN Convention on Contracts for the International Sale of Goods and other UNCITRAL texts.

542   Publication of awards helps develop a consistent jurisprudence for commercial usages and customs, which is particularly important in maritime law. This is why a number of institutions specialized in maritime arbitrations, such as the Tokyo Maritime Arbitration Commission of the Japan Shipping Exchange or the Society of Maritime Arbitrators, publish their arbitral awards in some form.[81]

543   A number of institutions also publish statistical data on caseloads, such as the ICC Court of International Arbitration, the SCC Arbitration Institute, the Hong Kong International Arbitration Centre, the German Institution for Arbitration and the Milan Chamber of Arbitration. Publication of such statistical data should not raise issues with confidentiality. Indeed, such published data usually include information on the number of cases, the number of issued awards, the nationality of the parties, and the nationality of the arbitrators, but no individual information on particular cases is disclosed. While this information can give an idea of the type and the amount of work done at a particular institution, and can be helpful when selecting institutional rules, it does not allow one to evaluate the quality of arbitral awards or assess the average duration of arbitral proceedings.

---

[77]From 1999 to 2004, this Journal was called the Stockholm Arbitration Report (SAR), and then from 2005 to 2009, the Stockholm International Arbitration Review (SIAR).

[78]The advantage of the publications of the Yearbook Commercial Arbitration and the ITA Arbitration Report is that they are searchable online on the Kluwer arbitration website.

[79]http://www.kluwerarbitration.com/ (last visited on 13 September 2018).

[80]http://www.kluwerarbitration.com/ (last visited on 13 September 2018).

[81]For more details, see the article of Kenji Tashiro, Quest for a Rational and Proper Method for the Publication of Arbitral Awards.

Finally, summaries of awards are made public through various online resources **544** and even by way of social networks. Most major awards are currently reported by the Global Arbitration Review.[82] Reports like these usually contain only the most essential information, such as a briefing on the nature of the dispute, the parties involved, the conclusions reached in the award, including the awarded or non-awarded amounts, the composition of the arbitral tribunal and the names of the parties' representatives. Confidentiality is, however, rarely an issue with these summary reports, because they are usually published with the parties' consent.

Thus, while arbitral awards are frequently published in some form, the publica- **545** tion is not systematic. This is not necessarily a problem from the point of view of confidentiality, but it makes it difficult for practitioners and researchers to analyse the characteristics of arbitral awards or trends in arbitration. First, only a small portion of institutional and *ad hoc* awards are published, which means that most arbitral awards remain unknown.[83] The awards are often deliberately selected for publication by responsible officials of the arbitration institutes. Second, arbitral awards are generally not published in full. It is often the reporter who selects extracts, choosing the passages relating to the issues in the award that the reporter considers the most relevant for publication.

These observations might explain the existing doubts among scholars about **546** whether the sample of published awards is representative.[84] Joshua Karton provides an illustrative example of why these doubts may be justified:

> International arbitral awards that rely on *lex mercatoria* or amiable composition are rare in practice. Their use was never internationally significant and is diminishing. Nevertheless, from the published awards, such decisions seem to be common. This is a result of a deliberate policy in favour of publishing such awards. A former Secretary-General of the ICC Court of International Arbitration observed of the ICC's own collection of published awards: 'Only those awards in which arbitrators have felt least constrained to apply national law have been published.'[85]

Given that the publication of arbitral awards is unsystematic, should it become **547** systematic? If yes, what form should it take? We will examine these questions in the next sections.

---

[82]http://globalarbitrationreview.com/news/ (last visited on 13 September 2018).

[83]See, e.g., Mourre (2013), pp. 63–64.

[84]Karton (2012), p. 475.

[85]Karton (2012), pp. 475–476, with further references.

4.4.5.2   Systematic Publication of Arbitral Awards?[86]

548   An increasing number of authors make the case for a systematic publication of arbitral awards.[87] It is interesting to analyse the arguments they advance, as well as possible counter-arguments. As a preliminary remark, it would be important to identify the various interests involved. As suggested by Joshua Karton,[88] two main groups of interests can be identified. On the one hand, we have the interests of the parties to a given dispute ('party interests' or interests of the international arbitration community), and, on the other hand, we have the interests of the system as a whole ('systemic interests'). As we will see, depending on the particular aspect to be improved, enhanced or developed, the interests of these groups may or may not coincide.

4.4.5.2.1   Consistent Arbitral Case Law

549   The main argument for systematic publication of arbitral awards is that it would create consistent and coherent arbitral case law—a step towards 'arbitral jurisprudence'. This case law would indicate general practices and attitudes without, however, creating a binding system of precedents.[89] The process would serve both the party and systemic interests. Indeed, it would benefit everyone by enhancing the principle of fairness, as similar situations would be treated similarly. Systematic publication would also help to develop a legally predictable environment for actual and potential users. Predictability of result is a common problem for litigation, and even bigger problem for international arbitration (as opposed to domestic litigation) because there is a big variety of possible applicable laws and no unified system of appellate courts.[90]

550   One could argue that creation of consistent arbitral jurisprudence is impossible because most arbitration cases are fact and contract driven, and because virtually every case has its own relevant law(s). As observed, however, by Julian D. M. Lew:

> Whilst every arbitration must be determined in the light of its particular facts and the relevant law, there remains nonetheless much that can be learnt from earlier awards, despite their differing facts.[91]

---

[86]We could examine the issue of systematic publication of arbitral awards in the section dealing with exceptions to the duty of confidentiality, but opted to do it while discussing the problem of tensions between confidentiality and publication of arbitral awards.

[87]*See, e.g.*, Born (2014), pp. 2822–2823; Mourre (2013); Buys (2003); Fernandez-Armesto (2012); Karton (2012); Lew (1982).

[88]Karton (2012), p. 457.

[89]Lew (1982), p. 226.

[90]Karton (2012), p. 462.

[91]Lew (1982), p. 226.

Guidance from past arbitral decisions could help clarify specific procedural   **551**
issues, such as determination of the applicable law or whether a given tribunal has
jurisdiction to resolve a dispute. Such issues require uniform solutions. This guidance might also help parties and arbitrators understand specific complex problems of
substantive law, as they could consult past decisions on cases with similar facts and
circumstances. In the international trade area, the *lex mercatoria* could also be
developed into a coherent body of rules through the publishing of arbitral awards.[92]

4.4.5.2.2 Enhancing Transparency of the Arbitration

Another reason to publish arbitral awards is to create a transparent system in which   **552**
the public is informed of reasoned decisions. This would also contribute to enhancing the legitimacy of international arbitration, *i.e.* its acceptance by the public as a
dispute resolution method. As emphasized by Cindy Buys, '[w]*hen the process has
consistency and predictability, its legitimacy is enhanced because parties know what
to expect.*'[93] Enhancing transparency of arbitration would thus serve the systemic
interests.

4.4.5.2.3 Improving the Quality of Arbitral Awards

Another argument for systematic publication is that it might improve the quality of   **553**
arbitral awards. The certainty of eventual publication would tend to give the arbitrators in a given dispute more control, which could encourage them to be particularly thorough, especially if the awards are published with their names attached. In
addition, all arbitrators could benefit from the previously published arbitral awards
and arguably would be better prepared to draft their awards. Improvement of the
quality of arbitral awards would serve both the party and the systemic interests.

4.4.5.2.4 Promotion of Arbitration as a Dispute Resolution Method

Systematic publication of arbitral awards would also promote the use of arbitration   **554**
in general. Since most awards are not publicly known, it is difficult for prospective
end users of arbitration to judge its advantages. If they could see the final products of
arbitration—arbitral awards—this could demonstrate to them that arbitration is a fair
and efficient method of dispute resolution.[94]

---

[92]Lew (1982), pp. 229–231.

[93]Buys (2003), p. 136.

[94]Lew (1982), p. 227.

4.4.5.2.5   Making Arbitrations More Accessible for Users

555   By distributing knowledge of arbitration issues more widely, systematic publication of arbitral awards could also serve party and systemic interests by reducing the cost of arbitration, thus making it more accessible to individuals and companies with more limited revenue (but who are nevertheless involved in cross-border transactions and seeking justice). Arbitrations are usually perceived as an expensive dispute resolution method accessible only to large companies. Although this is not true, arbitration proceedings come at a relatively high cost.

556   Only some law firms have an expertise in arbitration, and they charge relatively high fees to maintain the resources, expertise and networking tools they require. In other words, arbitration lawyers are still an elite group of insiders who benefit early from in their careers mostly from the experience of more senior colleagues. Publication of awards could help spread knowledge of arbitration to a more extended circle of legal professionals.

557   In countries where the English language is not extensively used, and where most lawyers may lack a good knowledge of English, the language barrier may also discourage some parties from choosing arbitration. Systematic publication of arbitral awards could mitigate this problem as it would enable translation of awards from English and study of awards in other languages.

4.4.5.2.6   Ad hoc v. Institutional Arbitrations and Choice of the Arbitration Institution

558   Systematic publication of arbitral awards would also help identify which form of arbitration would be better suited for a particular type of dispute. For instance, prospective parties would have more information to make a choice in favour of *ad hoc* or institutional arbitration. Also, in the case of institutional arbitration, publication of arbitral awards would allow the parties to compare the performance of different arbitration institutions, enabling them to select the institution best suited to their expectations regarding the conduct of proceedings.[95]

4.4.5.2.7   Appointing Arbitrators

559   If published awards also routinely indicated the names of the arbitrators having rendered the decision, this information would help prospective parties make a more informed decision when appointing an arbitrator. Currently, the parties usually have to rely on advice given by their counsel, who might know the relevant arbitrator by his reputation or through the personal experience.

---

[95]McIlwrath and Schroeder (2013), p. 95.

4.4.5.2.8 Execution of Arbitral Awards

One might also argue that systematic publication may facilitate enforcement (exe-   **560**
cution) of arbitral awards.[96] First, if the public is confident that the arbitration
process is fair, and that enforcement of the awards is efficient, it may contribute to
voluntary executions of the award. Second, if the relevant award is published, this
may put additional pressure on the losing party, who might want to avoid reputational risks related to non-execution of the award. However, in our view, the
publication of the award should not reveal the parties' names or allow to identify
them otherwise.

4.4.5.2.9 Privacy of the Parties

As to the arguments against systematic publication of arbitral awards, these mostly   **561**
revolve around the privacy of the parties to a given dispute.[97] Many parties wish to
keep the dispute and all related information and documents secret from the public.
The losing party, in particular, might not want details of its defeat to be known to the
public, especially if this party has been reproached for having behaved in bad faith or
dishonestly. Therefore, systematic publication of arbitral awards would arguably
take away one of arbitration's main advantages—confidentiality—thereby creating a
risk that users attracted by confidentiality would abandon arbitration for other
methods of dispute resolution.[98]

One can also argue that arbitration is a private system of dispute resolution, and so   **562**
there is no place for systematic publication of awards. The rationale would be that
since the arbitrators' jurisdiction is based on the parties' agreement, the arbitral
award is a contract that the parties have agreed, in advance, to perform. Publication
of such a private commercial contract would therefore be inappropriate.[99] This
position can, however, be easily challenged. An arbitral award is more than just a
contract: it is a final decision of a neutral body, which has the same effect as a court
decision.

4.4.5.2.10 Additional Costs

Another argument against systematic publication of awards is cost. As noted,   **563**
arbitration proceedings are already expensive, and publication could increase the
cost of disputes, depending on how the publication process is organised. All awards
will need to be prepared for publication, which will involve more time spent by

---

[96]Buys (2003), p. 136.
[97]See above Sect. 3.2.4.2.1 discussing the parties' interests to maintain the privacy of the dispute.
[98]Karton (2012), p. 480.
[99]Lew (1982), p. 225.

officials of the institutions and/or arbitrators to prepare the 'sanitized' texts. If the
parties are also involved in preparation of the published text, there might also be
additional direct costs for them as well. For example, if the parties need to agree on
the text of the award to be published, and there is a dispute, resolving such a dispute
will likely cause significant costs related mainly to parties' counsel fees.[100]

4.4.5.2.11 Intermediary Conclusions

564   Although systematic publication of arbitral awards would have many advantages for
the system as a whole, it might conflict with the interests of the parties to a given
dispute. While systemic interests are certainly more important in state court proceedings, the situation is different in arbitration because it is a private consent-based
system. As maintained by Joshua Karton:

> Since international arbitration is a private consent-based system, party interests in keeping
> awards confidential are likely to trump systemic interests in publishing them-even if those
> systemic interests align with the long-term interests of commercial parties generally.[101]

565   The real question is whether this conflict can be resolved so that the party interests
are not compromised. In particular, systematic publication of awards should not
compromise the parties' interests in the confidentiality of arbitral proceedings. We
think that this is achievable.

566   Some arbitration rules have specific regulations demonstrating that confidentiality of arbitration proceedings and publication of arbitral awards are compatible. For
example, the Milan Rules provide in Art. 8.1 that the arbitral proceedings and the
arbitral award are to be kept confidential. Further, Art. 8.2 specifies that the Chamber
of Arbitration may publish the arbitral award in anonymous format. The SIAC Rules
oblige the parties and the Tribunal to keep the arbitral award confidential,[102] but
allow SIAC to publish any award with the names of the parties and other identifying
information redacted.[103]

567   As observed by Rinaldo Sali, there is no contradiction between confidentiality of
arbitral proceedings and systematic publication of arbitral awards. He argues that
confidentiality should be maintained over the course of arbitral proceedings, but that
the systemic interest in publicity through publication of the award in anonymous
format should prevail once the proceedings are over.[104]

568   We agree that confidentiality of arbitral proceedings should not be an obstacle to
systematic publication of arbitral awards. Confidentiality can be protected if all
potentially sensitive information, as well as any information that would allow the

---

[100]Karton (2012), p. 482.

[101]Karton (2012), p. 447.

[102]Art. 39.1 SIAC Rules.

[103]Art. 32.12 SIAC Rules.

[104]Sali (2013), p. 73.

parties involved in the dispute to be identified, is removed from the published arbitral award. Restricted in this way, publication should not compromise the parties' interests in maintaining the privacy of their dispute. Below, we will further discuss how arbitral awards can be published in a way that avoids identification of the parties.

4.4.5.3 Form of Publication

As long as the parties' anonymity is protected, there should be no tensions between confidentiality and publication of the arbitral awards. Such protection depends on the form of publication, however, and it might prove difficult to find a form of publication which guarantees complete anonymity of the parties while keeping the award comprehensible to an external reader. Fortunately, the issue has been much discussed in the literature, where one can find relatively detailed recommendations. **569**

For example, the Milan Chamber of Arbitration has issued Guidelines for the Anonymous Publication of Arbitral Awards ('Milan Guidelines'). These were published in a recent treatise arguing for the rise of transparency in international arbitration.[105] The Milan Guidelines apply to the institutional arbitrations regulated by the Milan Rules.[106] They contain a set of general standards for publication; specific rules as to which information needs to be indicated/omitted; and the procedure for publication. Similar recommendations can also be found in a recent article of Joshua Karton.[107] **570**

The first question is whether arbitral awards should be published in full or in part. The reality is that only extracts or summaries of arbitral awards are usually made available. Published awards are redacted so that the reader does not have to read 'unnecessary' information, but can follow the reasoning of the arbitral tribunal regarding a specific issue.[108] The problem with this practice is that the redaction involves much external interference affecting the content of the published text of the award. The text is greatly influenced by the subjective views of those making the report. Publication of the full text would remove this problem. **571**

Another reality is that awards are often very lengthy (several hundreds of pages) and contain long discussions on fact findings which might not always be relevant for further discussions on legal issues of general applicability. From this point of view, partial publication of arbitral awards could be a good solution. The problem of subjectivity could be addressed by having the arbitrators who drafted the arbitral award also prepare the text to be published. **572**

It might also be argued that the parties *should* be able to influence the form of the published text of the award. In this view, it would be good to grant the parties the **573**

---

[105]Malatesta and Sali (2013), pp. 29–37.

[106]Malatesta and Sali (2013), p. 29, point 1 of the Preamble.

[107]Karton (2012), pp. 447–486.

[108]Lew (1982), p. 232.

right to review the text of the award resolving their dispute before its publication. They could also be granted various other rights with regard to the text of the award to be published: right of consultation, right to make corrections to the text, right to veto publication, etc. If the parties are vested with important powers regarding the text of the arbitral award to be published, there is a risk, however, that the parties could disagree. In case of disagreement, publication could turn into another full dispute in its own right.

4.4.5.3.1   Identification of the Parties

574   To protect the privacy of the parties in an arbitration, enough information should be redacted from the published text of the award so that the parties (and the dispute) are not recognisable. The names of the parties can easily be removed and replaced by X., Y. or any other letters, combination of letters, and/or signs. They can also be identified only as 'claimant' and 'defendant'. This might, however, be insufficient. If we imagine, for example, that a dispute is politically driven, and that it is over an important question for the economy of a given country, it might be difficult to publish the award in such a way that the parties cannot be identified.

575   As to what makes the parties recognisable or identifiable, a related question is how much some third parties already know. Third parties from the relevant industry/ area may be more able to identify the parties to a given dispute than third parties in general. People working in the relevant industry are usually aware of its ongoing disputes and might easily identify the involved parties when reading the arbitral award even if the names of the parties are removed. When publishing the award, it might thus be difficult to make the parties unrecognisable to everyone. Therefore, while such an effort should be made, it will not always be successful—depending on the nature of the dispute and the parties involved.

576   Another solution would be to postpone publication of the award for some period of time.[109] Postponed publication can even be considered necessary if an immediate publication could harm the parties' interests. The need for and delay of a postponement could be decided based on the particular circumstances of the case.

577   The Milan Guidelines provide that names and personal details of the parties should be omitted, but that their nationality is revealed. Any information that still renders a party recognisable must be indicated in general terms.[110]

578   Importantly, this 'sanitization' of the award must not prevent the reader from following the reasoning of the tribunal and from understanding the basis on which the tribunal reached a particular decision. Joshua Karton suggests that the arbitrators be instructed before they start drafting the award to do it in such a way so as to preserve the parties' confidentiality, while comprehensively setting out the legal issues of general applicability. More specifically, he recommends dividing the award

---

[109]Karton (2012), p. 479.
[110]Art. 2.4 of the Milan Guidelines.

into three parts: (i) recitation of the evidence and the facts found by the tribunal; (ii) applicable legal and procedural issues; and (iii) application of the law to the facts, and such matters as allocation of costs.[111]

4.4.5.3.2 Names of the Arbitrators

Another important issue is whether the awards should be published with the names **579** of the arbitrators. Many authors think that the names should be made public.[112] For example, Alberto Malatesta maintains that protecting privacy of arbitrators is not sufficient reason to remove the names of the arbitrators when publishing the award. He argues that there should be no obstacles to revealing the arbitrators' names, and makes the case for keeping them in the published arbitration awards.[113]

Julian D.M. Lew rightly argues that, when appointing an arbitrator, parties need **580** to know whether an arbitrator has the necessary experience and expertise for dealing with a particular case. The most appropriate and objective source of information evidencing the experience and expertise of a given arbitrator would be his arbitral awards.[114] Along these lines, Joshua Karton maintains that it is in the arbitrators' interests to reveal their names *'for promotional reasons or to demonstrate that they have nothing to hide'*.[115] He thinks that arbitrators will likely take advantage of the publication of their awards with their names—if this does not infringe on party autonomy.[116]

In general, the trend in opinion is clearly towards favouring the release of the **581** arbitrators' names. Thus, the ICC Court announced on 5 January 2016 that it will publish the names of the arbitrators sitting in ICC cases on its website, as well as their nationality and information on whether they were appointed by the Court or by the parties.[117] The ICC Court will also identify the chairman of the tribunal. The announcement specifies that '[i]*n order not to compromise expectations of confidentiality that may be important to the parties, the case reference number and the names of the parties and of counsel will not be published'*.[118] The Parties can nevertheless opt out of this limited disclosure.[119]

---

[111]Karton (2012), p. 478.

[112]See, *e.g.*, Malatesta (2013), p. 51; Karton (2012), p. 478; Lew (1982), p. 228.

[113]Malatesta (2013), p. 51.

[114]Lew (1982), p. 228.

[115]Karton (2012), p. 479.

[116]Karton (2012), p. 479.

[117]https://iccwbo.org/media-wall/news-speeches/icc-court-announces-new-policies-to-foster-trans parency-and-ensure-greater-efficiency/ (last visited on 13 September 2018).

[118]https://iccwbo.org/media-wall/news-speeches/icc-court-announces-new-policies-to-foster-trans parency-and-ensure-greater-efficiency/ (last visited on 13 September 2018).

[119]https://iccwbo.org/media-wall/news-speeches/icc-court-announces-new-policies-to-foster-trans parency-and-ensure-greater-efficiency/ (last visited on 13 September 2018).

582   This is a very important decision aimed at enhancing transparency for users and other stakeholders.[120] According to Alex Mourre, publication of the composition of ICC tribunals will help to promote *'regional, generation and gender diversity of arbitrators'*.[121] Publication will also be a useful tool for users of the ICC Court, as they will be able to see an arbitrator's experience in terms of the quantity of his ICC cases and to make a judgment on whether a particular arbitrator appears to be particularly busy.

4.4.5.3.3   Dissemination of Published Awards

583   As mentioned above, arbitral awards are published by a number of online and hard copy resources. While hard-copy reviews and texts of awards are helpful to academics and practitioners, online publication better enables them to do research and would probably be more welcome. For this, all awards would need to be properly catalogued and indexed.

4.4.6   Intermediary Conclusions

584   There is no systematic publication of arbitral awards, and current publication practices are quite diverse. This issue, like the more general issues of confidentiality and disclosure of arbitral awards, is mostly regulated by arbitration rules.[122] As indicated above, most arbitration rules and national arbitration laws impose a duty of confidentiality regarding arbitral awards, but they generally allow publication of arbitral awards with the parties' consent and/or if the text is 'sanitized'.[123] In addition, more and more arbitration rules allow the relevant institution to publish awards in a sanitized form even if there is no express consent from the parties. Finally, some arbitration rules and national arbitration laws unusually provide that arbitral awards are *not* confidential in the absence of the parties' agreement on the

---

[120]https://iccwbo.org/media-wall/news-speeches/icc-court-announces-new-policies-to-foster-trans parency-and-ensure-greater-efficiency/ (last visited on 13 September 2018).

[121]www.globalarbitrationreview.com/news/article/34453/icc-publish-arbitrator-names-crack-down-delay/ (last visited on 13 September 2018).

[122]See, for example, Arts 44(1) and 44(3) Swiss Rules; Arts 30(1) and 30(3) of the LCIA Rules; Art. 22(2) of the ACICA Rules; Art. 33 of the Abu Dhabi Rules; Art. 3 of the SCC Rules; Art. 12 of the Oslo Rules; Art. 34(5) of the UNCITRAL Rules; Art. 77 of the WIPO Rules.

[123]See, for example, Arts 44(1) and 44(3) Swiss Rules; Arts 30(1) and 30(3) LCIA Rules; Art. 22 (2) ACICA Rules; Art. 33 Abu Dhabi Rules; Art. 3 SCC Rules; Art. 34(5) UNCITRAL Rules; Art. 77 WIPO Rules; Art. 14B, Art. 2.1(b)(v) and (vi) NZAA; Art. 15(1) and 23C AIAA; Art. 26 of the Scottish Arbitration Act.

contrary.[124] While the last approach seems too radical, we support the idea of systematic publication of arbitral awards in a sanitized form even if there is no express consent to publication from the parties.

Whether state courts treat arbitral awards as confidential will primarily depend on **585** the general approach to confidentiality of arbitration in the relevant jurisdiction. If confidentiality of arbitration is recognised, this will generally extend to arbitral awards; the contrary is also true. Thus, in the absence of an express agreement on confidentiality, Swedish law considers that arbitral awards are not covered by confidentiality. In England, arbitral awards, like any other documents originating from arbitration proceedings, are in principle protected by confidentiality. This confidentiality, however, as we will see below, does not prevent the parties from making a legitimate use of arbitral awards outside of the arbitration proceedings.

We think that confidentiality of arbitral awards is not an obstacle to publication of **586** arbitral awards if the awards are published in such a form that the parties cannot be identified. In our view, systematic publication of arbitral awards would have many advantages. It would: create consistent arbitral case law and promote 'arbitral jurisprudence'; enhance transparency of arbitration; improve the quality of arbitral awards; promote the use of arbitration as a dispute resolution method; make arbitrations more accessible for users; enable users to make a more informed decision regarding the choice of arbitration institution and when appointing an arbitrator; and facilitate voluntary execution and enforcement of arbitral awards. For these reasons, systematic publication of arbitral awards should be the goal.

In our opinion, it would also be beneficial if the awards were published with the **587** names of the arbitrators. The arbitrators would promote their experience and expertise, and the parties would be able to make a more informed choice of arbitrator. And if the awards are published systematically with names, they will be properly catalogued and indexed so that researchers can easily search through them using online tools.

4.5 Confidentiality in Respect of Hearings

4.5.1 Introduction

Confidentiality in respect of hearings is another element of the duty of confidenti- **588** ality. It implies privacy of arbitration hearings, but also more generally confidentiality of all documents and information surrounding hearings. When using the term 'hearings', we mean both evidentiary and procedural hearings, unless we specifically refer to evidentiary hearings.

---

[124]Art. 12 of the Oslo Rules; Art. 5 of the Norwegian Arbitration Act of 14 May 2004; Art. 38(1) of the International Commercial Arbitration Law of Cost Rica.

589   Confidentiality regarding hearings means, first of all, that hearings are held in private. In principle, only the parties and the arbitrators can participate in a hearing, along with the parties' counsel, the secretary of the arbitral tribunal, and supporting staff (translators, court reporters providing live transcription, etc.). Third parties, the press, and the public are in principle not allowed to attend a hearing.[125] While fact and expert witnesses are being examined, they obviously have to attend the hearing, in person or sometimes via video conference. Once their own examination is over, they can also be allowed in the hearing room while other witnesses and experts are being examined (so that their testimony is not influenced by prior statements of other witnesses).

590   Confidentiality regarding hearings is, however, not limited only to privacy of hearings *per se*. Hearings generate many documents, such as transcripts of oral evidence or opening and closing submissions. Moreover, some information on the content of hearings is not documented but can be disclosed orally. The question is whether confidentiality of these documents and information should be maintained.

591   In this section, we will first examine how confidentiality of hearings is regulated in arbitration law and practice. We will see that while privacy of hearings is generally admitted, the confidentiality of information and documents surrounding hearings can be subject to controversy. Second, we will analyse whether there is a correlation between privacy of hearings and confidentiality of arbitration. We will see that such a correlation exists: privacy of hearings serves the goal of maintaining confidentiality of arbitration.

4.5.2   Arbitration Law and Practice on Confidentiality of Hearings

4.5.2.1   Privacy of Hearings

592   Privacy of arbitration hearings is not disputed. Most prominent writers agree that arbitration hearings are to be held in private.[126] State courts in several jurisdictions have also held that hearings are to be held in private. For example, the Swiss Supreme Court established that, unlike in state court proceedings, where the right to a public hearing is provided for by the ECHR and by the Federal Constitution,[127] the right to a public hearing is not guaranteed before arbitral tribunals.[128] The English High Court was even more explicit, stating in *Hassneh Insurance v. Mew* that privacy of hearings has been universal for hundreds of years and is thus undisputed:

---

[125]Born (2014), p. 2234.

[126]Born (2014), p. 2812; Poudret and Besson (2007), para 371; Blackaby et al. (2015), para 2.164.

[127]Art. 6(1) of the ECHR and Art. 30(3) of the Swiss Federal Constitution.

[128]TF 4A_612/2009, 10.02.2010, recital 4.1; Berger and Kellerhals (2015), para 1230.

If the parties to an English law contract refer their disputes to arbitration they are entitled to assume at the least that the hearing will be conducted in private. That assumption arises from a practice which has been universal in London for hundreds of years and [is], I believe, undisputed. It is a practice which represents an important advantage of arbitration over the Courts as a means of dispute resolution. The informality attaching to a hearing held in private and the candour to which it may give rise is an essential ingredient of arbitration.[129]

In its *Esso/BHP v. Plowman* decision (see the discussion of this case in Sect. 3.2.3.4), while rejecting the existence of an implied duty of confidentiality, the High Court of Australia held that the hearings were private in the sense that they were not open to the public.[130] It found that this privacy had its origins *'in the subject-matter of the agreement to submit disputes to arbitration'*, rather than attributing private character of the hearing to an implied term.[131] **593**

Many institutional arbitration rules have a specific provision regarding the privacy of hearings.[132] Most arbitration rules state that hearings would be held *'in private'*,[133] while some use the term *'in camera'*[134] (which has the same meaning). The ICC Rules have more explicit language, stating that *'persons not involved in the proceedings shall not be admitted'* to the hearings.[135] **594**

However, hearings can be attended by third parties or even by the public in some cases. Most arbitration rules allow an exception to the privacy of hearings rule if there is consent from the parties.[136] Some arbitration rules provide that this consent should be given in writing.[137] The ICC and the CEPANI Rules require approval from both parties and the arbitral tribunal for the hearing not to be held privately,[138] while the LCIA Rules require, alternatively, either agreement of the parties or directions of the arbitral tribunal.[139] **595**

---

[129]Hassneh Insurance Co v Mew [1993] 2 Lloyd's Rep 243.

[130]Esso Australia Resources Ltd. and Others v. Sidney James Plowman and Others, Arbitration International, Volume 11 No. 3, 1995, 241.

[131]Esso Australia Resources Ltd. and Others v. Sidney James Plowman and Others, Arbitration International, Volume 11 No. 3, 1995, 241.

[132]*See, e.g.*, ICC Rules (art 26.3), ACICA Rules (Art. 22.1), Swiss Rules (Art. 25.6), SCC Rules (Art. 32.3), LCIA Rules (Art. 19.4), WIPO Rules (Art. 55(c)), ICAC Rules (Art. 30.1), SIAC Rules (Art. 24.4), CEPANI Rules (Art. 23.6).

[133]SCC Rules (Art. 32.3), LCIA Rules (Art. 19.4), WIPO Rules (Art. 55(c)), ACICA Rules (Art. 22.1), SIAC Rules (Art. 24.4).

[134]Swiss Rules (Art. 25.6), ICAC Rules (Art. 30.1).

[135]ICC Rules (Art. 26.3).

[136]Swiss Rules (Art. 25.6), SCC Rules (Art. 32.3), WIPO Rules (Art. 55(c)), ACICA Rules (Art. 22.1), SIAC Rules (Art. 24.4), LCIA Rules (Art. 19.4).

[137]ACICA Rules (Art. 22.1), LCIA Rules (Art. 19.4).

[138]ICC Rules (Art. 26.3), CEPANI Rules (Art. 23.6).

[139]LCIA Rules (Art. 19.4).

4.5.2.2 Confidentiality of Documents and Information Surrounding Hearings

596   While privacy of hearings is a settled issue, confidentiality of the documents and information surrounding hearings can be subject to controversy. Some national arbitration laws expressly regulate this issue. Thus, the NZAA defines confidentiality so as to cover

> '*any notes made by the arbitral tribunal of oral evidence or submissions given before the arbitral tribunal*' and '*any transcript of oral evidence or submissions given before the arbitral tribunal*'.[140]

597   We think that not only privacy of hearings should be maintained, but also confidentiality of information and documents surrounding the hearings. In our opinion, this is necessary to maintain the confidentiality of the arbitration. Hearing documents and information should in principle be protected by confidentiality, as they are closely related to hearings and cannot be disclosed without opening the door to what was discussed at the hearing.

4.5.3 Correlation Between Privacy of Hearings and Confidentiality of Arbitration

598   Today, many authors emphasise that a distinction needs to be made between privacy of arbitration hearings and confidentiality of arbitration. We agree that privacy of hearings does not automatically imply that arbitration proceedings are confidential. On the other hand, it appears wrong to deny any correlation between confidentiality of arbitration and privacy of hearings.

599   This correlation has a long history in arbitration law. Arbitration proceedings have long been considered confidential, with no one seriously questioning the sources of this confidentiality, but the confidential nature of arbitration was sometimes attributed to the fact that arbitration hearings were held privately. Thus, in the previously cited *Hassneh Insurance v. Mew*, the English High Court held that the confidentiality duty over certain documents related to the arbitration proceedings was a natural extension of privacy of the hearing:

> If it be correct that there is at least an implied term in every agreement to arbitrate that the hearing shall be held in private, the requirement of privacy must in principle extend to documents which are created for the purpose of that hearing. The most obvious example is a note or transcript of the evidence. The disclosure to a third party of such documents would be almost equivalent to opening the door of the arbitration room to that third party. Similarly witness statements, being closely related to the hearing must be within the obligation of

---

[140]Art. 2(1) NZAA. Art. 15(1) AIAA contains a similar provision.

confidentiality. So also must outline submissions tendered to the arbitrator. If outline submissions, then so must pleadings be included.[141]

The High Court of Australia took an opposite view in *Esso/BHP v. Plowman*, **600** however, denying the overall confidentiality of the arbitration proceedings although admitting the private character of the hearing.[142] This ruling provoked much valuable questioning of the legal basis of confidentiality, and promoted recognition that privacy of hearings does not imply confidentiality of the whole arbitration process.

If not confidentiality, the question is what would be the reason for holding **601** hearings in private? One might argue that it is easier to organise a hearing if the number of participants is known in advance. Other than this argument of minor importance, we cannot find any other reasons to hold hearings privately. Confidentiality appears to be the main reason for private hearings. Indeed, arbitration hearings have been held privately for hundreds of years because the parties seek for discretion and do not want the details of their dispute to be known to outsiders. Thus, privacy of hearings is not just a rule of practical convenience: its main rationale is keeping confidentiality of the dispute.

4.6   Intermediary Conclusions

The content of the duty of confidentiality is very broad. It includes virtually any **602** information and documents relating to arbitration proceedings, arbitral awards, and hearings, including the existence of the arbitration itself. There are obviously exceptions to this general duty of confidentiality, that we will examine in Sect. 4.5.

First, any information regarding arbitration proceedings, including the mere **603** existence of an arbitration, can be subject to confidentiality. Whether a particular type of information is regarded as confidential will depend on various circumstances of the case, such as the reasons and consequences of the disclosure, rather than on which piece of information was disclosed. Indeed, if there was a legitimate reason for making disclosure, no breach of confidentiality can be admitted. On the contrary, a breach of the duty of confidentiality should be admitted if there was no legitimate reason for revealing the confidential information or document, and especially if the disclosure was made in bad faith with the purpose of damaging the other party's interest.

Second, any documents exchanged in the course of arbitration proceedings **604** should be subject to confidentiality. We agree with the extensive approach to confidentiality adopted by Art. 3.13 of the IBA Rules on Evidence, which stipulates that

---

[141]Hassneh Insurance Co v Mew [1993] 2 Lloyd's Rep 243.

[142]Esso Australia Resources Ltd. and Others v. Sidney James Plowman and Others, Arbitration International, Volume 11 No. 3, 1995.

'[a]*ny documents submitted or produced by a Party or non-Party in the arbitration ... shall be kept confidential ... and shall be used only in connection with the
arbitration'.*

We think that this solution encourages candour on the part of the persons
participating in arbitration proceedings and reinforces the principle of confidentiality
of arbitration. This confidentiality duty should, however, be limited to the documents
to which a person wishing to disclose them had access only because of the
arbitration.

605   *Third*, with regard to confidentiality of arbitral awards, most arbitration rules and
national arbitration laws regulating this issue impose a duty of confidentiality.
Confidentiality is, however, not an obstacle to a disclosure justified by a legitimate
use of arbitral awards outside of the arbitration proceedings. Confidentiality of
arbitral awards is also no obstacle to publication of arbitral awards if the parties
give their consent, or even without the parties' consent, if the awards are published in
such a form that the parties cannot be identified.

606   Today current publication practices are quite diverse, but there is no systematic
publication of arbitral awards. Systematic publication of arbitral awards can, however, result in many advantages, such as creating consistent arbitral case law,
enhancing transparency of the arbitration, improving the quality of arbitral awards,
promoting the arbitration as a dispute resolution method, making arbitrations more
accessible for the users, enabling users to make a more informed decision when
choosing an arbitration institution and appointing an arbitrator and facilitating
voluntary execution and enforcement of arbitral awards. For these reasons, we
think that a systematic publication of arbitral awards should be aimed in the future.

607   *Finally*, although privacy of hearings does not automatically imply that arbitration proceedings are confidential, there is a correlation between the two. The main
rationale for holding hearings privately is to prevent third parties from learning the
details of an arbitration dispute. Privacy of hearings thus primarily serves the goal of
maintaining confidentiality of arbitration. Since privacy of hearings is generally
admitted and is not subject to any controversy, it could be recognised, in our view,
as an autonomous *lex mercatoria* principle. In addition to privacy of hearings, all
information and documents surrounding hearings, such as transcripts of hearings,
opening and closing submissions, should also be subject to confidentiality.

Chapter 5
Exceptions and Limitations to the Obligation of Confidentiality

5.1 Introduction

According to the Cambridge Essential British Dictionary, 'exception' means 'something that is not included in a rule'.[1] If we assume that confidentiality is the rule, exceptions would be the cases derogating from the rule of confidentiality. There is, however, a controversy over whether the parties' obligation of confidentiality really exists in the absence of express contractual and other applicable provisions on confidentiality. If confidentiality is not the rule, the term 'exception' should arguably not be used.[2] We will still use the term 'exception' as we will assume for the purpose of our research that confidentiality is the rule in international commercial arbitration.　**608**

When analysing the problem of confidentiality, we conclude that there is no breach of confidentiality obligation as long as the conditions of one of the exceptions that we will describe below are met. However, one can also argue that (1) there is a confidentiality breach whenever confidential information or documents are disclosed, (2) but that such a breach can be justified by specific circumstances. These specific circumstances will be the cases of exceptions that we will set out below. Therefore, the result is the same under the two ways of reasoning, but the way to achieve this result is different. We think that the first way of reasoning is more logical and easier to understand, that is why we have adopted this approach.　**609**

As we will see, exceptions to the duty of confidentiality can be admitted in many cases. For example, Art. 23D AIAA contains a very detailed list of exceptions to the parties' and arbitral tribunal's obligation of confidentiality. According to this provision, confidential information in relation to arbitral proceedings may be disclosed in the following circumstances:　**610**

---

[1] http://dictionary.cambridge.org/ (last visited on 13 September 2018).
[2] Smeureanu (2011), p. 110.

© Springer Nature Switzerland AG 2019
E. Reymond-Eniaeva, *Towards a Uniform Approach to Confidentiality of International Commercial Arbitration*, European Yearbook of International Economic Law 7, https://doi.org/10.1007/978-3-030-19003-3_5

(i)   All the parties consent to disclosure;
(ii) The information is disclosed to a professional or other advisor;
(iii) The disclosure is necessary to ensure that a party to the arbitral proceedings has full opportunity to present its case;
(iv) The disclosure is necessary to establish or protect the legal rights of a party to the arbitral proceedings in relation to a third party;
(v)   The disclosure is necessary for enforcement of the award;
(vi) The disclosure is in accordance with an order made or a subpoena issued by a court;
(vii) The disclosure is authorized or required by another relevant law,[3] or required by a competent regulatory body, and the person making the disclosure gives written details[4] of the disclosure:

- to the other parties to the proceedings and the arbitral tribunal - if the person is a party to the arbitral proceedings;
- to all the parties to the proceedings - if the arbitral tribunal is making the disclosure.[5]

611   Even such a detailed list is, however, not exhaustive. Indeed, one cannot specify every possible situation when the use and disclosure of arbitration materials may potentially be necessary. There can be other circumstances when an arbitral tribunal and a court may make an order allowing disclosure of confidential information in relation to the arbitration proceedings (see Arts 23E, 23F and 23G AIAA).

612   These articles provide for the following distribution of competence between the arbitral tribunal and a state court. First, it is the arbitral tribunal which has the power to make an order allowing disclosure of confidential information, upon request of one of the parties (Art. 23E AIAA). Second, if the arbitral tribunal has granted such an order to one of the parties, the other party may request a court to make an order prohibiting disclosure of confidential information (Art. 23F AIAA). Finally, if the arbitral tribunal rejects the party's disclosure application or after termination of arbitral proceedings, a court has the power to make an order allowing disclosure of confidential information (Art. 23G AIAA).

613   While the AIAA provides no guidance as to how the arbitral tribunal should make its assessment when deciding whether a certain category of information should be disclosed (Art. 23E AIAA), it does provide such guidance to a court. When deciding on whether to allow or to prohibit the disclosure, a court will have to put on its balance, on the one side,

---

[3] Relevant law means: (a) a law of the Commonwealth, other than this Act; and (b) a law of a State or Territory and (c) a law of a foreign country, or of a part of a foreign country:

in which a party to the arbitration agreement has its principal place of business; or
in which a substantial part of the obligations of the commercial relationship are to be performed; or
to which the subject matter of the dispute is most commonly connected.

[4] The written details must include an explanation of the reasons for the disclosure.
[5] Art. 23D AIAA.

'*the public interest in preserving the confidentiality of arbitral proceedings*' and, on the other side, '*the public interest for the information to be disclosed*'

(Arts 23F and 23G AIAA).

Thus, the AIAA contains a detailed list of exceptions to the parties' and arbitral **614** tribunal's obligation of confidentiality, but also grants to the arbitral tribunal a large power of discretion to allow disclosure in the cases not mentioned in Art. 23E AIAA. If a party is not satisfied with the decision of the arbitral tribunal, it has an opportunity to appeal to a state court, which will render a final decision (Arts 23F and 23G AIAA).

Due to the multitude of exceptions to the duty of confidentiality, formulation of a **615** statutory provision on confidentiality is no easy task. When the possibility of introducing such a provision was discussed in England, no one disputed the desirability of establishing confidentiality as a general principle in the English Arbitration Act of 1996, but then concerns arose.[6] Predictably, the main ones involved 'the myriad exceptions to these principles [of confidentiality]', and in the end a provision on confidentiality was not included in the Act.[7]

If exceptions to the duty of confidentiality could be defined and classified, rule **616** making on confidentiality would be much easier. The English Court of Appeal tackled this challenge in the *Ali Shipping* case. In its decision, the Court of Appeal acknowledged the existence of a duty of confidentiality as well as exceptions to the 'broad rule of confidentiality', which it set out as follows:

1. Consent i.e. where disclosure is made with the express or implied consent of the party who originally produced the material;
2. order of the Court, an obvious example of which is an order for disclosure of documents generated by an arbitration for the purpose of a later court action;
3. leave of the court... which will be given in respect of...
4. disclosure when, and to the extent to which, it is reasonably necessary for the protection of the legitimate interests of an arbitrating party...
5. where the 'public interest' requires disclosure.[8]

While revising the Milan Arbitration Rules, the working group of the Milan **617** Chamber of Arbitration also faced a difficulty in formulating exceptions to the confidentiality rule.[9] Although the members of the working group agreed that the duty of confidentiality is not absolute, and that a number of exceptions should be provided for, they could not agree on an exhaustive list of such exceptions.[10] Finally, they reached an agreement on the following text, which provides: '*the parties [...] shall keep the proceedings and the arbitral award confidential, except in the case it*

---

[6]Report on the Arbitration Bill, paras. 11 to 16, in Merkin and Flannery (2014), pp. 433–444.

[7]Merkin and Flannery (2014), pp. 433–444.

[8]Ali Shipping v. Shipyard Trogir [1997] EWCA Civ 3054.

[9]Coppo (2013), p. 142.

[10]Coppo (2013), p. 142.

has to be used to protect one's rights.[11] This would include, for example, the cases when a party has to enforce the award or appeal against it.[12] Thus, instead of listing the specific cases of exceptions to the general rule of confidentiality, the Chamber of Milan chose to agree on a general provision opening the way to a number of exceptions.[13]

618   While exceptions to the duty of confidentiality can be classified in many ways, for purposes of this study we decided to use three main categories based on the persons bound by the confidentiality duty:

1. any persons having access to the information and documents from arbitration (Sect. 5.2. below);
2. only parties (Sect. 5.3. below);
3. only arbitrators (Sect. 5.4. below).

619   The first category mentioned above concerns cases when disclosure is required by the law, allowed by the parties, necessary to seek professional advice, or because the documents are already in the public domain. For the second and third categories, we will examine the most interesting developments in case law, as well as relevant provisions of some national arbitration laws and some arbitration rules.

5.2   General Cases of Exceptions to the Confidentiality

5.2.1   Disclosure Required or Authorised by Law or Regulation

620   The disclosure of confidential materials from an arbitration proceeding may be required or authorised by the applicable law. If this is the case and the person does not disclose more than what is required by law, he does not violate the confidentiality obligations of the arbitration. Some national arbitration laws and arbitration rules contain an express provision to this effect.[14] The specific cases when such disclosures can be authorised or allowed will depend on the applicable law and regulation. For example, listed companies typically have an obligation to disclose the existence of pending disputes, which would obviously include arbitration proceedings.[15]

---

[11]Art. 8(1) of the Milan Rules.

[12]Coppo (2013), p. 142.

[13]Coppo (2013), p. 142.

[14]See, for example, Art. 23D(2) AIAA; Rule 26(1)(a) of the Schedule 1 of the Scottish Arbitration Act of 2010; Art. 76(a) of the WIPO Rules; Art. 22.2 of the ACICA Rules; Art. 39.2 of the SIAC Rules; Art. 44(1) of the Swiss Rules.

[15]See, for example, Denoix De Sain Marc (2009), pp. 213–314, for more details.

5.2.2   *Disclosure Is Allowed by the Parties' Consent*

If the parties give their consent to the disclosure of the information or documents   **621**
relating to the arbitration proceedings, such information or documents can in principle be communicated outside of the arbitration proceeding. The disclosing party
should, however, respect the terms of the consent—and disclose only the information with respect to which the consent was given.

Several national arbitration laws and arbitration rules contain express rules   **622**
providing that the consent of all parties is a sufficient basis for disclosure of the
information relating to the arbitration proceedings[16] or for publication of the arbitral
award.[17] Some arbitration rules require that the consent be given in writing.[18] Thus,
if one of the parties needs to disclose the information or documents generated by or
exchanged in the course of an arbitration, a consent of the other party or parties will
be necessary. If someone else, e.g., an arbitrator or an arbitration institution, intends
to disclose this information or these documents, the consent of all parties is required.

Under English law, it is admitted that consent does not always have to be express;   **623**
it can also be implied as a matter of conduct.[19] An implied consent can be assumed,
for example, if one of the parties discloses information relating to the arbitration
proceedings in violation of its confidentiality obligations while the other party does
not raise any objection further to this disclosure.[20]

5.2.3   *Disclosure Is Necessary to Seek Professional Advice*

Undoubtedly, disclosure of confidential information should be allowed when it is   **624**
necessary to seek legal, accounting or other professional services.[21] The producing
party should, however, take all reasonable measures to ensure that the recipient
preserves the confidentiality of the disclosed information and documents.[22]

---

[16]See, for example, Art. 23D(2) AIAA; Rule 26(1)(a) of the Schedule 1 of the Scottish Arbitration
Act of 2010; Art. 76(a) of the WIPO Rules; Art. 22.2 of the ACICA Rules; Art. 39.2 of the SIAC
Rules; Art. 44(1) of the Swiss Rules.

[17]See, for example, Art. 30.3 of the LCIA Rules; Art. 77(i) of the WIPO Rules; Art. 30.3 of the
ICDR Rules; Art. 34.5 of the UNCITRAL Rules.

[18]See, for example, Art. 22.2 of the ACICA Rules; Art. 44(1) of the Swiss Rules; Art. 30.3 of the
LCIA Rules.

[19]Ali Shipping v. Shipyard Trogir [1997] EWCA Civ 3054; Department of Economic Policy and
Development of the City of Moscow v. Bankers Trust Co., [2003] EWHC 1377 (Comm); Lew
(2013), p. 447; Smeureanu (2011), pp. 113–114.

[20]Smeureanu (2011), p. 113.

[21]De Ly et al. (2012), p. 380.

[22]De Ly et al. (2012), p. 380.

5.2.4 Documents Are Already in the Public Domain

625   Although this may seem obvious, information and documents already in the public domain are not subject to confidentiality obligations. Some national arbitration laws and arbitration rules specifically provide this.[23] In fact, this is not an exception properly speaking, but rather an additional qualification to the definition of confidentiality.

626   By 'being in the public domain', it is generally meant that the information or documents are publicly accessible.[24] For example, the information published in a company's annual report or in other publicly accessible reports is considered to be in the public domain and thus non-confidential.[25] Sometimes, however, it is arguable whether a certain piece of information or a document is already in the public domain. In such a case, the burden of proof should in principle be on the party that claims that the information is already in the public domain.[26]

5.3 Exceptions to the Parties' Obligation of Confidentiality

5.3.1 Introduction

627   In addition to the cases described above, when disclosure of arbitration materials is generally allowed, there are other exceptions applicable only to the parties. These are mainly in cases when a party needs to disclose an arbitral award and/or other documents from arbitration in order to pursue its legitimate rights. This can happen, for example, when a party has to recognise, enforce or challenge an arbitral award before state judicial authorities. This can also happen when a party needs to disclose documents in parallel court or arbitration proceedings to support its case, or further to a court or arbitral tribunal's order. Such disclosures are, in principle, not considered as a violation of the parties' confidentiality obligations.[27]

628   Some national arbitration laws and arbitration rules specifically provide for such exceptions to the parties' duty of confidentiality.[28] For example, Art. 35(2) of the SIAC Rules provides that the parties will not disclose any materials relating to the proceedings and the award to a third party except '*for the purpose of making an application to any competent court of any State to enforce or challenge the award*'

---

[23]See, for example, Rule 26 of the Schedule 1 of the Scottish Arbitration Act of 2010; Art. 44(1) of the Swiss Rules; Art. 30(1) of the LCIA Rules; Art. 39.3 of the SIAC Rules.

[24]See, for example, Rohner and La Spada (2013), para 12.

[25]Smeureanu (2011), p. 111.

[26]Smeureanu (2011), p. 112.

[27]Born (2014), p. 2800.

[28]See, for example, Arts 23D(9) AIAA; Art. 14C(d) NZAA; Art. 44(1) of the Swiss Rules; Art. 30 (1) of the LCIA Rules; Art. 22(2)(d) of the ACICA Rules; Art. 33(1) of the Abu Dhabi Rules.

and *'for the purpose of pursing or enforcing a legal right or claim'*. Most national arbitration laws and arbitration rules, which contain a rule on the exceptions to the duty of confidentiality, have provisions with a similar language.[29]

In the present section, we will mainly examine the case law discussing disclosure **629** of arbitration materials outside of the arbitration proceeding. While these court decisions will demonstrate the specific cases when disclosures were or were not considered legitimate, we will see that each case should nevertheless be decided individually depending on the applicable law and the specific circumstances of the facts.

5.3.2 Recognition, Enforcement or Challenge of the Arbitral Award

5.3.2.1 In General

When a losing party does not voluntarily execute an arbitral award, the winning **630** party will have to disclose the arbitral award—and possibly other arbitration materials—in order to enforce it. As mentioned before, such disclosure is not considered as a violation of the party's duty of confidentiality. The same is true of disclosures made in the framework of a court action that a party can bring for the purpose of recognising or challenging an arbitral award.

As stated above, some national arbitration laws and arbitration rules specifically **631** allow exceptions to the parties' duty of confidentiality when the parties have to disclose documents from arbitration in order to enforce, recognise or challenge an arbitral award.[30] For example, Art. 22(2)(b) of the ACICA Rules provides, in particular, that the parties shall treat as confidential—and shall not disclose to a third party—all matters relating to the arbitration, the award, materials created for the purpose of the arbitration, and documents produced by another party in the proceedings except *'for the purpose of making an application to the court of any State to enforce the award'*.

National courts have consistently held that a party does not violate its duty of **632** confidentiality in disclosing arbitration materials in court proceedings tending to enforce or challenge an arbitral award.[31] For example, in the *Emmott case*, the

---

[29]See, for example, Arts 23D(5)-23D(6) AIAA; Art. 14C(b) NZAA; Section 18(2)(a) of the Hong Kong Arbitration Ordinance; Rule 26(1)(d) of the Schedule 1 of the Scottish Arbitration Act of 2010; Art. 44(1) of the Swiss Rules; Art. 30(1) of the LCIA Rules; Art. 22(2) of the ACICA Rules; Art. 39.2 of the SIAC Rules.

[30]See, for example, Arts 23D(5)-23D(6) AIAA; Art. 14C(b) NZAA; Section 18(2)(a) of the Hong Kong Arbitration Ordinance; Rule 26(1)(d) of the Schedule 1 of the Scottish Arbitration Act of 2010; Art. 44(1) of the Swiss Rules; Art. 30(1) of the LCIA Rules; Art. 22(2) of the ACICA Rules; Art. 39.2 of the SIAC Rules.

[31]Born (2014), p. 2800.

English Court of Appeal held that there were limits to the obligation of confidentiality, such as in cases when an award has to be enforced or challenged before a state court.[32]

5.3.2.2 No Frivolous Claims

633   Thus, there is no doubt that a party is allowed to disclose the award and, if necessary, other arbitration materials to the competent authority in order to recognise, enforce or challenge the arbitral award. Importantly, however, this exceptions to the parties' obligation of confidentiality do not cover the abuse of process. Abuse of process is defined in the Black's Law Dictionary as '[*t*]*he improper and tortious use of a legitimately issued court process to obtain a result that is either unlawful or beyond the process's scope*'. There may, for example, be cases when a party acts in bad faith, seeking not to pursue its legitimate rights, but rather to cause damage to the other party by disclosing confidential information.

634   Therefore, if an action to challenge an award is frivolous and does not pursue a legitimate goal, it can be considered as a breach of the confidentiality obligation. A party having made a frivolous claim can even be enjoined to pay damages caused to the other party as a result of the confidentiality breach.

635   Thus, in its decision of 18 February 1986, *G. Aïta v. A. Ojjeh*, the Paris Court of Appeal had to rule on the challenge of an arbitral award.[33] The award was rendered in England, and there was no request for an *exequatur* in France. As a basis for jurisdiction of the French Courts, the claimant invoked a provision in its arbitration agreement with the defendant stating that '*this agreement will be governed by the English law and the procedures in relation to its validity and execution can only be initiated in England, France and Switzerland*'. The claimant argued that, by this clause, the parties intended to extend jurisdiction for setting aside the arbitral award to English, French and Swiss Courts. On this basis, the claimant claimed jurisdiction of the French Courts and asked the French Court of Appeal to annul the arbitral award.

636   The defendant asked that the claimant's request for annulment of the arbitral award be considered inadmissible as filed before incompetent authorities. The defendant also filed a counterclaim in which he asked that the Court enjoin the claimant to pay FF 200,000 of damages for having initiated abusive proceedings. The Paris Court of Appeal followed the defendant's argument, disagreeing with the claimant's interpretation of the arbitration clause. The Court concluded that by filing his appeal with a manifestly incompetent authority, the claimant allowed a public debate of the facts that should have remained confidential. As a result of this

---

[32]Emmott v. Wilson & Partners Limited [2008] EWCA Civ 184.

[33]G. Aïta v. A. Ojjeh, Cour d'appel de Paris (1ère Chambre suppl.), 18 February 1986, in: Rev. Arb. 1986, 583. Also see Sects. 3.2.3.7 and 6.2.2.1 discussing this case.

wrongful behaviour, the Court enjoined the claimant to pay FF 200,000 of damages as well as the costs of the court proceedings.

5.3.2.3 Permissible Leaks of Information Because of Openness of Court Proceedings

5.3.2.3.1 Introduction

As we have seen, court proceedings tending to recognise, enforce or challenge an   **637** arbitral award can result in undesirable leaks of information. Given the generally admitted principle requiring court proceedings to be open to the public, there is always a risk that documents from confidential arbitration proceedings will become public. Indeed, if a party challenges the arbitral award before a state court, these proceedings will result in a court decision which will in most cases be publicly available. Unless such proceedings are filed, like in the *G. Aïta v. A. Ojjeh* case,[34] in bad faith, the parties do not violate their obligation of confidentiality by disclosing documents related to an arbitration before a state court.

Also, as we will see below,[35] in addition to the court proceedings tending to   **638** recognise, enforce and challenge an arbitral award, there can be various related court proceedings in which the information and documents from an arbitration can become part of the record. Given the principle of openness of court proceedings, disclosure of the arbitration materials in court proceedings can thus affect the principle of confidentiality of arbitral proceedings. Below, we will review what the principle of openness of the court proceedings generally implies with regard to arbitrations.

The principle of openness of court proceedings is firmly established in interna-   **639** tional and domestic law. It is an important element of the right to a fair trial, which is one of the fundamental human rights according to Art. 6(1) ECHR and Art. 14(1) of the International Covenant on Civil and Political Rights. The principle of openness of court proceedings aims to ensure the equal treatment of the parties, but also to allow citizens to control the independence, the impartiality and the proper adminis-tration of justice.[36] If we look into the law and practice of particular jurisdictions, we will see that most state court decisions are published and hearings are in principle held publicly.

In some jurisdictions, however, the parties may agree to exclude certain court   **640** actions from the principle of openness in order to preserve confidentiality of the arbitration proceedings (or for another reason).[37] In Switzerland, for example, parties wishing to avoid any publicity of their arbitration proceeding can agree to waive

---

[34] G. Aïta v. A. Ojjeh, Cour d'appel de Paris (1ère Chambre suppl.), 18 February 1986, in: Rev. Arb. 1986, 583; see above Sect. 3.2.3.7 for more details on this case.

[35] See Sect. 5.3.3.

[36] Würzburger (2014), para 4.

[37] Born (2014), p. 2801; see, for example, Art. 192 of the Swiss PILA.

their right to challenge the award (Art. 192(1) Swiss PILA). This rule applies only to arbitrations with a seat in Switzerland if none of the parties has its domicile, usual place of residence or place of business in Switzerland (Arts 176(1) and 192(1) Swiss PILA). The price to pay can, however, be too high as, once the parties have agreed on the waiver, a party wishing to challenge the award will not be able to do it as the award will be final once rendered by the arbitral tribunal.

641   We will further examine how the principle of openness of court proceedings is applied regarding 'arbitration claims' in Switzerland, England and the United States.

5.3.2.3.2   Swiss Law and Practice

642   The Supreme Court (*le Tribunal fédéral*) is the sole judicial authority which has competence to set aside the international arbitral awards rendered by arbitral tribunals with a seat in Switzerland (Art. 191 Swiss PILA). According to Art. 30(3) of the Swiss Federal Constitution, court hearings are public, and judgment should be rendered in public; exceptions to this rule can be provided by the law. In practice, however, appeal proceedings before the Swiss Supreme Court are conducted in principle only in writing. Documents submitted to the court, such as the arbitral award and written submissions, do not become part of the public record,[38] although they can be cited in court decisions.

643   Article 27 LTF provides that the Supreme Court must inform the public on its case law. According to the same provision, Supreme Court decisions are to be published in principle in anonymous form. Articles 57 to 64 of the Regulation on the Supreme Court[39] set out further details on the information that the Swiss Supreme Court must communicate to the public.

644   The Swiss Supreme Court decisions of principle (*arrêts de principe*), are published in the *Recueil officiel des arrêts du Tribunal fédéral* (ATF).[40] The decisions of principle resolve previously unresolved issues that are important for the application of the Swiss federal law (as opposed to the cantonal law). The decisions of principle also resolve issues that have to be re-examined because a clarification or a change of the case law becomes necessary.[41] By making the publication in the *Recueil officiel*, the Supreme Court shows that the relevant decisions have the value of a precedent.[42]

645   The Supreme Court decisions of principle can be found online on its website in the database 'ATF dès 1954 (Arrêts principaux)'.[43] As from 2007, all decisions of

---

[38]Habegger and Bühler (2009), p. 283.

[39]Règlement sur le Tribunal fédéral du 20 novembre 2006.

[40]Art. 58 of the Regulation on the Federal Supreme Court.

[41]Würzburger (2014), para 8.

[42]Würzburger (2014), para 8.

[43]http://www.bger.ch/fr/index/juridiction/jurisdiction-inherit-template/jurisdiction-recht.htm   (last visited on 13 September 2018).

the Supreme Federal Court rendered in 2000 and later are available in the database 'autres arrêts dès 2000'.[44] The decisions published in the *Recueil officiel* and those which are available online do not in principle mention the names of the parties or any other information that would allow the parties to be identified.[45]

According to Art. 59(1) LTF, the parties' arguments, if there are any, as well as the court deliberations and voting, should take place publicly. If the Supreme Court does not render its decision publicly, it has to make the conclusion of this decision available for a review by any person at the seat of the Supreme Court for a period of 30 working days (art. 59(3) LTF). Since the Supreme Court does not in principle render its decisions publicly, the title page (*le rubrum*) and the operative part (*le dispositif*) of all decisions of the Supreme Court are as a rule made available for the public consultation for a period of 30 working days after the judgment's notification. The names of the parties are not deleted, unless this is required by the law (Art. 60 of the Regulation on the Supreme Court). Only in very limited instances does the law allow deletion of the parties' names during the public consultation period of 30 days.[46] This is the case, for example, when the Act on assistance to the victims[47] applies.[48]

646

Therefore, when a party seeks to set aside an international arbitral award rendered by an arbitral tribunal with a seat in Switzerland, the Swiss Supreme Court will make available its decision upon request of any person. This consultation period will last 30 working days after notification of the decision to the parties. The decision is not available in full: only the title page indicating the names of the parties and the subject matter of the dispute, as well as the conclusion will be made available. The full version of the decision, with the names of the parties deleted, is later published online. Can the Supreme Court make exceptions to these rules taking into account the confidential nature of arbitration? The Swiss Supreme Court had to deal with this issue in its 19 June 2006 decision,[49] which we will review below.

647

The dispute was between two glass companies that concluded a licence agreement with an ICC arbitration clause.[50] The licensor initiated an ICC arbitration, claiming that the licensee developed products, which violated the terms of the licence agreement. In its second partial award, the Arbitral Tribunal issued a prohibition order against certain of the licensee's activities. The licensee challenged this arbitral award before the Swiss Supreme Court and made an application that the judgment on its motion to set aside the award should not be published. If the Court decision were to be published, the licensee—the appellant in this proceeding—asked

648

---

[44]Publication policy of the Federal Supreme Court case law, available at https://www.bger.ch/files/live/sites/bger/files/pdf/fr/urteilsveroeffentlichung_d.pdf (last visited on 13 September 2018).

[45]Würzburger (2014), para 7.

[46]Würzburger (2014), para 18.

[47]Loi fédérale sur l'aide aux victimes du 23 mars 2007.

[48]Würzburger (2014), para 18.

[49]TF 4P.74/2006, 19.06.2006.

[50]TF 4P.74/2006, 19.06.2006.

that the names of the parties and other information which could allow identification of the parties be deleted. The defendant and the Arbitral Tribunal supported the appellant's application for non-publication of the Supreme Court decision.[51]

649   The Supreme Court recalled that Art. 6(1) ECHR and Art. 30(3) of the Swiss Federal Constitution impose an obligation on the state courts to render their judgments publicly, but that neither of the legal texts specifies the manner in which this should be done.[52] As to the practice of the Swiss Supreme Court, it goes beyond the minimum required by the ECHR and the Constitution, because it publishes not only the conclusion of the decision, but also the reasoning section of judgments.[53]

650   The Swiss Supreme Court did not question the principle of confidentiality, admitting that the parties to arbitration have expectations of discretion.[54] The Supreme Court recalled that the principle of publicity of the Court decisions is the rule and that exceptions to this rule can be admitted only exceptionally, e.g., when justified by the parties' prevailing interest. Such an interest can be admitted, for example, if publication of a court decision, even in a sanitized form, allows identification of a person and puts safety of this person at risk.[55] In the given case, the Court considered that the parties failed to demonstrate a prevailing interest which would justify keeping this decision confidential.

651   Therefore, the Supreme Court did not allow any exceptions to the principle of publicity in this case, having rejected the application of non-publication of its decision. As in other cases, this Court decision was published after deletion of the names of the parties and other information that would allow the parties to be identified.[56] The Supreme Court also rejected the appellant's request to delete the names of the parties in the part of the judgment (title page and the conclusion) which were to be made available for consultation upon request for a period of 30 days after notification of the judgment.[57]

652   In addition to challenge proceedings before the Supreme Court, potential leaks of information can also take place because of enforcement proceedings before the courts of first instance. Indeed, in accordance with Art. 54(1) CPC, hearings are to be held publicly and judgments should be made accessible to the public. However, proceedings may be held in camera if required by public interest or by the legitimate interests of a person involved (art. 54(3) CPC). The principle of publicity is regulated by the CPC, i.e. a federal law,[58] but implementation of this principle and, in particular, the issue of how the decisions will be made accessible to the public is regulated by the cantons. Practices may vary from one canton to another.

---

[51] TF 4P.74/2006, 19.06.2006.

[52] TF 4P.74/2006, 19.06.2006, recital 8.4.1.

[53] TF 4P.74/2006, 19.06.2006, recital 8.4.1.

[54] TF 4P.74/2006, 19.06.2006, recital 8.4.1.

[55] TF 2C_677/2015, 31.03.2016, recital 4.3.

[56] TF 4P.74/2006, 19.06.2006, recital 8.5.

[57] TF 4P.74/2006, 19.06.2006, recital 8.4.2.

[58] Art. 122(1) of the Swiss Federal Constitution.

5.3.2.3.3 English Law and Practice

The principle of openness of court proceedings applies in England as well. As **653**
acknowledged by Justice Cooke in Department of Economic Policy and Development of the City of Moscow v. Banker Trust Co.,[59] '[t]he proper administration of
justice requires that not only is justice done but that it is seen to be done and that
therefore judgments should be open to public scrutiny'. Notwithstanding the principle of openness of court proceedings, there are major differences between Swiss
law and practice and the regulation provided by English law.

The English Civil Procedure Rules ('CPR') contain specific provisions on arbi- **654**
tration claims.[60] The CPR means by 'arbitration claims' the claims submitted before
the English courts which relate to arbitrations.[61] For example, proceedings tending
to enforce or challenge an arbitral award are considered as 'arbitration claims'.[62]
Provisions of the CPR preserve the confidentiality of arbitration with only a few
exceptions. Thus, arbitration claim forms, through which a party starts court proceedings, can be inspected by a non-party only with permission of the court.[63] In
other cases not relating to arbitration, the general rule is that a non-party may obtain a
copy of a statement of a case and a judgment or order made in public.[64] In addition,
arbitration claims will be heard in private unless there is a court order providing that
the hearings are to be held publicly.[65] There are also some exceptions when
arbitration claims will be heard in public.[66]

As to the conflict between confidentiality of arbitration and publication of **655**
judgments on arbitration claims, the English High Court set out the main principles
in the *Department of Economic Policy* case.[67] In this case, the court heard an
application challenging an award on the ground of serious irregularity—but did it
privately.[68] It was not until the moment when the court handed down the draft
judgment to the parties' lawyers for proofreading that a difference emerged between
the parties. The claimant stated that it wished the court decision to be made public,
while the other parties claimed that the judgment should stay unpublished.[69]

---

[59]Department of Economic Policy and Development of the City of Moscow v. Bankers Trust Co.,
[2003] EWHC 1377 (Comm).

[60]Part 62 of the CPR.

[61]Section 62.2 of the CPR.

[62]Section 62.2(1)(a) of the CPR and sections 66-68 of the English Arbitration Act 1996.

[63]Pendell and Richards (2009), p. 305, with further references.

[64]Pendell and Richards (2009), p. 305, with further references.

[65]Section 62.10 of the CPR.

[66]Section 62.10 of the CPR.

[67]Department of Economic Policy and Development of the City of Moscow v. Bankers Trust Co.,
[2003] EWHC 1377 (Comm).

[68]Department of Economic Policy and Development of the City of Moscow v. Bankers Trust Co.,
[2003] EWHC 1377 (Comm), paras 2, 4.

[69]Department of Economic Policy and Development of the City of Moscow v. Bankers Trust Co.,
[2003] EWHC 1377 (Comm), para 4.

656   The Court of Appeal acknowledged the principle of confidentiality of arbitrations. It also considered that there were many factors that militated against publication of the judgment, such as the parties' agreement to resolve their dispute through an arbitration; the parties' desire for privacy in arbitration; and the absence of any application for the hearing to be held publicly.[70] The Court held that its *judgment on the challenge of the award* should remain private and should not be available for publication.[71]

657   As to the *judgment on the application for publication*, the Court considered that this judgment should be published, as it raised matters of law and matters of wide interest. Moreover, it did not contain any confidential information. The existence of the dispute, the existence of the award and the existence of the earlier judgment on the challenge of the award had already been disclosed publicly.[72]

5.3.2.3.4   Law and Practice of the United States

658   In the United States, there is a presumption that judicial records are open to the public.[73] The public's right to access court records is based on both common law and the Constitution.[74] This right is, however, not absolute.[75] It is in the discretion of the court in charge of the post-award judicial proceedings to decide whether to permit access to a particular record, in light of the relevant facts and circumstances of the particular case.[76] In the proceedings related to recognition and enforcement of arbitral awards, court records open to the public comprise pleadings filed in these proceedings and exhibits thereto, including the award itself.

659   The practice of U.S. federal district courts is rather diverse, but, in most cases, the courts have been reluctant to protect confidentiality of the arbitration materials filed in the course of proceedings tending to recognise, enforce or challenge an arbitral award.[77] Two recent decisions, however, go against this trend.

660   *First*, the U.S. District Court for the Northern District of Texas issued an order protecting confidentiality of the post-award judicial materials in the case The Decapolis Group, LLC v Mangesh Energy, LLC et al.[78] In this case, the underlying

---

[70]Department of Economic Policy and Development of the City of Moscow v. Bankers Trust Co., [2003] EWHC 1377 (Comm), para 43.

[71]Department of Economic Policy and Development of the City of Moscow v. Bankers Trust Co., [2003] EWHC 1377 (Comm), para 55.

[72]Department of Economic Policy and Development of the City of Moscow v. Bankers Trust Co., [2003] EWHC 1377 (Comm), para 57.

[73]Nixon v. Warner Communications, Inc., 435 U.S. 589, 597 (1978).

[74]Tompkins (2017), p. 1, with further references.

[75]Nixon v. Warner Communications, Inc., 435 U.S. 589, 597 (1978).

[76]Nixon v. Warner Communications, Inc., 435 U.S. 589, 597-599 (1978).

[77]Tompkins (2017), p. 1, with further references; Drahozal, 32, with further references.

[78]The Decapolis Group, LLC v Mangesh Energy, LLC et al, 3:13-cv-1547-M (N.D. Texas 2014).

dispute related to payment of consulting fees by Mangesh Energy, Ltd ('Mangesh') to The Decapolis Group, LLC ('Decapolis') under a consulting agreement that the parties entered into in November 2006. This contract contained a confidentiality clause providing that the parties would not disclose confidential information, defined as '*information . . . relating to the business, products, affairs and finances of a Party and the Project for the time being confidential to that Party and trade secrets including, without limitation technical data and know-how relating to the business of the Party and the Project*'. The underlying contract also contained an arbitration clause with a choice of the ICC Rules.

The decision of the U.S. District Court for the Northern District of Texas **661** mentioned that the parties agreed that the arbitration proceedings would be confidential, but did not specify in which manner this confidentiality was agreed. On 25 April 2012, the Arbitral Tribunal rendered its final award finding that (1) the contract was valid and binding on the parties and (2) that in addition to attorney's fees and expenses, Decapolis would be entitled to the compensation described in the contract, including future payments for milestone events and a net profit interest. As Decapolis admitted, the defendants paid Decapolis' attorney's fees and costs for the first milestone before the proceedings for recognition of the arbitral award.

In April 2013, Decopolis filed a petition in the U.S. District Court for the **662** Northern District of Texas to recognize the arbitral award. Mangesh filed a motion to dismiss Decapolis' claim and a motion to seal Decapolis' petition, all exhibits thereto and all subsequent filings that may disclose the parties' confidential information. While the Court denied the motion to dismiss, it granted the motion to seal. The Court noted that the award contained extensive findings of facts, extending to sensitive information such as business strategies and developmental progress of Mangesh oil and gas exploration, and that the parties had expressly agreed on a confidentiality clause in their contract. The Court concluded that the public interest in the award was minimal and that it was counterbalanced by the parties' interest in confidentiality.

Second, in May 2016, Judge Valerie E. Caproni of the Southern District of **663** New York issued an order granting motion to seal arbitration materials.[79] In this case, both parties agreed that it was necessary to preserve confidentiality of their dispute and filed a joint motion to seal the Final Award. The judge agreed with the parties' arguments that the public right to access judicial documents is inapplicable when the documents relate to a private arbitration being subject to a strict confidentiality agreement.[80] Judge Caproni concluded that, in this particular case, the parties'

---

[79]Continental Insurance Company v Fairmont Premier Insurance Company, 16-cv-655 (S.D.N.Y. 2016).

[80]Continental Insurance Company v Fairmont Premier Insurance Company, 16-cv-655, 3 (S.D.N.Y. 2016).

interest in maintaining confidentiality of the Final Award were more important than any public interest in accessing the documents.[81]

5.3.2.3.5 Intermediary Conclusions

664   The principle of openness of court proceedings applies in all above-mentioned jurisdictions, subject to certain exceptions. In England, specific provisions on arbitration claims were introduced into the English Civil Procedure Rules to protect confidentiality of arbitration proceedings. In the United States, it has been admitted in several cases that the parties' interests in maintaining confidentiality of their arbitration proceedings were more important than any public interest in accessing the documents. At first sight, Swiss law appears to be less protective regarding arbitration claims as exceptions to publication of court decisions can be admitted only exceptionally, when justified by the parties' prevailing interest, and the parties' interest to maintain privacy of their arbitration proceedings does not seem to meet this condition.

665   There is, however, a fundamental difference in the way court decisions are published and regarding the materials made accessible to the public in the three jurisdictions. As a rule, in England and in the United States, the cases are identified by the names of the parties and non-parties may have access to written submissions and the award. By contrast, Swiss court decisions are generally published in a sanitized form, after the names of the parties and other information allowing to identify the parties have been deleted. Also, the arbitral award and written submissions do not become part of the public record. Since confidentiality of the parties can be preserved even if the court decision is published, the Swiss Supreme Court's restrictive practice regarding non-publication of its decisions appears rather reasonable.

5.3.3   Disclosure in Parallel or Related Arbitral and Court Proceedings

666   Today, it is common to see a party involved in a series of related court and arbitration proceedings. These proceedings do not necessarily have the same cause of action and do not involve all the same parties, but they can be related for various reasons. For example, several litigations may all relate to a dispute arising out of the same contract; or several proceedings may be directed against the same individual acting through different legal entities. Therefore, it can happen that certain materials from one arbitration will be voluntarily disclosed or will be produced as a result of a

---

[81]Continental Insurance Company v Fairmont Premier Insurance Company, 16-cv-655, 3 (S.D.N.Y. 2016).

compulsory disclosure process in a court proceeding or in another arbitration proceeding. For example, a party will need to disclose an arbitral award in a parallel court proceeding as a support of its argument on the *res judicata* effect of the existing arbitral award.

We will first clarify the use of the term 'disclosure', which can have two **667** meanings. First, it usually means the act or process of making known something that was previously unknown.[82] But 'disclosure' may also refer specifically to the process of *compulsory disclosure*, at a party's request, of information that relates to a litigation.[83]

In common law systems, *compulsory disclosure* (also called discovery or docu- **668** ment production) plays a very important role as part of adversary proceedings. Although the specific rules change depending on the jurisdiction, each party is generally under an obligation to produce all relevant evidence, even if a particular piece of evidence is detrimental to its own case.[84] By contrast, civil law jurisdictions are not familiar with broad-scope discovery, and the parties in principle do not have to produce the documents which can damage their case, subject obviously to the requirement that they not mislead the court.[85]

In both court or arbitration proceedings, compulsory disclosure is aimed at **669** assisting in finding the truth, and, as such, is essential for delivering justice. The discovery process will be efficient only if each party is cooperative and candid in its efforts to find documents responsive to the other party's document request. Lord Denning MR in *Riddick v. Thames Board Mills* explained the rationale for full and frank discovery this way:

> Discovery of documents is a most valuable aid in the doing of justice. The court orders the parties to a suit, both of them, to disclose on oath all documents in their possession or power relating to the matters in issue in the action. Many litigants feel that this is unfair. I have often known a party faced with such an order, saying to his solicitor: 'Need I disclose this document to the other side? I will damage our case greatly if they get to know of it.' The solicitor's answer is, and must be: 'Yes, you must disclose it, however much it damages your case.' Again I have known a party to say to his solicitor: 'But these are my own confidential papers, my own personal diary, our own inter-departmental memoranda. Must I disclose them?' The answer of the solicitor again is 'Yes, you must disclose them.' Confidential information has no privilege from disclosure [. . .] The court insists on your producing them so as to do justice in the case.

> The reason for compelling discovery of documents in this way lies in the public interest in discovering the truth so that justice may be done between the parties. That public interest is to be put into the scales against the public interest in preserving privacy and protecting confidential information. The balance comes down in the ordinary way in favour of the public interest of discovering the truth, i.e. in making full disclosure. . . . The thing to do in

---

[82]Definition of 'disclosure' from the Black's Law Dictionary.

[83]Definition of 'discovery' from the Black's Law Dictionary.

[84]Kaufmann-Kohler and Bärtsch (2004), p. 14.

[85]Kaufmann-Kohler and Bärtsch (2004), p. 14.

every case is to weigh the competing public interests and see which way the scales come down.[86]

670 International arbitration proceedings were influenced by both common law and civil law systems. Today there is hardly any international arbitration proceeding that does not involve a document disclosure, but the scope of such disclosure is more limited in arbitration proceedings than it is in the court proceedings of common law jurisdictions.[87] Art. 3 of the IBA Rules on Evidence is the result of a compromise between common law and civil law systems; it contains generally admitted rules on the document production in international arbitration proceedings. Today, in many arbitrations, the parties and arbitrators choose to apply the IBA Rules on Evidence— at least as guidelines.

671 Relying on Art. 3 of the IBA Rules on Evidence, therefore, one can give a brief description of the document production process in arbitration proceedings. First, each party addresses a document production request to the other party identifying the documents it would like the other party to produce. Second, each party responds to the other party's document production request, either by accepting to produce the requested documents or by objecting to the request. Third, the Tribunal issues a ruling on the requests on which the parties could not agree. Finally, each party has to produce the documents it agreed to produce voluntarily or in accordance with the order of the Tribunal.

672 In the present section, we will examine the following situations regarding the use and disclosure of documents in parallel or related arbitration and court proceedings. Let us assume an arbitration between A and B ('First Arbitration') and a subsequent or parallel arbitration or court proceeding between A and C ('Second Proceeding'). In the first scenario, A would like to use certain documents from the First Arbitration in the Second Proceeding. In the second scenario, C would like A to disclose certain documents from the First Arbitration in the Second Proceeding. Therefore, in the first scenario, A already has the documents it wants to use in its possession. In the second scenario, C does not have the documents in its possession and wants to use the document production to obtain these documents from A.

673 The cases we will discuss below fall under one of the above scenarios. Most of these cases were adjudicated by the English courts. Only one of the cases is from another jurisdiction: the state of Delaware.

674 Several courts have had to deal with the issue of disclosure of arbitration materials from one proceeding in another proceeding, and we provide summaries of their decisions. The decisions are very important to understand which exceptions to the parties' duty of confidentiality have been effectively admitted by state courts. However, one must keep in mind that even in the presence of defined rules and principles, each case is addressed in its context, depending on the specific factual

---

[86]Riddick v. Thames Board Mills [1977] 3 ALL ER 677, at 687-688.

[87]Kaufmann-Kohler and Bärtsch (2004), p. 14.

circumstances. For example, here is what the English Court of Appeal ruled in the Emmot case[88]:

> The second point to be stressed is that it is particularly important that what has been said about the possible exceptions to confidentiality must read in context. I take two examples. First, if a court decides in the context of a summons (as it did in *London and Leeds Estates Ltd v Paribas Ltd* (No 2)) that the 'public interest' may outweigh the confidentiality of arbitration documents, it does not necessarily follow that a party may voluntarily disclose documents to third parties on the ground that it is in the 'public interest.' Second, it does not follow from the fact that a court refers to the possibility of an exception for the order of the court or leave of the court in a case where it has the power to make the order or give leave (as in *Dolling-Baker v Merrett* or *Glidepath BV v Thompson*) the court has a general and unlimited jurisdiction to consider whether an exception to confidentiality exists and applies.[89]

Thus, in the Emmot case, the English Court of Appeal emphasized the importance of the context and a very broad discretionary power of the Court.   **675**

In 1988, in the case *Shearson Lehman Hutton Incorporated and Another v. Maclaine Watson & Co. Ltd and Others*,[90] the English High Court had to consider whether the documents submitted in the course of an arbitration could be disclosed in a subsequent public litigation between different parties. The claimants sought production of the pleadings, the award, documents produced by way of evidence, and the transcript of the evidence in arbitration proceedings between the first defendant and a third party. The defendants objected to disclosure of the requested documents, arguing that they had been generated and exchanged in the course of a private arbitration. The defendants claimed confidentiality and privacy of arbitration, relying on a number of authorities whose main reasoning, as summarised by Justice Webster, was that: **676**

> [I]t would be contrary to the interests of justice if parties were to be discouraged from making full and frank discovery in an action because of their apprehension that documents disclosed might be used by or for the purposes of persons not parties to the litigation in question.[91]

Justice Webster did recognise that arbitrations are private and confidential.[92] He did not agree, however, with the above-cited considerations and concluded that the documents in the custody of the first defendant, arising out of its arbitration with a third party, were to be disclosed to the claimants as they were relevant to the issues in   **677**

---

[88]Emmott v. Wilson & Partners Limited [2008] EWCA Civ 184.

[89]Emmott v. Wilson & Partners Limited [2008] EWCA Civ 184 at para 87.

[90]Shearson Lehman Hutton Incorporated and Another v. Maclaine Watson & Co. Ltd. [1988] 1 WLR 946.

[91]Shearson Lehman Hutton Incorporated and Another v. Maclaine Watson & Co. Ltd. [1988] 1 WLR 948; Lew (2013), p. 443.

[92]Shearson Lehman Hutton Incorporated and Another v. Maclaine Watson & Co. Ltd. [1988] 1 WLR 948.

this court proceeding.[93] He rejected the application seeking confidentiality of arbitration materials by reasoning that there is no risk that the parties to arbitration will be discouraged from making a full and frank discovery because there is no involuntary disclosure in arbitration:

> Discovery is a process of involuntary disclosure. Parties to litigation are obliged to give disclosure of documents in their possession. But documents adduced or evidence given in an arbitration are in no sense adduced or given involuntarily, and I see no significant risk that parties to arbitrations would be inhibited in their conduct of them by apprehension about the possible subsequent use of documents or evidence relied upon by them in those arbitrations by other parties.[94]

678   While Justice Webster's decision rejecting the confidentiality application seems fair, we would like to comment on his reasoning. Indeed, Justice Webster is not entirely correct when he states that the parties are never compelled to disclose documents in the course of arbitration proceedings. Involuntary disclosure is also part of arbitration proceedings.[95] While it is true that the parties submit their supporting evidence, i.e. exhibits, voluntarily, there is a document production process as well, requiring the parties to produce documents responsive to the request of the adverse party. If there is a dispute between the parties on whether a specific document or a certain category of documents has to be produced, the arbitral tribunal will issue an order. A party can thus be compelled by the tribunal's order to disclose certain documents. Also, the documents produced in the course of compulsory disclosure can be submitted by either party as exhibits. This means that documents produced involuntarily can become part of the evidence.

679   Consequently, contrary to Justice Webster's statement, parties to arbitration could be discouraged from making a full and frank disclosure '*by apprehension about the possible subsequent use of documents or evidence relied upon by them in those arbitration by other parties*'. In any case, we think that even the documents produced as a result of voluntary disclosure should be protected by confidentiality. In our opinion, Justice Webster could have justified his decision by the public interest exception. We think he could have reasoned, for example, that, in this particular case, the public interest of finding the truth overrode the private interest of the parties to arbitration of keeping the materials from arbitration confidential. We will discuss the public interest exception below.

680   Almost 10 years later, in the *Ali Shipping* case, the English Court of Appeal had to deal with the issue of whether the documents submitted in the course of an arbitration can be disclosed in subsequent arbitrations between different parties.[96] The disputed issue was very similar to that of the previously discussed *Shearson Lehman*

---

[93]Shearson Lehman Hutton Incorporated and Another v. Maclaine Watson & Co. Ltd. [1988] 1 WLR 946.

[94]Shearson Lehman Hutton Incorporated and Another v. Maclaine Watson & Co. Ltd. [1988] 1 WLR 948.

[95]See, for example, Art. 3.7 of the IBA Rules on Evidence.

[96]Ali Shipping v Shipyard Trogir [1997] EWCA Civ 3054.

case. The main difference was that one party sought disclosure of the arbitration documents in subsequent arbitrations, and not in a public litigation as in *Shearson Lehman*. Below, we set out a summary of the facts and the legal issues that the *Ali Shipping* case raised before the Court of Appeal.

Ali Shipping Corporation ('Ali'), Leman Navigation Inc. ('Leman'), Lavender **681** Shipping Limited ('Lavender'), and Leeward Shipping Limited ('Leeward) were owned by Greenwich Holdings Limited ('Greenwich'). In four separate contracts, Shipyard Trogir ('the Yard') undertook the obligation to build vessels with each of the four companies owned by Greenwich: vessel Hull 202 for Ali ('the Hull 202 Agreement'); vessel Hull 204 for Lavender ('the Hull 204 Agreement'); vessel Hull 205 for Leeward ('the Hull 205 Agreement'); and vessel Hull 206 for Leman ('the Hull 206 Agreement').[97]

Following Yard's failure to complete vessel Hull 202 in accordance with the Hull **682** 202 Agreement, Ali rescinded the contract and claimed substantial damages before an arbitral tribunal composed of a sole arbitrator ('First Arbitration'). The Yard sought to defend Ali's claim by arguing, in particular, that Leman, Lavender and Leeward did not pay the first instalments of the contract price for Hulls 204-206. The Yard claimed that the performance of Hull 202 Agreement had become dependent on performance of the subsequent contracts with Leman, Lavender and Leeward, and that the corporate veil should be pierced since all four companies were owned by Greenwich. In the First Arbitration, the sole arbitrator awarded Ali a sum of USD 21,594,391 plus interest and costs.[98]

The Yard initiated arbitrations under Hulls Nos. 204-206 Agreements against **683** Leman, Lavender and Leeward and applied for interim awards seeking payment of the first instalments of the contractual price which were not paid by each of the three companies. In these arbitrations, the Yard sought to submit certain documents from the First Arbitration: the Award, the written opening submission for Ali, and transcripts of the oral evidence given by certain witnesses for Ali. However, the Yard was precluded from doing so by Justice Longmore on the basis that use of the materials would amount to breach of the Yard's implied obligation of confidentiality in respect of the First Arbitration. After Justice Clarke discharged Justice Longmore's injunction, Ali made an appeal to the Court of Appeal seeking to protect the confidentiality of the arbitration materials from the First Arbitration.[99]

The Court of Appeal confirmed the existence of an implied obligation of confi- **684** dentiality, but acknowledged that it could be subject to exceptions. As mentioned above, these exceptions are: consent of a party who originally produced the materials, order or leave of the Court, and a public interest exception. Regarding the order or leave of the Court, the Court of Appeal noted that it was the practical scope of this exception, i.e., the grounds on which such leave or order is to be granted, which gave rise to difficulty. It considered that the test to be applied is that of a 'reasonable

---

[97] Ali Shipping v Shipyard Trogir [1997] EWCA Civ 3054.
[98] Ali Shipping v Shipyard Trogir [1997] EWCA Civ 3054.
[99] Ali Shipping v Shipyard Trogir [1997] EWCA Civ 3054.

necessity'.[100] Thus, the issue to be resolved is whether the disclosure is 'reasonably necessary' for the establishment or protection of the legitimate interests of an arbitrating party.

685   Before focusing on the 'reasonable necessity' test, the Court of Appeal had to review and reach a conclusion on another argument raised by the parties. Since Ali, Leman, Lavender and Leeward were all owned by the same company, the Yard argued that Leman, Lavender and Leeward were not 'third party strangers' regarding the arbitration materials concerning Ali and should be allowed access to these materials.[101] In essence, the Court had to decide whether another exception to the rule of confidentiality could be admitted: the one allowing a party to disclose the arbitration materials to the parties who are in the same beneficial ownership as the entity objecting to the disclosure.

686   The Court of Appeal decided resolutely that the fact that the Yard contemplated disclosure to the parties who were in the same beneficial ownership and management as Ali should not be a ground to allow disclosure. Disclosure could be allowed only if a recognised exception to the rule of confidentiality was proven or if the stance of the objecting party could be shown to be fraudulent or in the nature of an abuse of process.[102]

687   As to the reasonable necessity test, the Court of Appeal held that that disclosure should be 'reasonably necessary' for the protection of the party's legal rights; the fact that the documents were merely helpful was not sufficient to order disclosure. Also, it considered that a Court applying the 'reasonable necessity' test should take a flexible approach *taking account of the nature and purpose of the proceedings for which the material is required, the powers and procedures of the tribunal in which the proceedings are being conducted, the issues to which the evidence or information sought is directed and the practicality and expense of obtaining such evidence or information elsewhere'*.[103]

688   The Court of Appeal agreed that the use of the materials from the First Arbitration could save time and expense and reduce the risk of inconsistent findings between the Hull 202-204 arbitrators and the sole arbitrator in the First Arbitration. However, it considered that the convenience and good sense were in themselves not sufficient to satisfy the test of 'reasonable necessity'. For this reason, the Court of Appeal held that the injunction originally granted by Justice Longmore precluding the Yard from the use of the materials from the First Arbitration should be made final.

689   The English Courts acknowledged that an exception to the general rule of confidentiality can be admitted when the interests of justice justify the use of evidence from one arbitration in another arbitration or court proceeding. For example, in the *London & Leeds Estate v Paribas Ltd* case,[104] the English High Court held

---

[100] Ali Shipping v Shipyard Trogir [1997] EWCA Civ 3054.

[101] Ali Shipping v Shipyard Trogir [1997] EWCA Civ 3054.

[102] Ali Shipping v Shipyard Trogir [1997] EWCA Civ 3054.

[103] Ali Shipping v Shipyard Trogir [1997] EWCA Civ 3054.

[104] London & Leeds Estate v Paribas Ltd [1995] 2 EG 134.

that the risk of potential inconsistencies in a witness's evidence was something that would justify an exception to the general rule of confidentiality in the interests of justice. In this case, it was argued that the evidence provided by an expert in a rent review arbitration was not consistent with the evidence he had submitted in earlier arbitrations. Justice Mance stated, in particular:

> [I]f a witness were proved to have expressed himself in a materially different sense when acting for different sides, that would be a factor which should be brought out in the interest of individual litigants involved and in the public interest.[105]

In the *Ali Shipping* case,[106] the English Court of Appeal agreed with the reasoning of Justice Mance in the above-mentioned case and agreed that an exception to confidentiality should be admitted if there was a risk that a witness provided inconsistent testimony in different proceedings. The Court reasoned that the interests of justice required that a judicial decision be reached on the basis of truthful or accurate evidence. It considered, however, that in this case the proper term should have been 'the interests of justice' rather than the 'public interest exception':

> As a matter of terminology, I would prefer to recognise such an exception under the heading 'the interests of justice' rather than 'the public interest' in order to avoid the suggestion that use of that latter phrase is to be read as extending to the wider issue of public interest contested in the Esso Australia case.[107]

In the Emmot case,[108] the English Court of Appeal held that the interests of justice justified disclosure of arbitration materials when the purpose was to prevent courts from being misled. Thus, the English Court of Appeal allowed disclosure of certain arbitration pleadings in subsequent court proceedings before the New South Wales and the British Islands courts. This disclosure was permitted in order to prevent the New South Wales and the British Islands courts from being misled about the nature and the scope of the issues already adjudicated in a previous arbitration. The Court of Appeal held, in this decision, that the interests of justice were not confined to the interests of justice in England, but could also be extended to the justice done overseas.[109]

In the *Westwood Shipping Lines* case,[110] the claimants asked for disclosure of the documents from a previous arbitration, which could arguably establish unlawful conduct and unlawful actions. The English High Court held that this disclosure would serve not only the individual interests of the claimants, but also the interests of justice. The court reasoned that '*the court should not allow confidentiality of*

690

691

692

---

[105]London & Leeds Estate v Paribas Ltd [1995] 2 EG 134.

[106]Ali Shipping v Shipyard Trogir [1997] EWCA Civ 3054.

[107]London & Leeds Estate v Paribas Ltd [1995] 2 EG 134. See below for a discussion of "the Esso Australia case" to which the Court refers.

[108]Emmott v. Wilson & Partners Limited [2008] EWCA Civ 184.

[109]Emmott v. Wilson & Partners Limited [2008] EWCA Civ 184.

[110]Westwood Shipping Lines Inc and another v Universal Schiffahrtsgesellschaft MBH and another [2012] EWHC 3837.

arbitration materials in any sense to stifle the ability to bring to light wrongdoing of one kind or another'.[111]

693   The English Privy Council[112] were called to decide on whether the terms of an express confidentiality agreement precluded the disclosure of an award in a further arbitration between the same parties.[113] The same parties, Associated Electric Gas Insurance Services Ltd ('Aegis') and European Reinsurance Company of Zurich (European Re), were involved in two arbitrations under the same reinsurance agreement. In the first arbitration, the parties and the arbitrators agreed on a general duty of confidentiality:

> The parties, their lawyers, and the Court of Arbitration agree as a general principle to maintain the privacy and confidentiality of the arbitration. In particular they agree that the contents of the brief or other documents prepared and filed in the course of the proceeding, as well as the contents of the underlying claim documents, testimony, affidavits, any transcripts, and the arbitration result will not be disclosed at any time to any individual or entity, in whole or in part, which is not a part to the arbitration between AEGIS and European Re.[114]

694   In the first arbitration, the Arbitral Tribunal rendered an award in favour of European Re and European Re sought to rely on this award in the second arbitration. Aegis argued that such a disclosure would violate the principle of private nature of the arbitration proceedings and would result in breach of the express confidentiality agreement. The Privy Council held that legitimate use of an earlier award in a later arbitration between the same parties did not constitute violation of the confidentiality agreement. According to the Privy Council, if confidentiality agreements were to be construed without limitation, any award would be unenforceable. This would be fundamentally inconsistent with the purpose of the arbitration. In this case, the Privy Council found that the purpose of the confidentiality agreement was to prevent disclosure of confidential information to third parties having interests adverse to Aegis and European Re, but not the use of arbitral award in a subsequent arbitration between the same parties.

695   In the United States, in *United States v. Panhandle Eastern Corp.*, the District Court of Delaware judges addressed the issue of disclosure of the materials originating from an arbitration in a subsequent court litigation.[115] As explained in more

---

[111]Westwood Shipping Lines Inc and another v Universal Schiffahrtsgesellschaft MBH and another [2012] EWHC 3837.

[112]The Judicial Committee of the Privy Council is the court of final appeal for the UK overseas territories and Crown dependencies, and for those Commonwealth countries that have retained the appeal to Her Majesty in Council or, in the case of Republics, to the Judicial Committee (http://jcpc.uk/).

[113]Associated Electric Gas Insurance Services Ltd v European Reinsurance Company of Zurich [2003] UKPC 11.

[114]Associated Electric Gas Insurance Services Ltd v European Reinsurance Company of Zurich [2003] UKPC 11.

[115]United States v Panhandle Eastern Corporation 118 FRD 346 (D Del 1988).

detail above,[116] Panhandle Eastern Pipe Line Co. ('PEPL') sought to preserve confidentiality of the documents relating to an earlier arbitration.

The Delaware District Court recalled the standards for issuing a protective order **696** on confidentiality under Rule 26(c) of the Federal Rules of Civil Procedure. First, Rule 26(c) places the burden of persuasion on the party seeking the protective order. Second, according to the same rule, '*the party seeking the protective order must show good cause by demonstrating a particular need for protection*' and '*must provide specific examples of the hard that will be suffered because of the disclosure of information.*'[117]

On the one hand, the Court concluded that there was no confidentiality obligation **697** in the absence of a specific provision in the arbitration rules and since there was no express agreement on such an obligation between the parties. On the other hand, the Court, assuming that an understanding of confidentiality existed, found that PEPL failed to provide specific examples of the hardship that it will suffer as a result of disclosure.

5.3.4 Public Interest Exception

Another exception to the general rule of confidentiality is the public interest excep- **698** tion, which should be admitted where arbitral proceedings affect third parties' interests or involve the functioning of a state.[118] This exception is fully justified in investor-state disputes where the fact that a state is party to the dispute calls for a greater transparency.[119] The public interest can, however, be invoked in commercial arbitrations as well. For example, a state can have interests in a commercial arbitration because a party to this arbitration is a state-owned entity. Or the public interest could be justified in commercial arbitrations by the fact that the dispute is over an asset that is particularly important for the economy of a particular region.

For a commercial arbitration case involving the public interest, one can consider **699** the *Esso/BHP* case.[120] As explained in more detail above,[121] Esso/BHP entered into two agreements for the sale of natural gas (Sales Agreement) to two public utilities, GFC and SEC. At some point, Esso/BHP sought an increase in the price. They justified the price increase by the imposition of a new tax. Under the Sales Agreements, Esso/BHP were required to provide the details justifying any price increase; they agreed to disclose this information provided that the two public utilities

---

[116]See above Sect. 3.2.3.5 for more details on the case.

[117]United States v Panhandle Eastern Corporation 118 FRD 349 (D Del 1988).

[118]See, for example, Tweeddale (2005), p. 69; Gu (2004), p. 7; Tjio (2009), p. 13.

[119]Kinnear et al. (2013), p. 108.

[120]Esso Australia Resources Ltd. and Others v. Sidney James Plowman and Others.

[121]See above Sect. 3.2.3.4.

undertook not to communicate this information to the Minister, the Government and the people of Victoria.

700   The High Court of Australia rejected the defence arguments of Esso/BHP based on the existence of an implied duty of confidentiality in private arbitrations. It held that there was no implied duty of confidentiality in the absence of an express agreement and upheld the declaration according to which GFC and SEC were not restricted from disclosing information to the Minister and third persons obtained from Esso/BHP in the course of or by reason of the arbitration.[122]

701   The decision was rendered by five judges of the High Australian Court with one judge, Justice Toohey, providing a dissenting opinion. Justice Toohey maintained that confidentiality was an implied term in the agreement to arbitrate. He admitted, however, that it was easier to express a non-confidentiality rule as there were too many potential exceptions to this principle. Justice Toohey expressed a concern that a principle subject to too many exceptions would hardly be a principle:

> In terms of formulation, it is easy enough to express a principle of non-confidentiality. In effect, that is what the Minister has done in declarations 6C and 6F which he seeks to uphold. But it is much harder to express a principle of confidentiality which accepts, as it must, that there are significant exceptions. And this has been the appellants' difficulty from the outset of this litigation. A principle of confidentiality, expressed to be subject to 'all exceptions' or the like, is a principle so nebulous as to be hardly a principle at all.[123]

702   The difficulty of formulating exceptions to the principle of confidentiality could have contributed to the decision of the majority of Justices on the non-confidentiality rule. We think that the judges could have reached the same decision without rejecting the principle of confidentiality. In this case, GFC and SEC were public utilities supplying gas and electricity to the households of Victoria. Thus, the disclosure of information on the price increase to the Minister of Energy, the Government and the people of Victoria was responding to the public interest of the people of Victoria. Therefore, in our opinion, the judges could have allowed the disclosure of materials by acknowledging the confidentiality of arbitration and by admitting a public interest exception in this particular case.

703   As already mentioned, in the meantime, provisions on the confidentiality of arbitral proceedings were introduced into the AIAA (Arts 23C, 23D, 23E, 23F, 23G). These provisions apply in the proceedings arising from all arbitration agreements concluded from 14 October 2015 onwards, unless the parties decide to 'opt-out'.[124] Art. 23G AIAA contains a provision on the public interest exception. According to Art. 23G AIAA, the court may make an order allowing a party to disclose confidential information if it is satisfied that the public interest in preserving

---

[122]Esso Australia Resources Ltd. and Others v. Sidney James Plowman and Others, Arbitration International, Volume 11 No. 3, 1995, p. 238.

[123]Esso Australia Resources Ltd. and Others v. Sidney James Plowman and Others, Arbitration International, Volume 11 No. 3, 1995, p. 259.

[124]Art, 22(2) AIAA; Nottage (2017), pp. 1–2; Shirlow (2015), p. 2.

the confidentiality of arbitral proceedings is outweighed by other considerations that render it desirable in the public interest for the information to be disclosed.

The English courts, which rendered important decisions on the exceptions to the **704** parties' duty of confidentiality, have not yet had a chance to establish detailed rules on the public interest exception. As mentioned earlier, in the *London & Leeds Estate v Paribas Ltd* case,[125] Justice Mance held that the public interest exception to the general rule of confidentiality should be admitted when there was a risk of potential inconsistencies in a witness's evidence. In fact, as noted later by the English Court of Appeal in the *Ali Shipping* case,[126] the proper term in this judgment should have been 'the interests of justice' rather than the 'public interest exception'. As to the public interest exception, Justice Potter stated in the *Ali Shipping* case that '*it may well fall to the English Court at a future time to consider some further exception to the general rule of confidentiality based on wider considerations of public interest*'.[127]

5.4 Exceptions and Limitations to the Scope of the Arbitrators' Duty of Confidentiality

5.4.1 Introduction

As discussed earlier, no one disputes the existence of the arbitrators' duty of **705** confidentiality. The scope of this duty is very broad—it covers practically any information that the arbitrators learn in the course of arbitral proceedings—but it can obviously not be unlimited. In certain cases, arbitrators will be allowed or even obliged to disclose confidential information.

We will examine three main areas where exceptions to the arbitrators' duty of **706** confidentiality can potentially be admitted. First, we will examine whether arbitrators can be exempted from their duty of confidentiality due to their duty to testify before a state court. Second, we will address exceptions to the confidentiality of deliberations and, in particular, dissenting opinions. Finally, we will explore whether the arbitrators' duty of confidentiality will preclude the arbitrators from disclosing cases involving serious criminal behaviour.

---

[125]London & Leeds Estate v Paribas Ltd [1995] 2 EG 134.

[126]Ali Shipping v Shipyard Trogir [1997] EWCA Civ 3054.

[127]Ali Shipping v Shipyard Trogir [1997] EWCA Civ 3054.

5.4.2 Conflict Between the Arbitrators' Duty of Confidentiality and the Duty to Testify

707   Let us assume there is a setting-aside proceeding or another court proceeding where an arbitrator is compelled as a witness in relation to the matter he arbitrated or is arbitrating. Can arbitrators be exempted from their duty to testify given their obligation of confidentiality? The answer can change depending on the applicable law, as there is no uniform approach in different jurisdictions.

708   For example, in Kazakhstan, arbitrators are in principle exempted from the duty to testify before the court. Thus, the Law of the Republic of Kazakhstan on International Arbitration exempts arbitrators from being compelled as witnesses:

> Confidentiality meaning that *arbitrators* shall not disclose information, which became known to them in the course of arbitral proceedings, without prior consent of the parties or their legal successors, and *may not be interrogated as witnesses with respect to circumstances that became known to them in the course of arbitral proceedings, save in the cases where the law explicitly provides for the duty of a citizen to report information to a relevant body* (italics added).[128]

Kazakh laws on civil and criminal law procedures also implement the arbitrators' exemption from their duty to testify. Thus, the Code of Civil Procedure and the Code of Criminal Procedure of the Republic of Kazakhstan contain provisions exempting arbitrators from the duty to testify about the facts that became known to them by reason of their office.[129] Although the Kazakh regulation exempting arbitrators from a duty to testify appears to be progressive, other laws can provide for exceptions to this rule. Thus, the real meaning and content of this exemption will depend on the exceptions provided for in other laws.

709   Swiss law does not expressly exempt arbitrators from being compelled as witnesses in either civil or criminal proceedings. Art. 166(1) of the Code of Civil Procedure and Arts 170(1) and 171(1) of the Code of Criminal Procedure provide, in particular, that two categories of persons are allowed to refuse to testify: (1) those who are bound by professional secrecy (lawyers, notaries, doctors, etc.); and (2) officials—regarding the facts entrusted to them by reason of their office.

710   Even if arbitrators are 'lawyers' within the meaning of the above-mentioned articles, it is unlikely that these provisions will exempt arbitrators from the duty to testify.[130] Indeed, when the 'lawyers' act as arbitrators, this type of activity is not covered by these provisions.[131] Unlike judges, arbitrators are not officials, which means that Art. 166(1)(c) of the Code of Civil Procedure and Art. 170(1) of the Code

---

[128] Art. 4(5) of the Law of the Republic of Kazakhstan on International Arbitration.

[129] Art. 79 (3-1) of the Code of Civil Procedure of the Republic of Kazakhstan, Art. 82 (2.1-1) of the Code of Criminal Procedure of the Republic of Kazakhstan.

[130] Zurich Court of Appeals, decision of 7 September 2000, ASA Bulletin 2/2001, 322–324.

[131] Jeandin (2011), CPC commenté, Art. 166 para 11; Jolles et al. (2013), pp. 140–141.

of Criminal Procedure do not apply to them either. It can, however, be argued that because arbitrators, like judges, have an adjudicator role, and because arbitral awards have effects similar to state court's decisions, legal provisions exempting judges from a duty to testify should apply by analogy to arbitrators. Nevertheless, this interpretation has not been confirmed by the Swiss Supreme Court.

Art. 156 of the Swiss Code of Civil Procedure can potentially be used to exempt **711** the arbitrator from the obligation to testify:

> If taking evidence puts at risk interests worthy of protection of a party or a third party, particularly their trade secrets, the court orders the necessary measures.

There is, however, a major inconvenience related to the use of this provision: unless the court issues a protective measure, the arbitrator has a duty to testify, notwithstanding a conflict with his duty of confidentiality.[132] Thus, exemption from the duty to testify will depend on the court's discretion.[133]

Therefore, *de lege ferenda*, it would be justified for arbitrators to be exempted as **712** judges are from the duty to testify and to collaborate in the meaning of Art. 166(1)(c) of the Code of Civil Procedure and Art. 170(1) of the Code of Criminal Procedure.[134] This exemption would, in its scope of application, include the facts that became known to arbitrators by reason of their service as arbitrators.

As to the specific issue of arbitrators' testimony in setting-aside proceedings, the **713** regulation also varies significantly depending on the jurisdiction. For example, in England, the court can call arbitrators to testify in setting-aside proceedings.[135] The arbitrators' testimony should, however, be used as the last recourse, when no other means of evidence can prove the relevant fact.[136] By contrast, in France and in the U. S., the courts consider that the arbitrators' testimony is not an admissible way of evidence.[137] Thus, the Paris Court of Appeal held that the courts cannot call the arbitrator to testify because the arbitrator assumes the status of a judge.[138]

In Switzerland, there is no prohibition for an arbitrator to testify in setting-aside **714** proceedings. As a person who directly witnessed relevant facts and as a non-party to proceedings, an arbitrator can thus be called to testify (Art. 169 of the Code of Civil Procedure). As discussed above, an arbitrator is not entitled to refuse to cooperate under Art. 166(1)(c) of the Code of Civil Procedure. However, if he can prove that his evidence will put at risk interests of a party or of a third party worthy of

---

[132]Jolles et al. (2013), p. 141.

[133]Jolles et al. (2013), p. 141.

[134]Jolles et al. (2013), p. 141.

[135]Besson (2011), p. 100, with further references.

[136]Besson (2011), p. 101, with further references.

[137]Besson (2011), pp. 101–102, with further references.

[138]Consorts Rouny v. Soc. Anonyme Holding, Cour d'appel de Paris, 29 May 1992, in: Rev. Arb. 1996, 408.

protection, the arbitrator will be exempted by the court from his obligation to testify (Art. 156 of the Code of Civil Procedure).

5.4.3   Exceptions to the Confidentiality of Deliberations?

715   Some arbitration rules contain specific provisions on the exceptions to the confidentiality of deliberations. Thus, the LCIA Rules and the Abu Dhabi Rules provide that arbitrators can be compelled to disclose the confidentiality of deliberations if so required by the applicable law.[139] These provisions are sufficiently general to respect potentially existing mandatory provisions of the *lex arbitri*. For example, if an arbitrator is called by the competent state court to testify in a setting aside proceeding, he might be called to disclose the content of the deliberations if the *lex arbitri* does not exempt him from his obligation to testify. Also, arbitrators will not violate the confidentiality of deliberations if they have to disclose the fact that another arbitrator on the panel refuses to participate in the deliberations because he becomes unable or unfit to act.[140]

716   While dissenting opinion is not the subject of our study,[141] the issue deserves brief examination to the extent that there is a risk that dissenting opinions may violate the confidentiality of deliberations.

717   There is no uniform solution in international arbitration regarding dissenting opinions. Thus, neither the drafters of the UNCITRAL Model Law nor the drafters of the UNCITRAL Arbitration Rules could reach a consensus on this issue.[142] As a result, neither of these texts contains a provision on dissenting opinions. Moreover, the explanatory note to the Model Law expressly admits the absence of regulation, indicating that '*the Model Law neither requires nor prohibits "dissenting opinions*"'.[143]

718   Jean-François Poudret provides another good example of the lack of consensus on this issue in his article dedicated to dissenting opinions in arbitration.[144] He and the other two pillars of international arbitration, Claude Reymond and Pierre Lalive, carried out a collective study on international and domestic arbitration in Switzerland.[145] The three authors could reach agreement on almost all problematic issues, but not on the right of an arbitrator to make a dissenting opinion in the absence of

---

[139]LCIA Rules, Art. 30.2; Abu Dhabi Rules, Art. 33(2).

[140]LCIA Rules, Art. 30.2; DIAC Rules, Art. 41.2.

[141]For a detailed analysis of the dissenting opinion, see, for example, Manuel Arroyo, Dealing with Dissenting Opinions in the Award, Jean-François Poudret, Légitimité et opportunité de l'opinion dissidente dans le silence de la loi ?, Smit (2004).

[142]Arroyo (2008), p. 438.

[143]Explanatory Note to the Model Law, para 43.

[144]Jean-François Poudret, Légitimité et opportunité de l'opinion dissidente dans le silence de la loi ?

[145]Lalive et al. (1989).

relevant regulation in the national law, of institutional rules, or of the parties' express agreement.[146]

Manuel Arroyo also conducted a comparative law survey on the admissibility of   **719**
dissenting opinions, sharing the results of this survey in an article published in ASA Bulletin in 2008.[147] According to this survey, 24 out of 107 arbitration laws permit dissenting opinions, while the remaining national arbitration laws have no provision on the subject.[148] For example, such jurisdictions as Bulgaria, Estonia, Lithuania, Norway, Poland, Portugal, Romania, Spain and Turkey permit dissenting opinions.[149]

In some cases, solutions are proposed by domestic courts.[150] For example,   **720**
according to the Swiss Supreme Court, a dissenting opinion is not considered to be part of the arbitral award.[151] In the absence of a specific regulation in the parties' agreement or applicable institutional rules, the dissenting opinion can be communicated to the parties only if the majority of arbitrators agree to such a communication.[152]

In an exemplary case before the French Court of Appeal, the Secretariat of the   **721**
ICC Court of Arbitration sent a dissenting opinion to the parties before communication of the arbitral award.[153] The French Court of Appeal found that this disclosure violated the confidentiality of deliberations as it could potentially affect the arbitrators' freedom of decision.[154] This breach, however, was not considered to be a sufficient ground for annulment of the award.[155]

Given the nature of a dissenting opinion, its revelation may constitute a violation   **722**
of the confidentiality of deliberations, if not unanimously allowed by all members of the tribunal.[156] Therefore, dissenting opinions should be carefully drafted not to reveal the substance of deliberations, but to limit comments to alternative views of the facts and law.[157] However, if the court finds that an arbitrator has breached the secrecy of deliberations, it is generally admitted that such a breach will not be a

---

[146]Poudret (2004), p. 243.

[147]Arroyo (2008), pp. 437–466.

[148]Arroyo (2008), pp. 439–440.

[149]Arroyo (2008), pp. 439–440, with further references.

[150]Arroyo (2008), pp. 439–440.

[151]ATF of 11 May 1991, in: ASA Bull. 266 (1992), 2b.

[152]ATF of 11 May 1991, in: ASA Bull. 266 (1992), 2b.

[153]Uzinexportimport Romanian Co. c/Attock Cement C, Cour d'appel de Paris (1ère Ch. C), 7 July 1994, in : Rev. Arb. 1995, 107.

[154]Uzinexportimport Romanian Co. c/Attock Cement C, Cour d'appel de Paris (1ère Ch. C), 7 July 1994, in: Rev. Arb. 1995, 107.

[155]Uzinexportimport Romanian Co. c/Attock Cement C, Cour d'appel de Paris (1ère Ch. C), 7 July 1994, in: Rev. Arb. 1995, 107.

[156]Kunz (2013), pp. 18–19.

[157]Mosk and Ginsburg (2000), p. 31.

sufficient ground for annulment of the award.[158] If an arbitrator has caused damage to the arbitrators-members of the same panel, they can pursue him for damages. As discussed above,[159] the nature of the arbitrators' duty of confidentiality regarding the content of deliberations is contractual as the arbitrators-members of the same panel are bound between each other by a contract of "société simple". Thus, a contractual claim will be available in the case of a breach of the secrecy of deliberations.

5.4.4   Conflict Between the Arbitrators' Duty of Confidentiality and the Duty of Disclosure in Cases of Serious Criminality

723   There appears to be an increasing concern about the use of arbitration to further criminal activities, such as money laundering or corruption.[160] In this connection, the question is whether the arbitrator has a duty of disclosure in cases of serious criminality—which would prevail over his duty of confidentiality. English arbitration practitioners have raised this question, calling on the arbitration community to ensure that arbitral proceedings are not used to further criminal activities:

> [I]f the parties' trust is simply that the arbitral tribunal act as a mute observer of a criminal offence, then it should not be respected. There needs to be more reflection in this area but it seems wrong that the confidential nature of arbitral proceedings and the ultimate enforceability of an award should be open to abuse by international crime. The arbitration community must therefore be vigilant to ensure that it does not unwittingly assist such crime.[161]

724   By contrast, the ICC Working Group on Criminal Law and Arbitration came to the conclusion that it would be contrary to the parties' expectations if the arbitrators were required to disclose the offences found:

> It appeared contrary to the nature of arbitration, contrary in particular to the trust that the parties place in the arbitrator, for an arbitral tribunal to report to the authorities the offences found [...].[162]

725   We think that a balance should be found in order to avoid the use of arbitrations to further criminal activities while preserving the arbitrators' duty of confidentiality. In our opinion, the arbitrators' duty of confidentiality should remain the rule, while exceptions to this rule should be clearly provided by the applicable law.

726   Therefore, we agree with Prof. Lew's opinion that arbitrators do not have a duty of disclosure unless there are legislative rules, applicable at the seat of the arbitration

---

[158]Poudret (2004), p. 250, with further references.

[159]See above Sect. 3.3.3.2.

[160]Blackaby et al. (2015), para 5.82; Cremades and Cairns (2003), pp. 65–91; Lew (2011), pp. 113–115.

[161]Blackaby et al. (2015), para 5.86.

[162]ICC Report Working Group on Criminal Law and Arbitration (Doc 420/492).

or to the members of the tribunal, requiring the tribunal to disclose certain informa-tion to the relevant authorities.[163] Indeed, the arbitrator's role is not to investigate or to sanction crimes—like the police or courts do.[164] A tribunal has its own means to avoid the use of arbitration for furthering criminal activities. For example, if it concludes that the arbitration is a sham dispute used for money-laundering purposes, the tribunal can refuse to grant substantive relief and dismiss the claim.[165] If the tribunal finds that the contract in dispute is tainted by corruption, it can also decide that the contract is void.[166]

5.5 Intermediary Conclusions

As seen above, there are many cases when information relating to the arbitration proceedings can be disclosed. We call these cases 'exceptions' or 'limitations' to the duty of confidentiality. Some arbitration rules and national arbitration laws provide a list of such exceptions. The most common exceptions to the duty of confidentiality are: (1) disclosure is authorised or required by the law; (2) the parties have consented to the disclosure; (3) disclosure is necessary to seek professional advice; (4) the documents are no longer confidential as they are already in the public domain; (5) disclosure is necessary to pursue the parties' legitimate rights. As to the latter, this exception has a broad scope of application and has given rise to an abundant case law.   **727**

As consistently held by national courts, the parties do not violate their duty of confidentiality by disclosing the arbitral award and other arbitration materials for the purpose of recognising, enforcing or challenging an arbitral award. A party can initiate court proceedings without fear of being accused of a breach of confidential-ity, if the goal is to pursue its legitimate interests. By contrast, if a party abuses the process by bringing a frivolous claim with the purpose of disclosing confidential information, this action can be considered as a breach of the confidentiality duty. There is even a risk, as in the case *G. Aïta v. A. Ojjeh*, that a party having made a frivolous claim will be enjoined to pay damages caused to the other party as a result of the confidentiality breach.   **728**

When a party to arbitration decides to go to a court, it must be remembered that the principle of publicity and transparency generally applies in state court proceed-ings. Although some jurisdictions may treat arbitration claims with more confiden-tiality, many jurisdictions do not. Thus, when disclosed information or documents from arbitration become part of the record in court proceedings, there is a risk that confidential information can become publicly available. This means that the hearings   **729**

---

[163]Lew (2011), p. 115.
[164]Lew (2011), p. 115.
[165]Lew (2011), p. 115.
[166]Lew (2011), p. 115.

may be held publicly and that court decisions relating to arbitrations, and sometimes also the arbitration award as well as other materials related to arbitration filed in the state court proceeding, may be rendered public and/or be published.

730   As to the disclosure of arbitration materials in other arbitration or court proceedings, the main conclusion is that each case needs to be addressed in context. There are, however, some common cases when disclosure will generally be allowed. For example, the confidentiality of arbitral proceedings will not be an obstacle when the interests of justice and the public interest require disclosure of the arbitration materials.

731   English and U.S. courts differ significantly in how they treat the disclosure of arbitration materials in a court proceeding. The main reason is that English law recognises that there is an implied duty of confidentiality, while U.S. jurisdictions require an express agreement or a specific provision in the applicable arbitration rules in order to admit confidentiality. Since confidentiality is the rule in English law, a party requesting disclosure of arbitration materials from the other party must prove the necessity of such a disclosure in another proceeding. By contrast, confidentiality is not the rule in U.S. jurisdictions. Thus, the disclosure process will take place as usual unless the party resisting the disclosure is able to prove the hardship it will suffer as a result of this disclosure.

732   As to exceptions to the arbitrators' duty of confidentiality, we see that there is no uniform approach in different jurisdictions. These differences relate, in particular, to the arbitrators' duty to testify and the arbitrators' duty of disclosure in cases of serious criminality. Each situation should be resolved by referring to the applicable law and depending on the context of the specific circumstances. The arbitrators' duty of confidentiality should, however, remain the rule, while exceptions to this rule should be allowed only when they are required by the law.

733   Regarding the confidentiality of deliberations, the only exception that can be admitted is when disclosure is required by the applicable laws and regulations. A dissenting opinion should not reveal the substance of deliberations, but should only express alternative views of the facts and law. It can only be disclosed to the parties if the majority of arbitrators agree to such a disclosure.

734   Finally, we think that notwithstanding the multitude of exceptions, confidentiality of arbitration should still be the rule. Although it will be impossible to formulate all exceptions to the rule of confidentiality, a limited number of exceptions can be identified. These can be the most common cases of exceptions described above: (1) disclosure is authorised or required by the law; (2) the parties have consented to the disclosure; (3) disclosure is necessary to seek professional advice; (4) the documents are no longer confidential as they are already in the public domain; (5) disclosure is necessary to pursue the parties' legitimate rights; (6) disclosure is justified by the public interest; (7) disclosure is justified by the interests of justice. As to the implementation of these rules, each case will be resolved depending on the applicable law and in light of the specific circumstances.

Chapter 6
Remedies and Sanctions in Case of Confidentiality Breach

6.1 Introduction

We will see that a number of remedies and sanctions are available against the persons   **735**
having breached their confidentiality duties. These are, for example, confidentiality
order and injunctive relief, claim for compensation of damages, criminal and disciplinary sanctions, termination of the contract and reputational damage. We will
examine the problem of remedies and sanctions in the same order we proceeded in
the section dealing with the persons bound by a duty of confidentiality. We will
review the remedies and sanctions available against the parties, the arbitrators, the
arbitration institution, the counsel and third persons.

6.2 Remedies in Case of Confidentiality Breach by the Parties[1]

6.2.1 Confidentiality Orders[2]

A confidentiality order is an interim measure that can be granted at the request of a   **736**
party in order to preserve confidentiality regarding the arbitration. A confidentiality
order can also be issued by state courts in the form of injunctive relief. First, we will
examine who has competence to issue an order regarding confidentiality of the
arbitration. Second, we will review two cases in which a state court and an arbitral
tribunals had to grant interim measures regarding confidentiality of the arbitration
proceedings.

---

[1]For developments on the problem of the parties' obligation of confidentiality, see above Sect. 3.2.

[2]Also see above Sect. 2.5 discussing confidentiality order as a source of confidentiality obligations.

© Springer Nature Switzerland AG 2019
E. Reymond-Eniaeva, *Towards a Uniform Approach to Confidentiality of
International Commercial Arbitration*, European Yearbook of International
Economic Law 7, https://doi.org/10.1007/978-3-030-19003-3_6

6.2.1.1 Competence of Arbitral Tribunals and State Courts to Issue a Confidentiality Order

737 Both arbitral tribunals and state courts can have competence to issue confidentiality orders. The arbitral tribunal's competence is generally admitted in the arbitration literature.[3] Also, Art. 17(2)(b) of the UNCITRAL Model Law provides that the arbitral tribunal has power to order a party to

'[t]*ake action that would prevent, or refrain from taking action that is likely to cause, current or imminent harm or prejudice to the arbitral process itself*'.

Confidentiality orders prohibiting parties to disclose confidential information would fall into the scope of this provision.

738 Although the ICC Rules do not contain provisions on the parties' obligation of confidentiality, they stipulate in Art. 22(3) that the arbitral tribunal may make orders concerning the confidentiality of arbitration proceedings upon the request of any party. The SIAC Rules impose on the parties a duty of confidentiality in Rule 35. In order to provide for an efficient enforcement of this Rule, they vest an arbitral tribunal with the power '*to take appropriate measures, including issuing an order or award for sanction or costs*' if a party breaches its confidentiality obligations under this Rule.

739 In Switzerland, arbitral tribunals are vested with competence to make orders on confidentiality based on Art. 183 of the Swiss PILA, which allows arbitral tribunal to order provisional measures. Indeed, there are no restrictions as to the nature of provisional measures that can be ordered by an arbitral tribunal as long as these measures are closely related to the dispute.[4] Therefore, a tribunal can issue confidentiality orders, for example, in the form of an injunction ordering a party to refrain from making publications relating to the dispute the tribunal is to resolve.[5]

740 In England, the arbitral tribunal's competence over confidentiality disputes was established by case law. The English Court of Appeal held in the *Emmott* case that a dispute over the limits of the parties' obligation of confidentiality should ordinarily be decided by the arbitral tribunal and not by a court.[6] The reason for this is that the confidentiality duty finds its origins in the parties' agreement to arbitrate as an implied obligation.[7] There are, however, limits to what an arbitral tribunal can determine. Thus, such limits may be with regard to deciding on such exceptions to

---

[3]See, for example, Blackaby et al. (2015), para 5.28; Born (2014), p. 2813; Hwang and Chung (2010), Confidentiality in arbitration, 1 [of the electronic version]; Tjio (2009), pp. 14–15.

[4]Bucher (2011), Commentary of Art. 183 LDIP, para 2.

[5]Bucher (2011), Commentary of Art. 183 LDIP, para 3.

[6]Emmott v Wilson & Partners Limited [2008] EWCA Civ 184; Tjio (2009), pp. 14–15.

[7]Emmott v Wilson & Partners Limited [2008] EWCA Civ 184; Tjio (2009), pp. 14–15.

the confidentiality obligations as the public interest exception or on an exception for the interests of justice.[8]

The arbitral tribunal's powers are, however, limited as it cannot directly obtain a forced execution of its confidentiality order from the parties.[9] This is a reason why it can be preferable in some cases to refer a matter directly to a state court.   **741**

6.2.1.2   Cases in Which State Court and Arbitral Tribunal Issued Confidentiality Orders

The purpose of confidentiality order is to protect confidential information. A party   **742** can ask the arbitral tribunal or a state court to enjoin the other party not to disclose certain information and documents if there is an imminent threat that it will reveal confidential information regarding the arbitration. This happened, for example, in *Bleustein et autres v. Société True North et Société FCB International*[10] in a dispute opposing shareholders of a company (Publicis). The value of this company dropped as a result of disclosure of the existence of an arbitration proceeding. The Paris Commercial Court held that the defendants in this case, True North Inc. and FCB International, disclosed information in breach of their obligation of confidentiality and issued an injunction banning future disclosure:

> To prohibit to the companies True North Inc. and FCB International any communication disclosing to the public information on the existence, the content and the subject-matter of the dispute opposing them to SA Publicis, which is now subject to an arbitration, unless these companies have duly proved legal obligations to report.[11]

In another dispute between a Swiss company (the claimant) and an Italian   **743** company (the defendant) in ICC case No. 12242,[12] the defendant learnt about disclosure of the information relating to the arbitral proceedings because it was contacted by a journalist. The journalist working for a newspaper asked the defendant's representative to review a draft of an article regarding the defendant's dispute with the claimant.[13] Because the draft contained detailed information on the claims, the defendant deduced that the journalist had obtained the information from the claimant. Some of the information was erroneous and the defendant could rectify it, but it could not prevent the article from being published. On 9 July 2003, it requested that the Tribunal urgently enjoin the defendant to stop violating the confidentiality of

---

[8]Tjio (2009), pp. 14–15.

[9]Bucher (2011), Commentary of Art. 183 of LDIP, para 10.

[10]Bleustein et autres v. Société True North et Société FCB International, Tribunal de commerce de Paris (Ord. réf.), 22 February 1999, in: Rev. Arb. 2003, Issue 1, 189–194. For more details on this case, see above Sects. 3.2.3.7 and 4.2.2.3.

[11]Loose translation of Bleustein et autres v. Société True North et Société FCB International, Tribunal de commerce de Paris (Ord. réf.), 22 February 1999, in: Rev. Arb. 2003, Issue 1, p. 192.

[12]Jolivet (2011), pp. 40–42.

[13]Jolivet (2011), p. 40.

arbitral proceedings.[14] Having examined the defendant's arguments and having heard on 10 July 2013 the claimant, the Tribunal issued a Procedural Order on 11 July 2013.[15]

744   In its decision, the Tribunal came to the conclusion that the Parties were not bound by a strict duty of confidentiality such as it is established, for example, in the WIPO Rules.[16] It found, however, that confidentiality is one of the customary principles that contributed to the success of the international commercial arbitration. The Tribunal considered that Art. 20.7 of the 1998 ICC Rules, allowing the Tribunal to take measure for protecting confidential information, was a sufficient legal basis to enjoin a party to respect confidentiality of the arbitral proceedings.[17]

745   The Tribunal found that the claimant did not entirely respect its duty of discretion given that it disclosed to the press not only the fact of the ongoing arbitration, but also provided too many details on the dispute.[18] In addition, some of the information communicated by the claimant was apparently erroneous. Thus, the Tribunal held that by providing to the press too many details on the arbitration dispute, the claimant had violated the principle of confidentiality. The Tribunal invited the parties to rectify, wherever possible, the information provided to the press and to avoid in the future any disclosure of the information on the arbitral proceedings other than joint communications.[19]

6.2.2 Damages

6.2.2.1 In General

746   As in the case of any other breach of obligation, a party who suffered damages as a result of the other party's breach of confidentiality obligation should be entitled to sue the breaching party for damages. If we assume that the basis of the confidentiality obligation is contractual because flowing from an implied term in the arbitration agreement or originating from an express agreement on confidentiality, a contractual claim is available.

747   In the famous *G. Aïta v. A. Ojjeh* case,[20] the Paris Court of Appeal took a revolutionary decision when it enjoined a party to pay damages for having violated its confidentiality duty regarding the arbitration. In this case, the Court found that

---

[14]Jolivet (2011), p. 40.

[15]Jolivet (2011), pp. 40–42.

[16]Jolivet (2011), p. 42.

[17]Jolivet (2011), p. 42.

[18]Jolivet (2011), p. 42.

[19]Jolivet (2011), p. 42.

[20]G. Aïta v. A. Ojjeh, Cour d'appel de Paris (1ère Chambre suppl.), 18 February 1986, in: Rev. Arb. 1986, 583. For more details on this decision, see above Sects. 3.2.3.7 and 5.3.2.2.

confidentiality was an obligation implied in the arbitration agreement on which the parties expressly agreed.[21] The Paris Court of Appeal held that the claimant filed his motion to set aside the arbitral award in bad faith with a manifestly incompetent authority. By filing this motion, he allowed public disclosure of facts which were to be maintained confidential.[22] For these reasons, the claimant was awarded to pay FF 200,000[23] in damages and FF 20,000 for costs of the proceedings.[24]

In *G. Aïta v. A. Ojjeh*, the Paris Court of Appeal found that there was an implied **748** obligation of confidentiality flowing from the arbitration agreement. As discussed, however, in earlier sections, all jurisdictions do not recognise the existence of an implied duty of confidentiality. Therefore, for asserting a claim regarding confidentiality, it can be challenging to prove the existence of a confidentiality obligation in the absence of express agreement or express provision on confidentiality in the applicable arbitration rules or law.

In certain cases, a claim in tort could be available against a party violating its **749** confidentiality duty. Under Swiss law, for a tort liability under Art. 41 CO, the following conditions have to be met: (1) unlawful act (art. 41(1) CO) or act contrary to morality (art. 41(2) CO), (2) committed wilfully or negligently, (3) damage, and (4) causal link between the unlawful act and the damage.[25] It can be problematic though to show that the breach of confidentiality constitutes an unlawful act or an act contrary to morality. In some cases, this condition can be met.

If someone infringes one's *droits absolus*, such as property right or personality **750** right, this will constitute an unlawful act.[26] The infringement of personality rights of natural and legal persons is prohibited by Art. 28 CC. Legal persons are entitled to all personality rights for enjoyment of which it is not necessary to be a natural person.[27] Protection of the privacy of a legal person is one of the personality rights protected by Art. 28 CC.[28]

In order to provide a definition of privacy, a distinction needs to be made between **751** three areas, which were originally attributed to natural persons, but can also be extended to legal persons. These are (1) intimate personal life, (2) private life and

---

[21]G. Aïta v. A. Ojjeh, Cour d'appel de Paris (1ère Chambre suppl.), 18 February 1986, in: Rev. Arb. 1986, 584. Here is the exact wording in French of the Court's arguments: 'Qu'il est en effet de la nature même de la procédure d'arbitrage d'assurer la meilleure discrétion pour le règlement des différends d'ordre privé ainsi que les deux parties en étaient convenues'.

[22]G. Aïta v. A. Ojjeh, Cour d'appel de Paris (1ère Chambre suppl.), 18 February 1986, in: Rev. Arb. 1986, 583.

[23]Approximately, 30,000 Euros.

[24]G. Aïta v. A. Ojjeh, Cour d'appel de Paris (1ère Chambre suppl.), 18 February 1986, in: Rev. Arb. 1986, 584. According to Serge Lazareff, 200,000 Francs equaling to approximately 30,000 Euros was not sufficient to cover the injured party's damages (Lazareff 2009, p. 88).

[25]Werro (2012a), Commentary of Art. 41 CO, para 6.

[26]Werro (2012a), Commentary of Art. 41 CO, para 75.

[27]ATF 138 III 337, recital 6.1.

[28]ATF 138 III 337, recital 6.1.

(3) public life.[29] The intimate personal life area includes the information that should remain secret from everyone, except regarding persons to whom this information was specifically provided (for example, a lawyer or a doctor).[30] The private life area includes the remaining information about the private life, i.e. the information that a person shares with a restricted number of persons, such as friends and relatives.[31] As opposed to public life area, a person would not want this information to be known publicly as he wants to keep privacy of his life.[32]

752   Infringement of a personality right is, however, not always unlawful. According to Art. 28(2) CC, an infringement can be justified in three cases: if there is a consent of the person whose rights are infringed, if there is an overriding private or public interest or if such an infringement is authorised by the law.

753   Not every breach of confidentiality will be considered as an infringement of a personality right. It will be decided on a case-by-case basis, depending, in particular, on the circle of persons who became aware of the information, the type of disclosed information and how the disclosure affected the injured person. As an example, let's assume that a private bank A learns as a result of its arbitration proceeding with a private bank B that the finances of B were rather poor in 2016. A reveals this information to a newspaper which publishes it. B's difficult situation was temporary and in 2017, it completely recovered, but because of A's revelation to the press, its reputation as a stable and a reliable bank has been damaged and some of its clients left in 2017. Unless the competent authority decides that there was an overriding public or private interest in revealing this information, such a disclosure can be considered as an infringement of a personality right of B.

754   In addition, if the purpose of A's disclosure was to damage the reputation of its competitor, it may also constitute an unlawful act under Art. 2 of the Act on Unfair Competition. Also, A's disclosure committed intentionally with the purpose of injuring B's interest could be a basis for claiming damages as an act contrary to morality under Art. 41(2) CO. Although the application of this provision is very restrictive, it can be applied to the acts hurting the moral sense and committed wilfully if there is no other legal provision prohibiting such a behaviour.[33]

755   As to the specific problems related to asserting a claim for damages, difficulties may arise when attempting to prove (1) that the other party is responsible for the document's disclosure and (2) that disclosure caused a certain amount of damages.[34] As noted by Emmanuel Gaillard and John Savage, '[i]t *will never be easy to establish which party is responsible for the document's release, and it may be*

[29]ATF 138 III 337, recital 6.1.

[30]ATF 138 III 337, recital 6.1.

[31]ATF 138 III 337, recital 6.1.

[32]ATF 138 III 337, recital 6.1.

[33]Werro (2012a), Commentary of Art. 41 CO, paras 99–100; ATF 124 III 297, JdT 1999 268, recital 5.

[34]Brown (2001), p. 1016; Gaillard and Savage (1999), p. 692; Müller (2005), pp. 232–233.

difficult for the disclosing party to prove that it suffered loss as a result of any breach by its adverse party'.

Regarding the first point, confidential information can be disclosed by oral or **756** written transmission of the information. If the confidential information was disclosed in an email, a briefing note or another form allowing to have documentary evidence of such a disclosure, the leak can be easily identified. It is more problematic if the confidential information was transmitted orally, without leaving any documentary evidence.

Regarding the second point, it can be problematic to prove that (1) there was **757** quantifiable damage, (2) to demonstrate the causal link between the confidentiality breach and the suffered damage and (3) to assess the amount of the damages. In most cases, it will be very difficult to prove the damage without having an expert report.

Thus, in the case *Bleustein et autres v. Société True North et Société FCB* **758** *International*,[35] Mr Bleustein and other claimants asked the court to designate an expert to evaluate, outside of court proceedings, the impact of the press releases by True North on the share price of Publicis and thus, the amount of damages suffered by claimants, shareholders of Publicis. As explained above[36], the value of Publicis' shares dropped as a result of press releases by True North. The purpose of this request was to obtain evidence of the suffered damages, probably in preparation to future court proceedings. The court rejected this application as it considered that such an expertise was to be carried out in the proceedings on the merits.

We do not know whether such an expert report was prepared, but if it had been, **759** the role of the expert would have been to compare the value of the shares before and after the press releases. Indeed, in most legal systems, including France, Switzerland and England, the purpose of damages is to restore an injured party to the position the party was in before being harmed.[37] Thus, damages are often calculated as a difference between the state of affairs before and after the harmful event.[38] If a confidentiality breach caused a drop in the value of shares or had a negative impact on the revenues, the theory of difference can apply.

If there is no material damage which can be quantified by applying the theory of **760** difference, but reputation of a person has been damaged as a result of a confidentiality breach, can there be a compensation for non-pecuniary damage? This should be allowed by most legal systems, but it will be difficult to determine the amount of these damages. In *G. Aïta v. A. Ojjeh*, Mr Ojjeh succeeded in convincing the court that he suffered damages as a result of the confidentiality breach by Mr Aïta. Out of the claimed amount of FF 500,000, Mr Ojjeh was awarded FF 200,000, i.e. 40% of what he claimed. It is, however, not clear from the text of the decision how the court determined this amount.

---

[35]Bleustein et autres v. Société True North et Société FCB International, Tribunal de commerce de Paris (Ord. réf.), 22 February 1999, in: Rev. Arb. 2003, Issue 1, 189–194.

[36]See above Sect. 4.2.2.3.

[37]Gilliéron (2011), pp. 121–122.

[38]Gilliéron (2011), pp. 121–122.

6.2.2.2   Penalty Clause or Liquidated Damages

761   There exists, however, a legal solution allowing to avoid the problem with proving the damages. Christophe Müller suggests that the parties include in their agreement on confidentiality a penalty clause providing for a fixed amount or for a method allowing to easily determine the amount of the damages.[39] In our opinion, this could be a solution to the problem of proving the damages. A penalty clause is enforceable in Swiss law and in most civil law jurisdictions. One should be aware, however, that penalty clauses are typically unenforceable in common law jurisdictions. Thus, under English law, only a clause fixing liquidated damages can be enforced. We will examine below the regulation provided by Swiss and English laws regarding the agreements fixing in advance the amount to be paid in the event of a contract breach.

762   Swiss contract law permits the parties to enter into agreements on penalty.[40] For a creditor, agreeing on a penalty clause would usually result in two benefits. On the one hand, a creditor does not need to prove the damages. Indeed, the penalty amount must be paid even if the creditor has not suffered any loss or damage.[41] If, however, the amount of the suffered damage exceeds the penalty amount, the creditor may claim additional compensation if he can prove that the debtor is in negligent breach of his obligations.[42] Therefore, penalty clause makes it easier to remedy the harm caused by non-execution or by defective execution of a contractual obligation.[43] On the other hand, penalty clause aims to deter a debtor from the breach as he knows in advance that he will have to pay the penalty amount in case of the breach.[44]

763   Under Swiss law, the parties are free to determine the amount of the contractual penalty.[45] They can, for example, agree on a fixed amount or on a method which allows calculating the penalty amount easily.[46] By contrast, a penalty clause cannot leave it to the discretion of the creditor to fix the penalty amount.[47] The validity of a penalty clause can be contested only if its purpose is to ensure execution of unlawful or immoral undertaking, or if execution of the obligation became impossible because of the circumstance beyond the debtor's control.[48]

764   If the penalty amount is excessive, this will not affect the validity of the penalty clause, the court may only reduce the penalty amount.[49] When reducing the penalty amount, a judge must act with restraint, as the parties' autonomy should in principle

---

[39]Müller (2005), p. 233.

[40]Arts 160–163 CO.

[41]Art. 161(1) CO.

[42]Art. 161(2) CO.

[43]Mooser (2012a), Commentary of Art. 160 CO, para 2.

[44]Mooser (2012a), Commentary to Art. 160 CO, para 2.

[45]Art. 163(1) CO.

[46]Mooser (2012b), Commentary to Art. 163 CO, para 1.

[47]Mooser (2012b), Commentary to Art. 163 CO, para 1.

[48]Art. 163(2) CO.

[49]Art. 163(3) CO; Mooser, Commentary to Art. 163 CO, para 5.

be respected.[50] A judge can reduce the penalty amount only if the amount is unreasonably excessive and manifestly incompatible with the law and equity.[51] The fact that the penalty amount is higher than the amount of damages to which the creditor could have been entitled in the case of non-performance should not be a sufficient ground for reducing the penalty amount.[52]

By contrast, English law allows enforcing agreements on liquidated damages, but **765** not on penalty.[53] Thus, if the parties agree that the contract-breaker will pay a specified sum in case of a breach, English judge may qualify this sum either as a penalty (which is irrecoverable) or as liquidated damages (which are recoverable).[54]

In its landmark decision of 4 November 2015, the English Supreme Court has **766** introduced a new test for deciding when a contractual provision will be considered penal.[55] Before this decision, an agreement was enforceable if the fixed amount corresponded to a genuine pre-estimate of the likely loss.[56] If the amount was not strictly speaking a pre-estimate of the likely loss, it could still be recovered if the agreed amount was '*commercial justifiable, provided always that its dominant purpose was not to deter the other party from breach*'.[57]

Under the new rule, a contractual provision will be considered penal and therefore **767** unenforceable under English law if the contractual remedy for breach imposes a detriment on the contract-breaker out of all proportion to the innocent party's legitimate interest in enforcing the counterparty's obligations under the contract.[58] Thus, the first step is to consider whether any legitimate business interest is served and protected by the clause. If so, the second step is to examine whether the provision made for that interest is extravagant, exorbitant or unconscionable.[59]

Since this landmark decision of the English Supreme Court, the regulation in **768** England is less far apart from that of Switzerland. In both cases, the judge will have to examine whether the fixed amount is not exorbitant in view of the interest of the innocent party to enforce the counterparty's obligation. Thus, it is in the discretion of judges to decide which amount will be considered as exorbitant or unreasonably excessive. We will need to see how English judges will apply the new case law to understand whether this test is applied very differently in the two jurisdictions. As to

---

[50]Mooser (2012b), Commentary to Art. 163 CO, para 7.

[51]Mooser (2012b), Commentary to Art. 163 CO, para 7.

[52]Mooser (2012b), Commentary to Art. 163 CO, para 7.

[53]Beale (2015), para 26-178.

[54]Beale (2015), para 26-178.

[55]Cavendish Square Holding BV v Talal El Makdessi and ParkingEye Limited v Beavis [2015] UKSC 67.

[56]Beale (2015), para 26-178.

[57]Beale (2015), para 26-178, with further references.

[58]Cavendish Square Holding BV v Talal El Makdessi and ParkingEye Limited v Beavis [2015] UKSC 67, para 32.

[59]Cavendish Square Holding BV v Talal El Makdessi and ParkingEye Limited v Beavis [2015] UKSC 67, para 152.

the result of this exercise, they are still fundamentally different. If a Swiss judge finds the fixed amount unreasonably excessive, he will reduce the penalty amount. In the same situation, an English judge will qualify the contractual provision as a penalty clause and will consider it unenforceable. Consequently, the parties need to be particularly careful when fixing the amount of liquidated damages if there is a risk that English law will apply or that the clause will need to be enforced in England.

769   The parties willing to agree on a fixed amount to be paid by the party breaching its confidentiality obligation need to be aware of the differences in regulation of this issue in different jurisdictions. When fixing the amount, the parties will take into account, in particular, the type of activities they are engaged in, their revenues, the nature and value of the contract. Each party will need to decide whether confidentiality is an important point in its relations with the counterparty and how a breach of confidentiality should be sanctioned. It might be that the parties do not attribute the same importance to the obligation of confidentiality, in which case they will have to find a compromise.

6.2.3   Termination of the Arbitration Agreement

770   Breach of confidentiality could potentially be regarded as a fundamental breach of the arbitration agreement. If so, the aggrieved party will be entitled to terminate the arbitration agreement. In case it has chosen this option and provided there is no existing arbitration agreement at the time the arbitral award is rendered, such an arbitral award could be considered as void. That was the conclusion of the Stockholm City Court in the case *Bulgarian Foreign Trade Bank Ltd. v. A.I. Trade Finance Inc.*[60]

> Confidentiality comprises a basic and fundamental rule in arbitration proceedings... [B] reach of confidentiality, as a main rule, must be regarded as a fundamental breach of the arbitration agreement. The City Court does not consider that it is of any material importance what has become known concerning the arbitration proceedings or in which manner it took place.

> The breach of contract, which was thereby fundamental, constituted valid ground for Bulbank to avoid the contract. Bulbank has avoided the contract on 11 November 1997. The City Court concludes that there was no valid arbitration agreement on the date when the arbitration award was rendered. Therefore the City Court declared that award rendered on 22 December 1997 void.[61]

771   However, the Swedish Court of Appeal annulled this decision. It considered that '*a party cannot be deemed to be bound by a duty of confidentiality, unless the parties*

---

[60]Judgment of the Supreme Court of Sweden rendered in 2000 in Case N T 1881–99: The Bulbank Case, in: Stockholm Arbitration Report, Volume 2, 2000, pp. 137–147. See above Sect. 3.2.3.6 for a more detailed description of the case.

[61]Judgment of the Supreme Court of Sweden rendered in 2000 in Case N T 1881–99: The Bulbank Case, in: Stockholm Arbitration Report, Volume 2, 2000, 139–140.

have concluded an agreement concerning this.[62] Thus, it declared valid the arbitral award and overturned decision of the Stockholm City Court.[63]

This issue of the repudiatory breach of the arbitration agreement was also developed in the Singapore case *AAY and others v. AAZ AS*.[64] The High Court held that in any arbitration with a seat in Singapore, the obligation of confidentiality will apply absent the parties' express agreement on the contrary. In this case, no breach of confidentiality obligations was established. The High Court discussed, however, the possibility of a repudiatory breach for the sake of argument. As summarised by Michael Hwang and Kevin Lim: **772**

> Assuming *arguendo* that the obligation of confidentiality prohibited the disclosures referred to above, and AAZ was consequently in breach of the arbitration agreement, the court held that such breach was not repudiatory in nature, such that it had the effect of discharging the Plaintiffs from all future performance of the arbitration agreement (including the assessment of damages pursuant to the Partial Award). This was because the parties did not make confidentiality a condition of the arbitration agreement. It was also not the case that the Plaintiffs had been deprived of substantially all the benefit of the arbitration agreement.[65]

Thus, even in the presence of a confidentiality obligation and its breach, the High Court concluded that the breach of confidentiality was not repudiatory in nature because the parties did not make confidentiality a condition to the arbitration agreement, nor it caused a substantial deprivation of the benefits of the arbitration agreement to any party. We agree with the reasoning of the Singapore High Court as it seems unreasonable to allow a party to terminate the arbitration agreement whenever there is a breach of confidentiality obligations. Such a solution would result in absurd situations enabling the parties to use this mean for improper purposes. **773**

Let us briefly examine how the issue of repudiatory breach is regulated by general contract law. We will use for these purposes the regulation provided by the CISG, the UNDROIT Principles and the PECL. Although the CIGS applies only to international contracts of sale of goods, it has the benefit of expressing a general consensus on the contract law as it was ratified in 84 countries.[66] **774**

According to Art. 51(2) CISG, a seller is entitled to avoid the contract in its entirety only if the buyer's non-performance *'amounts to a fundamental breach of the contract'*. Art. 25 CISG defines the fundamental breach as follows: **775**

---

[62] Judgment of the Supreme Court of Sweden rendered in 2000 in Case N T 1881–99: The Bulbank Case, in: Stockholm Arbitration Report, Volume 2, 2000, 147.

[63] Judgment of the Supreme Court of Sweden rendered in 2000 in Case N T 1881–99: The Bulbank Case, in: Stockholm Arbitration Report, Volume 2, 2000, 147.

[64] AAY and others v AAZ AS, High Court, Suit [Y], Case No. [2009] SGHC 142, 15 June 2009.

[65] Michael Hwang and Kevin Lim, AAY and others v. AAZ AS, High Court, Suit [Y], Case No. [2009] SGHC 142, 15 June 2009, A contribution by the ITA Board of Reporters, Kluwer Law International, 6.

[66] http://www.uncitral.org/uncitral/fr/uncitral_texts/sale_goods/1980CISG_status.html, last visited on 13 September 2018.

A breach of contract committed by one of the parties is fundamental if it results in such detriment to the other party as substantially to deprive him of what he is entitled to expect under the contract, unless the party in breach did not foresee and a reasonable person of the same kind in the same circumstances would not have foreseen such a result.[67]

776   Similarly, the UNIDROIT Principles and the PECL provide that a party may terminate the contract if the other party's non-performance is fundamental.[68] The UNIDROIT Principles provide a more detailed regulation, as compared to the two other sources. They also indicate other factors, not mentioned in the CISG, that will be taken in consideration when determining whether a failure to perform an obligation amounts to a fundamental non-performance:

(c) the non-performance is intentional or reckless;

(d) the non-performance gives the aggrieved party reason to believe that it cannot rely on the party's future performance;

(e) the non-performing party will suffer disproportionate loss as a result of the preparation or performance if the contract is terminated.[69]

777   If we apply some of the above-mentioned provisions by analogy, a party to an arbitration should be entitled to avoid the arbitration agreement if (1) the other party breached its confidentiality obligation intentionally or recklessly, (2) this violation gives the aggrieved party reason to believe that it cannot rely on the adversary party's future performance or (3) violation of the confidentiality obligation substantially deprives the aggrieved party of what it was entitled to expect under the arbitration agreement. Thus, any breach of the duty of confidentiality cannot be regarded as a fundamental breach. To be considered as fundamental, we take a view that a breach of confidentiality needs to meet at least one of the three above-mentioned conditions.

778   In which case a party to an arbitration can be considered to be substantially deprived of what it was entitled to expect under the arbitration agreement? In our opinion, it should be the case if the parties have agreed to make confidentiality a condition of the arbitration agreement. Also, the competent authority can deduce that confidentiality was an essential obligation for the execution of an arbitration agreement by having recourse to the contract interpretation rules. The fundamental breach should, however, be construed narrowly to avoid that the parties have abusive or excessive recourse to the avoidance of contract.[70]

---

[67] Art. 25 of the CISG.

[68] Art. 7.3.1(1) UNIDROIT Principles and Art. 9:301(1) PECL.

[69] Art. 7.3.1(2) of the UNIDROIT Principles.

[70] Liu (2005), point 6.

Therefore, we think that breach of confidentiality obligations can result in **779** repudiation of the arbitration agreement only if the parties agreed that confidentiality was a condition to the arbitration agreement or if there are other serious reasons to believe that such a breach results in a substantial deprivation of the benefits of the arbitration agreement to any party. The parties can also expressly agree on a remedy in their confidentiality clause by specifying, for example, that in the case of confidentiality breach by one of the parties, the other party is entitled to terminate the arbitration agreement.

Another important point is that termination of the arbitration agreement will take **780** effect only for the future. This means that a possible termination of the arbitration agreement will only prevent commencement or continuation of the pending arbitration proceedings. Since avoidance does not have a retroactive effect, it should not be possible to annul an arbitral award based on the confidentiality breach. In any case, we think that annulment of the arbitral award is a too drastic measure and that it is disproportionate to the purpose it intends to achieve.

6.2.4   Other Remedies

In addition to other available remedies, an arbitral tribunal can take into account **781** confidentiality breach by any of the parties when allocating the arbitration costs. Tribunal's power to allocate the arbitration costs depending on the parties' conduct during the proceedings is recognised, for example, in Art. 38 of the ICC Rules:

> 4) The final award shall fix the costs of the arbitration and decide which of the parties shall bear them or in what proportion they shall be borne by the parties.
>
> 5) In making decision as to costs, the arbitral tribunal may take into account such circumstances as it considers relevant, including the extent to which each party has conducted the arbitration in an expeditious and cost-effective manner.

Therefore, if a tribunal finds that any of the parties delayed the proceedings by **782** revealing confidential information from the proceedings, it can penalize the party having breached its confidentiality duty by obliging it to pay a more significant part of the arbitration costs.[71]

---

[71]Lew (2013), Confidentiality in Arbitrations in England, para 21–35.

6.3   Remedies and Sanctions in Case of Confidentiality Breach by Arbitrators

783   If arbitrators are bound by a duty of confidentiality regarding the arbitration they need to adjudicate, there should be remedies and sanctions for the breach of their duty. A competent state court can issue an injunctive relief against an arbitrator to prohibit disclosure of confidential information. In some jurisdictions, arbitrators can face criminal sanctions if they breach their professional duty of confidentiality. For example, the French Criminal Code provides in Art. 226-13 that a person having disclosed the confidential information that was entrusted to him because of his profession or temporary mission will be punished by one-year in prison and a EUR 15,000 fine.[72] By contrast, the Swiss Criminal Code provision on violation of the professional obligation of confidentiality, Art. 321 of the Swiss Criminal Code, does not apply to arbitrators.[73] Indeed, the list of persons subject to the professional obligation of confidentiality is exhaustive and cannot be extended to other persons. Art. 321 of the Swiss Criminal Code mentions lawyers, but when a lawyer acts as an arbitrator, this type of activity is not covered by this provision.[74]

784   Where the duty of confidentiality is breached, a *contract claim* is available to the parties because the nature of their relationship with the arbitrators is contractual.[75] In some jurisdictions, such as England and the U.S. jurisdictions, however, arbitrators benefit from an arbitral immunity, which protects them from all or some civil liability claims regarding their activities accomplished under the arbitrators' mandate.[76]

785   As discussed above, the arbitrator's duty of confidentiality exists not only vis-à-vis the parties, but also vis-à-vis the witnesses, as well as his colleagues arbitrators on the panel. While an arbitrator does not have a contractual relationship with the witnesses, the question is less clear-cut regarding the relationship between arbitrators-members of the same panel. As discussed above, we think that there is a contractual relationship between arbitrators-members of the arbitral tribunal.[77] In our opinion, the arbitrators-members of the same panel form a partnership that could be qualified under Swiss law as a contract of *société simple*.[78] The duty of confidentiality is an extension of the duty of loyalty that the partners of a *société simple* owe to each other.[79] Thus, if an arbitrator discloses information on deliberations outside of

---

[72]Loquin (2015), L'arbitrage du commerce international, para 327.

[73]Ritz (2007), p. 187.

[74]Jeandin (2011), CPC commenté, Art. 166 para 11; Jolles et al. (2013), pp. 140–141.

[75]Gaillard and Savage (1999), p. 598; Schöldström (1998), pp. 25–27; Furrer (2008), p. 811; Jolles et al. (2013), pp. 136–137.

[76]Smahi (2016), Part I, 890–894.

[77]See above Sect. 3.3.3.2.

[78]Arts 530–531 CO.

[79]TF 4A_619/2011, 20.03.2012, recital 3.6; Philippin (2013), p. 125.

the panel thus causing harm to his colleagues on the panel, they are in principle entitled to file a contractual claim.

If a contract claim filed against an arbitrator by a party or by a colleague arbitrator **786** is successful, generally available legal remedies are termination of the contract and compensation for damages. The latter is also available in case of a successful tort claim. For example, under Swiss law, a breach of confidentiality by an arbitrator can result in a claim for damages based on Arts 97 ff (bad performance of the contract) and Arts 41 ff (tort liability) CO.[80] A tort claim can be available,[81] in particular, if the arbitrator violates one's personality rights by disclosing confidential information. As discussed above,[82] under Swiss law, protection of the privacy of a person is one of the personality rights protected by Art. 28 CC.[83]

In addition, a person whose personality rights have been or can be unlawfully **787** infringed can also request an injunction to stop or prevent a harmful disclosure based on Art. 28 CC. As to criminal liability and disciplinary sanctions, there are none under Swiss law. Indeed, arbitrators are not under the supervision of the state, nor do they have the status of officials.[84]

Regarding a claim for compensation of damages, it must be emphasized that **788** many arbitration rules contain provisions limiting arbitrators' liability. Thus, Art. 31.1 of the LCIA Rules excludes arbitrators' liability for any act or omission. However, this exclusion of the arbitrator's liability does not apply if (1) the wrongdoing is intentional or (2) if such limitation of liability is prohibited by any applicable law. Similarly, Art. 40 of the ICC Rules provides that arbitrators shall not be liable to any person for any act or omission unless such limitation of liability is prohibited by applicable law.

Some agreements also tend to exclude any contractual liability. However, some **789** national laws consider such contracts void in case of gross negligence or deliberate wrongdoing. For example, an agreement excluding liability for unlawful intent or gross negligence in advance is regarded as void in accordance with Art. 100(1) CO. In line with Art. 100(1) CO, Art. 45(1) of the Swiss Rules excludes liability of arbitrators unless the act or omission is shown to constitute intentional wrongdoing or gross negligence.

Finally, reputational damage is a very efficient sanction against breaching the **790** duty of confidentiality, even if it is a non-legal sanction. Given the growth in media coverage and the use of social media tools, the name of an arbitrator having breached his confidentiality duty will likely become publicly known - at least among professionals working in arbitration.

---

[80]Ritz (2007), p. 187; Jolles et al. (2013), p. 141.

[81]See above Sect. 6.2.2.1 regarding in particular the conditions to be met for a tort liability under Swiss law.

[82]See above Sect. 6.2.2.1 discussing the protection of personality rights.

[83]ATF 138 III 337, recital 6.1.

[84]Ritz (2007), p. 187.

6.4 Remedies in Case of Confidentiality Breach by Arbitration Institution

791 As discussed above, the nature of relationship between the parties and the relevant arbitration institution is contractual. The following legal consequences may result from the fact that there is a contractual relationship between the parties and the relevant arbitration institution.

792 *First*, if we admit that confidentiality is an obligation the performance of which is important for the existing contractual relationship, the parties should be entitled to terminate their contract with the relevant arbitration institution in case of a confidentiality breach. It can indeed be argued that by violating its duty of confidentiality the arbitration institution breaches the relationship of confidence necessary to maintain the contract with the parties. Since confidentiality is one of the reasons why the parties decided to use the relevant arbitration institution, violation of confidentiality appears to be a fundamental breach of the contract.

793 *Second*, there is a possibility to enforce the contractual obligation of confidentiality by requiring a competent court to issue an injunction.

794 *Third*, if one of the parties suffered losses as a result of the confidentiality breach, such a party can sue the arbitration institution for damages under a contractual claim. A possibility to seek for damages can also be available under a tort claim.[85]

795 It is, however, important to bear in mind that most institutional rules contain a limitation of liability clause. Thus, Art. 40 of the ICC Rules excludes the liability of the Court and its members, the ICC and its employees for any act or omission in connection with the arbitration, '*except to the extent such limitation of liability is prohibited by applicable law.*' As discussed above in the section dealing with the arbitrators' liability,[86] the limitation of liability clauses will be interpreted in accordance with the rules of the applicable law, which will in most cases prohibit limitation of liability in the case of intentional wrongdoing and gross negligence.

796 Finally, since arbitration institutions do not exercise an activity supervised and regulated by the state, disciplinary or criminal sanctions are generally not available against them.

---

[85]See above Sect. 6.2.2.1 discussing some aspects of tort liability under Swiss law.

[86]See above Sect. 6.3.

6.5   Remedies and Sanctions in Case of Confidentiality Breach by Counsel

The lawyer breaching his professional secrecy may be subject, in addition to the client's claim for compensation of damages, to criminal and disciplinary sanctions. In France, for example, a lawyer breaching his confidentiality duties may be subject to imprisonment of one year and a fine of EUR 15,000.[87]   **797**

In Switzerland, professional secrecy is mainly imposed by two legal provisions, Art. 321 of the Criminal Code and Art. 13 LLCA.[88] While both provisions sanction the breach of professional secrecy by a lawyer, their *ratione personae* scope is different. As set out earlier,[89] under Art. 321 of the Criminal Code, lawyers practising in the framework of a monopoly, legal counsel (*avocats-conseil*) and foreign lawyers are subject to sanction, but not in-house lawyers. The scope of Art. 13 LLCA is more restricted as it includes only the lawyers practising in the framework of a monopoly.[90]   **798**

Art. 321 of the Swiss Criminal Code stipulates that the breach of professional secrecy offence will be punished by imprisonment of up to 3 years or a pecuniary sanction.[91] The lawyer is liable only if he committed the offence wilfully and if there is a complaint from the person to whom the lawyer owes his professional duty of secrecy.[92] If a lawyer violates Art. 13 LLCA, he can be subject to disciplinary sanctions that vary from a formal warning notice to a permanent ban on practising law, depending, in particular, on the seriousness of the fault.[93] Disciplinary sanctions can also be imposed by the lawyers' cantonal bar associations on their members.[94]   **799**

If the lawyer's breach of confidentiality caused the party he is representing to suffer loss, such a party can seek to be compensated in damages by asserting a contractual claim. If there is no contractual relationship with the lawyer, in certain cases, a tort claim can also be available to a person having suffered damages as a result of the lawyer's breach of confidentiality.[95] Under Swiss law, a tort claim can be brought by a person who has suffered harm as a result of his personality rights violation by a lawyer who wrongly disclosed information that was accessible before   **800**

---

[87]Art. 226-13 of the French Criminal Code.

[88]For more details, see above Sect. 3.5.4.2.1.

[89]See above Sect. 3.5.4.2.3.

[90]See above Sect. 3.5.4.2.3.

[91]Art. 321 of the Swiss Criminal Code.

[92]Arts 321 and 12(1) of the Swiss Criminal Code; Maurer and Gross (2010), p. 210.

[93]Art. 17 LLCA; Maurer and Gross (2010), p. 211.

[94]Art. 31 of the Swiss Code of Deontology.

[95]Under Swiss law, for example, provisions on contractual and tort liability can be found in Arts 97 ff (bad performance of the contract), Arts 394 ff (agency contract), Art. 41 (tort liability) CO and in Arts 27–28 CC (tort liability for violation of personality rights). See above Sect. 6.2.2.1 discussing the conditions to be met for a tort liability.

to a restricted group of persons.[96] A party can also terminate its contract with the lawyer in case of a confidentiality breach as the relationship of confidence is essential for the contractual relationship between a party and his lawyer. Finally, there is a possibility to request a competent state court to issue an injunction prohibiting the lawyer to disclose confidential documents and information.

801   As to the breach of confidentiality regarding persons other than the client, as discussed before, a lawyer does not have a direct relationship with them as long as he acts on behalf of his client.[97] In other cases, although a lawyer has no contractual relationship with the adverse party, the arbitrators or other persons involved in an arbitration proceeding, he is obviously not allowed to violate these persons' personality rights by disclosing confidential documents or information.

6.6 Remedies in Case of Confidentiality Breach by Third Persons[98]

802   As we demonstrated above,[99] in some cases, a contract can be the basis for a duty of confidentiality for third persons, such as secretary to the arbitral tribunal, fact witnesses, expert witnesses appointed by the parties or by the tribunal, translators and interpreters, court reporters, etc. In this case, a third person can be sued for damages if he violates his contractual obligation of confidentiality causing thus damages to his contractual counterparty. Also, if the confidentiality obligation was essential for performance of the contract, there is a possibility to terminate the contract with a third person. In addition to contractual claim, a claim in tort[100] can also be available against a third person which caused harm by revealing confidential information.

803   Regarding damages, on the basis of a contractual or a tort claim, it can, however, be problematic to prove the exact amount of the damages and the causal link between the disclosure of the confidential information and the suffered damages. Finally, a competent state court can issue an injunction prohibiting to a third person to disclose confidential information.

---

[96]Art. 41 (tort liability) CO and Arts 27–28 CC (tort liability for violation of personality rights). For more details on protection of personality rights, see above Sect. 6.2.2.1.

[97]See above Sect. 3.5.1.

[98]For the remedies which are common in case of confidentiality breach by third persons and by the parties, see above Sect. 6.2.

[99]See above Sect. 3.6.

[100]See above Sect. 6.2.2.1 discussing some aspects of tort liability under Swiss law.

6.7 Intermediary Conclusions

A number of remedies are available against the persons breaching their confidentiality duty with regard to arbitration proceedings. *First*, it would be common to call for an order on confidentiality to stop or prevent a breach of confidentiality. An arbitral tribunal has power to issue a confidentiality order, which will be binding upon the parties. As arbitral tribunal does not have competence to issue a binding order upon arbitrators, arbitration institutions, counsel and third persons, an injunction prohibiting disclosure of confidential information needs to be issued by a competent state court. **804**

Second, the injured person can seek compensation for damages on the basis of a contractual or a tort claim. One should, however, be aware that some institutional rules contain clauses limiting liability of the relevant arbitration institution and the arbitrators adjudicating the relevant case. It can also be difficult to prove the fact of having suffered certain damages and the measure of these damages. There is, however, at least one known court case, *G. Aïta v. A. Ojjeh* case, where such damages were successfully awarded. **805**

Third, national laws can provide for criminal and disciplinary sanctions on the lawyers violating their statutory obligations of confidentiality regarding their client's affairs. While the lawyer's activity is ordinarily regulated and supervised by the state, it is not always the case with regard to arbitrators. Criminal and disciplinary sanctions against the arbitrators exist only in some jurisdictions. **806**

Fourth, there is a possibility to terminate the contract where confidentiality is an essential obligation for performance of the contract. There is an anxiety over a possibility of termination of the arbitration agreement and annulment of the arbitral award since the decision of the Stockholm City Court in the case *Bulgarian Foreign Trade Bank Ltd. v. A.I. Trade Finance Inc.*[101] This decision was, however, annulled by the Swedish Court of Appeal which declared valid the arbitral award because it considered that there could not be a duty of confidentiality in the absence of a parties' express agreement. **807**

In our opinion, breach of confidentiality obligations can result in repudiation of the arbitration agreement only if the parties agreed that confidentiality was a condition to the arbitration agreement or if there are other serious reasons to believe that such a breach results in a substantial deprivation of the benefits of the arbitration agreement to any party. Even if a confidentiality breach results in termination of the arbitration agreement, this should not provoke annulment of the arbitral award. Indeed, termination of the arbitration agreement should take effect only for the future. **808**

---

[101] Judgment of the Supreme Court of Sweden rendered in 2000 in Case N T 1881–99: The Bulbank Case, in: Stockholm Arbitration Report, Volume 2, 2000, pp. 137–147. See above Sects. 3.2.3.6 and 6.2.3 for a more detailed description of the case.

809   *Fifth*, the arbitral tribunal can penalize the party having breached its confidentiality duty, if such a breach has delayed or hindered the proceedings, by obliging it to pay a more significant part of the arbitration costs.

810   *Finally*, although it is not a legal remedy, it should be remembered that there is a risk of reputation damages for counsel and arbitrators.

811   The issue of remedies in case of a confidentiality breach is mostly problematic with regard to the parties. The difficulty for the courts and tribunals is to find a remedy which would be sufficiently severe to dissuade the parties from disclosing confidential information. Annulment of the arbitral award seems to us a too drastic measure, disproportionate to the purpose it intends to achieve. It can also be counterproductive if the losing party breaches its confidentiality duty and can thus walk away from its responsibilities. In order to encourage the parties to respect their mutual confidentiality obligations and to avoid the problem of finding an adequate remedy, the parties can agree on contractual remedies in case of breach of confidentiality obligations. This can be done, for example, in the main contract alongside the arbitration and confidentiality clauses.

812   Thus, one solution for the parties would be to fix in advance the amount to be paid in the event of a contract breach. Such a clause would have the benefit of resolving the problem of proving the amount of the suffered damages. In addition, this amount would be adapted to the parties' financial situation and their expectations as to what they are ready to pay. The parties should, however, be cautious as penalty clauses are generally unenforceable in common law jurisdictions.

Chapter 7
Possibility of Uniform Rules on Confidentiality

7.1 Introduction

Confidentiality of international commercial arbitration is one of the most controversial topics in arbitration. Our analysis has shown, however, that not all aspects of confidentiality are controversial. The two main controversial issues are: (1) the existence of parties' implied duty of confidentiality; and (2) publication of arbitral awards. In the present section, we will first demonstrate that a consensus is possible on both issues. Second, we will propose a solution in the form of uniform rules on confidentiality. The purpose of such rules would be to ensure legal predictability and increase transparency of arbitration.   **813**

7.2 Consensus on Confidentiality Is Possible

7.2.1 Parties' Implied Duty of Confidentiality and the Myriad of Exceptions

Legal practice varies in different countries, and legal scholars are greatly divided on whether the parties to an arbitration are bound by a duty of confidentiality in the absence of specific regulation and express agreement on confidentiality. Based on an analysis of regulation in several jurisdictions, we have seen that the existence of an implied duty of confidentiality is undisputed in England and Singapore; denied in Sweden, the U.S. and Australia (if the parties opt-out from the AIAA confidentiality provisions and in the absence of express agreement on confidentiality); and still   **814**

© Springer Nature Switzerland AG 2019
E. Reymond-Eniaeva, *Towards a Uniform Approach to Confidentiality of International Commercial Arbitration*, European Yearbook of International Economic Law 7, https://doi.org/10.1007/978-3-030-19003-3_7

under discussion in France and in Switzerland.[1] What are the reasons for this divergence?

815   *First*, there are historical reasons. In our opinion, lawmakers in the countries where arbitration is commonly used missed some historical opportunities to introduce rules on confidentiality of arbitration, subject to a number of exceptions. This would have stopped the debate over the existence of an implied duty of confidentiality and could have thus prevented the Australian and Swedish courts from ruling against confidentiality in the famous *Esso/BHP and Bulbank* decisions.

816   Thus, in the *Esso/BHP* case,[2] when denying the existence of an implied duty of confidentiality, the Australian High Court reasoned, in particular: (1) that there was no decision supporting the existence of an obligation of confidence in Australia and in the U.S.; (2) that legal scholars and practitioners had conflicting views on whether the parties were bound by an obligation of confidentiality; and (3) that if a confidentiality obligation had formed part of the law, one would have expected it to be recognised long before the English High Court decision in *Dolling-Baker*.[3] Similarly, in the *Bulbank* decision, when denying the existence of an implied duty of confidentiality, the Supreme Court of Sweden reasoned that there was no clear and well-founded view on the duty of confidentiality either in Sweden or elsewhere.[4]

817   *Second*, there is a practical reason for the divergence in legal practice on confidentiality. Jurists are apparently reluctant to recognise the existence of a duty of confidentiality because they find it hard to determine exceptions to the duty of confidentiality. Indeed, there appear to be a wide range of possible exceptions to the duty of confidentiality. Thus, when the issue of including an obligation of confidentiality to the Arbitration Act 1996 was discussed in England, such codification was considered premature because of an important number of possible exceptions to the general principle of confidentiality.[5] Similarly, the Singapore High Court explained that the absence of a provision on obligation of confidentiality was due, in particular, to the existence of many exceptions to the duty of confidentiality.[6] In the Australian *Esso/BHP* case, when denying the existence of an implied duty of confidentiality, the High Court reasoned that complete confidentiality could not be achieved, particularly because an arbitration award may be subject to judicial

---

[1]See above Sects. 3.2.3 and 3.2.4.3.3

[2]See above Sect. 3.2.3.4 for a detailed analysis of the case.

[3]Esso Australia Resources Ltd. and Others v. Sidney James Plowman and Others, Arbitration International, Volume 11 No. 3, 1995, 243-244. The Australian High Court referred to an English High Court decision Dolling-Baker v. Merrett [1990] 1 WLR 1205.

[4]Judgment of the Supreme Court of Sweden rendered in 2000 in Case N T 1881-99: The Bulbank Case, in: Stockholm Arbitration Report, Volume 2, 2000, p. 147. See above Sects. 3.2.3.6 and 6.2.3 for a detailed analysis of the case.

[5]Report on the Arbitration Bill, in Merkin and Flannery (2014), pp. 433–444.

[6]AAY and others v AAZ AS, High Court, Suit [Y], Case No. [2009] SGHC 142, 15 June 2009, 54. See above Sect. 3.2.3.3.

review, and because there may be other circumstances allowing a party to disclose information regarding the arbitration to a third party.[7]

In our opinion, if exceptions to the duty of confidentiality had been clearly identified sooner, this could have allowed state courts to admit the existence of an implied duty of confidentiality in the Australian *Esso/BHP* case and in the French *Nafimco* case.[8] In *Esso/BHP*, the Australian High Court could have affirmed the existence of an implied duty of confidentiality while recognising a public interest exception. In *Nafimco*, the Paris Court of Appeal could have held in favour of the existence of an implied duty of confidentiality while holding that a party was allowed to disclose certain arbitration materials to pursue its legitimate rights.   **818**

7.2.2   Confidentiality Is Not an Obstacle to Publication of Arbitral Awards

Jurists also differ over publication of arbitral awards. This lack of consensus appears to be an obstacle to a uniform regulation on confidentiality of arbitration proceedings. Some legal scholars argue that confidentiality of arbitration is not compatible with the general tendency towards transparency and that confidentiality contradicts the principle of openness of court proceedings.[9] Significantly, in the UNCITRAL Model Law, the question of confidentiality was intentionally left open with regard to publication of the arbitration awards, in order to avoid regulation of an overly controversial issue.[10]   **819**

Notably, Norwegian lawmakers included a provision on non-confidentiality of arbitration[11] in the Norwegian Arbitration Act because they wanted to provide more transparency to arbitral proceedings through publication of awards when the Act was revised in 2004. In the end, the ultimately-adopted text went even further, stipulating non-confidentiality of arbitral proceedings as a general principle.[12]   **820**

In our opinion, publication of awards revealing the names of the parties should be allowed only with the parties' consent, or if there is a legitimate reason for such publication. On the contrary, as discussed above, publication of awards in a form that does not allow the parties to be identified should be generally allowed.[13]   **821**

---

[7]Esso Australia Resources Ltd. and Others v. Sidney James Plowman and Others, Arbitration International, Volume 11 No. 3, 1995, 244.

[8]See above Sect. 3.2.3.7 for more details on this case.

[9]See, for example, Fernandez-Armesto (2012), p. 583; Müller (2005), pp. 233–234.

[10]Rapport du Secrétaire général sur les éléments éventuels de la Loi type sur l'arbitrage commercial international, Annuaire de la Commission des Nations Unies pour les droit commercial international, Volume XII, 1981, deuxième partie, 95–96.

[11]Art. 5(1) of the Norwegian Arbitration Act.

[12]Nisja (2008), p. 190.

[13]See above Sects. 4.4.5.3.1 and 4.4.6.

7.3 Towards a Uniform Approach Through Harmonization of National Arbitration Laws

822   As we have shown above, the main controversial issues on confidentiality of arbitration proceedings can be resolved. In other words, a uniform approach to confidentiality is possible. It would benefit all arbitration users and, more generally, the general public—by increasing legal predictability and transparency of arbitration.

823   According to certain authors, confidentiality should be dealt with in arbitration rules rather than in a Model Law.[14] We disagree with this opinion. In our view, introducing a provision on confidentiality in a Model Law would undoubtedly be a step forward. Moreover, in our opinion, the most efficient way of moving towards a uniform approach on confidentiality would be to adopt rules on confidentiality in national arbitration laws. This is so for three reasons:

1. This will end the debate on the existence of an implied duty of confidentiality.
2. Arbitration rules do not apply to all arbitrations.
3. Arbitration rules do not apply to third parties.

824   *First,* if a rule on confidentiality is contained in national arbitration law, this will put an end to the debate on the existence of an implied duty of confidentiality. There would be a specific provision having a binding legal effect on all persons involved in arbitration proceedings.

825   *Second,* unlike provisions on confidentiality in arbitration rules, provisions on confidentiality in national arbitration laws would apply to all arbitrations. Provisions on confidentiality in institutional arbitration rules would not ensure a uniform approach, as they would not apply to *ad hoc* arbitrations. Introducing provisions on confidentiality into non-institutional arbitration rules, such as the UNCITRAL Arbitration Rules, would not guarantee a uniform approach either, as not all arbitrations are regulated by arbitration rules. By contrast, every arbitration will necessarily be governed by some national law.

826   *Third,* institutional arbitration rules have a binding effect only on the parties, on the arbitration institutions, and on arbitrators. National arbitration laws, as the *lex arbitri,* would also have a binding effect on counsel and on third parties, such as fact and expert witnesses, third party funders, interpreters, and court reporters. Introducing rules on confidentiality to national arbitration laws would thus resolve the problem of third parties' duty of confidentiality. Indeed, as explained above, in the absence of an express provision on confidentiality, there are not many sources which can impose a duty of confidentiality on third parties, e.g., on witnesses in an arbitration.[15] Parties' representatives should, however, be required to inform the

---

[14]Sanders (2005), pp. 456, 476; Dimolitsa (2009), p. 13.
[15]See above Sect. 3.6.3.4.

third parties involved in arbitration proceedings of their duty of confidentiality. This should be done at the very first contact with the third parties.

Therefore, if every jurisdiction makes an effort to adopt provisions on confiden-   **827** tiality, and if these provisions have a similar content, this will result in a more uniform approach to confidentiality. While globalization of arbitration procedure is not a goal in itself, harmonization of rules on confidentiality appears to be necessary. According to Gabrielle Kaufmann-Kohler, globalization of arbitration procedure materialises principally through national arbitration laws:

> The globalization of arbitration occurs primarily under the auspices of national arbitration laws, in a classical fashion. Globalization is made possible thanks to the freedom that various national legislation grants to the parties and to the arbitrators.[16]

At the same time, this author emphasizes that national arbitration laws should   **828** give enough freedom to the parties and to the arbitrators. While we think that all legislators should aim to have a uniform approach on confidentiality, the rule on confidentiality should be non-mandatory. The parties should be free to derogate from this rule and agree on a non-confidentiality regime regarding any aspect of their arbitration. Also, we do not think that this harmonization process should extend to the regulation of remedies in case of a confidentiality breach. In our opinion, the issue of remedies should be resolved by national legislators according to the particularities of each legal system.

How will this harmonisation process occur, and is it at all realistic? We think that   **829** the process will advance, albeit slowly. The issue of confidentiality is often raised when national arbitration laws are revised, which occurs regularly. If provisions on confidentiality are introduced into the UNCITRAL Model Law the next time it is revised, for example, this will guide and inspire lawmakers in revising national arbitration laws. This will certainly take time. However, if at least the most commonly used arbitration jurisdictions adopt provisions on confidentiality, the risk of legal uncertainty will significantly decrease. This will be a big step towards adopting a uniform approach with regard to confidentiality of arbitration.

As demonstrated by the Australian example, notwithstanding the existence of   **830** common law rules denying an implied duty of confidentiality, it is possible to rule in favour of confidentiality in national arbitration law. Thus, the way to move forward should be towards greater confidentiality and this can be achieved through introducing confidentiality provisions into national arbitration law.

With regard to Swiss law, we think that proposed rules on confidentiality can be   **831** introduced into Chapter 12 of the Swiss Private International Law Act. The proposed provisions are compatible with the Swiss Rules and, in particular, with Art. 25(6) on confidentiality of hearings and Art. 44 on confidentiality of arbitration proceedings. Even if the parties choose arbitration rules which provide that the arbitration proceedings are not confidential, they would still be compatible with the amended Swiss

---

[16]Kaufmann-Kohler (2003), p. 1333.

PILA as the proposed provisions are of non-mandatory nature and the parties can derogate from them.

7.4 Proposed Text for the Rules on Confidentiality

832 As to specific language for the rules on confidentiality to be introduced into national arbitration laws, we propose the following text:

1. Persons Bound by the Duty of Confidentiality
The parties, the arbitrators, the secretary of the arbitral tribunal, the arbitration institution and its members and the staff, the fact and expert witnesses, the party representatives and their auxiliaries, third party funders and any other third persons having access to the information and documents relating to the arbitration shall be bound by a duty of confidentiality.

2. Scope of the Duty of Confidentiality
The duty of confidentiality will extend to (1) all information relating to the arbitration, including the existence of an arbitration, (2) all documents submitted or produced by a party or non-party in the arbitration, to which the person wishing to disclose the document had access only because of the arbitration and (3) all awards and orders.

3. Confidentiality of Hearings

1. All hearings shall be held in private, unless access is allowed by the arbitral tribunal.
2. All documents and information surrounding hearings, including any notes made by the arbitral tribunal of oral evidence or submission given before the arbitral tribunal and any transcript of oral evidence or submissions given before the arbitral tribunal, are subject to confidentiality.

4. Exceptions to the Duty of Confidentiality

1. Disclosure of confidential information and documents is permitted if (1) disclosure is authorised or required by the law; (2) the parties have consented to the disclosure; (3) disclosure is necessary to seek legal, accounting or other professional services; (4) the documents are in the public domain; (5) disclosure is necessary to pursue the parties' legitimate rights; (6) disclosure is justified by the public interest; (7) disclosure is justified by the interests of justice.
2. In cases other than those mentioned under 7.4(1), the arbitral tribunal, after giving each of the parties an opportunity to be heard, may allow disclosure of confidential information and confidential documents where there is a demonstrated need to disclose that outweighs any party's legitimate interest in preserving confidentiality.
3. The disclosure shall be limited to what is reasonably required to serve the purpose justifying such a disclosure.

5. Publication of Arbitral Awards

1. Publication of arbitral awards is allowed only with the consent of the parties.
2. Such consent is not necessary if the award is published with the names of the parties and other identifying information redacted.

6. Non-mandatory Nature of Confidentiality Provisions

Unless the parties agree otherwise in writing, Arts 1 to 5 apply to every arbitration for which the place of arbitration is, or would be, state X.

Chapter 8
Conclusions

We can now summarise our main recommendations on how to approach confiden-   **833**
tiality of arbitration. We hope that these ideas will help overcome the lack of
consensus between different legal systems and within the arbitration community.

8.1 Persons Bound by a Duty of Confidentiality

The parties' duty of confidentiality is the most controversial category of persons   **834**
involved in arbitration proceedings. There is no agreement on whether the parties are
bound by a duty of confidentiality in the absence of an express legal or contractual
basis. This divergence results in a significant risk of legal uncertainty for the parties
to an arbitration proceeding. Therefore, we think it would be more judicious to have
a uniform approach on the parties' obligation of confidentiality in most, if not all
jurisdictions.

In our opinion, this uniform approach should be based on universally recognising   **835**
the parties' duty of confidentiality. Indeed, we have seen that denying confidentiality
might have a negative impact on attractiveness of arbitration as one of the reasons the
parties submit their dispute to arbitration is because they believe it to be confidential.
A complete confidentiality can obviously not be achieved, but this does not mean
that confidentiality cannot be the rule, subject to certain exceptions.

There is much less controversy regarding the duty of obligation owed by arbitra-   **836**
tors, arbitration institutions and counsel. Their duty of confidentiality will in most
cases exist due to the duty of discretion owed to the parties, which is in turn due to
the existence of a contractual relationship. Moreover, as for counsel's duty of
confidentiality, a lawyer's activity is generally regulated by the state, and so domestic law rules on a lawyer's professional conduct will regulate his duty of
confidentiality.

© Springer Nature Switzerland AG 2019   217
E. Reymond-Eniaeva, *Towards a Uniform Approach to Confidentiality of
International Commercial Arbitration*, European Yearbook of International
Economic Law 7, https://doi.org/10.1007/978-3-030-19003-3_8

837   Confidentiality provisions which can be contained in arbitration rules are not directly binding on third persons having access to the information and documents relating to arbitration proceedings, such as fact and expert witnesses, third party funders, arbitral tribunal's secretary, court reporters and interpreters. For this reason, our recommendation here is that an agreement on confidentiality be entered into with any third person to whom information or documents relating to an arbitration are provided. *De lege ferenda*, we also propose to impose, in *national arbitration laws*, a duty of confidentiality on parties, arbitrators, arbitration institutions, counsel and all third persons having access to information and documents relating to arbitration.

8.2   Content of the Duty of Confidentiality

838   More generally, we recommend that the content of the duty of confidentiality should be broad. It should cover: (i) all information relating to the arbitration, including the fact of existence of the arbitration; (ii) all documents submitted or produced by a party or non-party in the arbitration; (iii) all awards and orders; and (iv) information and documents surrounding hearings. In the context of this recommendation for broad coverage, we would like to make four specific points.

839   *First*, regarding the information relating to the arbitration, we think that the parties should be protected from bad faith disclosures, i.e., from disclosure of any information regarding the arbitration by one party aiming to cause damage to the other party. This will also prevent disruptions to the conduct of arbitration proceedings, thus allowing the arbitrators and the parties' representatives to focus on substantive issues of the dispute.

840   *Second*, we agree with the extensive approach to confidentiality adopted by Art. 3.13 of the IBA Rules on Evidence stipulating that

> '[a]*ny documents submitted or produced by a Party or non-Party in the arbitration . . . shall be kept confidential . . . and shall be used only in connection with the arbitration'*.

We think that this solution encourages the candour of the persons participating in arbitration proceedings and reinforces the principle of confidentiality of arbitration. The confidentiality duty should, however, be limited to the documents to which the person wishing to disclose the document had access only because of the arbitration.

841   *Third*, confidentiality of the awards that reveal the identity of the parties should be protected. Publication of such awards should be allowed only with the parties' consent. On the contrary, publication of awards in a sanitized form, in which the parties' identity is not revealed, should be generally allowed. In our opinion, systematic publication of arbitral awards should be the goal, in order to create consistent arbitral case law, improve the quality of arbitral awards, promote arbitration as a dispute resolution method, make arbitrations more accessible for the users, enable the users to make a more informed decision regarding the choice of arbitration institution and when appointing an arbitrator and facilitate voluntary execution and enforcement of arbitral awards.

Fourth, privacy of hearings is generally recognised. In addition, we think that all information and documents surrounding hearings, such as transcripts of hearings, or opening and closing submissions, should also be subject to confidentiality. Confidentiality of these documents and information should be maintained as their disclosure would be equivalent to opening the door to the hearing room.   **842**

8.3 Handling Exceptions to the Duty of Confidentiality

In advocating for a broad duty of confidentiality of arbitration, we do not mean to minimize exceptions. It is important to determine a list of exceptions to the duty of confidentiality as the difficulty in clearly identifying such exceptions appears to mainly explain the reluctance to recognise the existence of a duty of confidentiality. Based on our analysis of existing regulations and state court decisions, we think that disclosure of confidential information and documents should be allowed in the following cases: (i) disclosure is authorised or required by the law; (ii) the parties have consented to the disclosure; (iii) disclosure is necessary to seek professional advice; (iv) the documents are no longer confidential as they are already in the public domain; (v) disclosure is necessary to pursue the parties' legitimate rights; and (vi) disclosure is justified by the public interest; (vii) disclosure is justified by the interests of justice.   **843**

It is impossible to anticipate every possible case where disclosure should be allowed. Thus, an arbitral tribunal should also have the power to allow disclosure of confidential information and documents in the cases not mentioned above. The tribunal should take its decision after giving each of the parties an opportunity to be heard and should allow disclosure where there is a demonstrated need to disclose that outweighs any party's legitimate interest in preserving confidentiality.   **844**

National courts have provided abundant case law on disclosures made by parties with the purpose of pursing their legitimate rights. The courts have consistently held that the parties do not violate their duty of confidentiality by disclosing arbitral awards, or by disclosing other arbitration materials for the purpose of recognising, enforcing or challenging an arbitral award. However, when a party does not pursue its legitimate rights, but abuses the process by making a frivolous claim, this action can be considered as a breach of the confidentiality duty. There is even a risk, as in the *G. Aïta v. A. Ojjeh* case, that a party making a frivolous claim will be enjoined to pay damages caused to the other party as a result of the confidentiality breach.   **845**

Importantly, in the case of a legitimate disclosure of information or documents relating to an arbitration, one must remember that the principle of publicity and transparency applies in state court proceedings. Thus, when disclosed information or documents from an arbitration become part of the record in a court proceeding, there is a risk that confidential information can become publicly available. Hearings may   **846** be held publicly and court decisions relating to arbitrations may be rendered publicly and/or be published.

847   Exceptions to the duty of confidentiality of arbitrators must be particularly regulated, given the adjudicator role of arbitrators similar to that of court judges. There is no uniform approach to the arbitrators' duty to testify in different jurisdictions. *De lege ferenda*, we think that national legislators should aim to provide arbitrators with the same prerogatives that court judges enjoy regarding their duty to testify. Like court judges, arbitrators should be generally exempted from their duty to testify. Thus, we would recommend that Swiss lawmaker include arbitrators in the list of persons exempted from the duty to testify and to collaborate on setting the meaning of Art. 166(1)(c) of the Code of Civil Procedure and Art. 170(1) of the Code of Criminal Procedure. This exemption would extend to any facts that became known to the arbitrators by reason of their service as arbitrators.

8.4   Remedies and Sanctions for Breach of the Duty of Confidentiality

848   A number of remedies are available against persons breaching their duty of confidentiality regarding arbitration proceedings. In our opinion, such remedies should *not* be subject to harmonisation at the level of national arbitration laws as existing arbitration law and domestic law provisions already provide the necessary regulation. It should also be remembered that not only direct sanctions can motivate to respect confidentiality obligations. Thus, for counsel and arbitrators, there is primarily a risk of reputational damages.

849   *First*, a party can seek a confidentiality order as a remedy. This is a quite common way to stop or prevent a breach of confidentiality. Since it is generally recognised that an arbitral tribunal has the power to issue confidentiality orders, there is no need to have a specific provision on confidentiality orders.

850   *Second*, the injured person can seek compensation for damages on the basis of a contractual or a tort claim. Each legal system has its own provisions on contractual and tort responsibility. Significantly, however, some institutional rules contain clauses limiting liability of the relevant arbitration institution and of the arbitrators adjudicating the relevant case. Also, when seeking compensation for damages, it can be difficult for a claimant to prove that he suffered damages and to measure these damages. There is, however, at least one known court case, the *G. Aïta v. A. Ojjeh* case, in which such damages were awarded.

851   To avoid the problem of proving damages, the parties could fix the amount to be paid in the event of a contract breach in advance. They should, however, be cautious as penalty clauses are generally unenforceable in common law jurisdictions. For example, under English law, only liquidated damages are recoverable. If the contractual remedy for breach imposes a detriment on the contract-breaker out of all proportion to the innocent party's legitimate interest in enforcing the counterparty's obligation, such a contractual provision will be considered penal and therefore unenforceable under English law. Under Swiss law, if a judge considers that the agreed amount is unreasonably excessive, he will reduce the penalty amount, but the penalty clause will still be valid.

Third, national laws can provide for criminal and disciplinary sanctions against **852** lawyers who violate their statutory obligations of confidentiality regarding their client's affairs. Some jurisdictions provide for criminal and disciplinary sanctions against arbitrators as well. Quite obviously, this area cannot be harmonized at the level of national arbitration laws.

Fourth, an injured party can be entitled to terminate an arbitration agreement for **853** breach of confidentiality. Since the decision of the Stockholm City Court in the *Bulbank* case, the arbitration community has become concerned about the possibility of termination of an arbitration agreement and annulment of an arbitral award. We think that a breach of confidentiality can result in termination of an arbitration agreement only if: (i) the parties agreed that confidentiality was a condition to the arbitration agreement; (ii) there are other serious reasons to believe that such a breach has resulted in a substantial deprivation of the benefits of the arbitration agreement to any party; or (iii) the parties expressly agreed on termination of their arbitration agreement as a remedy in case of a confidentiality breach by one of the parties. Thus, if a confidentiality obligation is essential for the parties, they can agree on a mechanism to terminate the arbitration agreement in case of a confidentiality breach. As to annulment of the arbitration agreement, we do not think that it should be possible because termination of the arbitration agreement should take effect only for the future.

Fifth, an arbitral tribunal can penalize the party which breached its confidentiality **854** duty by obliging it to pay a more significant part of the arbitration costs if a confidentiality breach disrupted the conduct of the arbitration proceeding and caused additional costs.

8.5 Final Conclusions

Our opinion is that a uniform approach to confidentiality of international commercial **855** arbitration is possible. The best way to achieve it would be through harmonization of national arbitration laws. We propose that rules on confidentiality be introduced into the UNCITRAL Model Law and into national arbitration laws.[1] Switzerland could set a good example by introducing these rules into the Chapter 12 of the Private International Law Act. We have proposed language for the text of such national laws.[2]

---

[1] A proposed text of rules on confidentiality can be found in Sect. 7.4.

[2] See above Sect. 7.4.

856   As stated above, the advantage of introducing such rules into national arbitration laws (rather than into arbitration rules) is that: (i) arbitration rules do not apply to all arbitrations; (ii) arbitration rules do not apply to third parties; and (iii) introducing an express provision on confidentiality into national arbitration laws will put an end to the debate on the existence of an implied duty of confidentiality. The proposed rules will not be mandatory, and the parties will be able to derogate from the confidentiality regime.

857   Subject to certain exceptions, we think that all persons involved in arbitration proceedings should be bound by a duty of confidentiality regarding all information and documents relating to the arbitration. The duty of confidentiality should also extend to arbitral awards and orders, as well as to all information and documents surrounding hearings. In terms of exceptions, the list of exceptions will remain open, as the arbitral tribunal will be able to allow disclosure in the cases not specifically mentioned by our proposed rules on confidentiality. Confidentiality regarding arbitral awards should, however, not be an obstacle to publications of awards that do not reveal the identity of the parties. Moreover, systematic publication of awards in a sanitized form should be the aim going forward.

858   In the meantime, as long as confidentiality has not become the universally recognised rule in international commercial arbitration, we recommend that parties seeking predictability on the issue of confidentiality enter into a tailor-made agreement[3] or adopt institutional rules containing provisions on confidentiality of arbitration proceedings.[4] As long as the law governing an arbitration does not contain mandatory provisions on confidentiality, the parties' agreement will always prevail.

859   Some aspects of confidentiality, such as privacy of hearing and secrecy of deliberations of arbitral tribunal are not subject to any controversy and thus could be recognised, in our view, as autonomous *lex mercatoria* principles.

---

[3]See above in Sect. 2.2 model confidentiality or non-confidentiality clauses.

[4]See above Sect. 2.3 analysing regulation of the confidentiality issue by several arbitration rules.

Table of Cases

ICC Arbitration Awards and Procedural Orders

- Final Award in Cases No. 2745 and no. 2762 of 1977. In: Jarvin S, Derains Y (1990) Collection of ICC Arbitral Awards 1974–1985, Kluwer Law and Taxation Publishers, pp 326–331
- Final Award in Case No. 6032 of 1992. In: Arnaldez JJ, Derains Y, Hascher D (1997) Collection of ICC Arbitral Awards 1991–1995. Kluwer Law International, pp 560–567
- Procedural Order No. 5082 of 1994. In: Hascher D (1997) Collection of Procedural Decisions in ICC Arbitration 1993–1996. Kluwer Law International, pp 68–75
- Procedural Order of 1994 in ICC Case No. 7893. In: Journal du droit international 1998
- Arbitral Award in Case No. 8694 of 1996. In: Arnaldez JJ, Derains Y, Hascher D (2003) Collection of ICC Arbitral Awards 1996–2000, Kluwer Law International, pp 470–474
- Partial Arbitral Award in Case No. 7983 of 1996. In: Arnaldez JJ, Derains Y Hascher D (2009) Collection of ICC Arbitral Awards 2001–2007, Kluwer Law International, pp 567–574
- Procedural Order of 11 July 2003 in Case No. 12242. In: Jolivet E (ed) (2011) Decisions on ICC Arbitration Procedure. A Selection of Procedural Orders issued by Arbitral Tribunal acting under the ICC Rules of Arbitration (2003–2004), 2010 Special Supplement, International Chamber of Commerce, pp 40–42
- Final Award in Case No. 11961 of 2006. In: Arnaldez JJ, Derains Y, Hascher D (2013) Collection of ICC Arbitral Awards 2008–2011, Kluwer Law International, pp 135–178
- Procedural Order of 2006 in an ICC case between two European parties. In: Derains Y, Evidence and Confidentiality, pp 67–68

© Springer Nature Switzerland AG 2019
E. Reymond-Eniaeva, *Towards a Uniform Approach to Confidentiality of International Commercial Arbitration*, European Yearbook of International Economic Law 7, https://doi.org/10.1007/978-3-030-19003-3

Iran-United States Claims Decisions

Investment Arbitration Decisions and Procedural Orders

National Decisions

Australia

England

- Derby Magistrates' Court, ex parte B [1996] AC 487
- Dolling-Baker v Merrett [1990] 1 WLR 1205
- Emmott v Wilson & Partners Limited [2008] EWCA Civ 184
- Hassneh Insurance Co v Mew [1993] 2 Lloyd's Rep 243
- Leeds Estates Limited v Paribas Limited (2) [1995] E.G. 134
- Lincoln National Life Insurance Co v Sun Life Assurance Co of Canada [2004] EWCA 1660
- Oxford Shipping Co. Ltd. v Nippon Yusen Kaisha (The Eastern Saga), High Court of Justice, Queen's Bench Division (Commercial Court), [1984] 2 Lloyd's Rep. 374; 3 All ER 835, 26 June 1984, Journal of International Arbitration, Kluwer Law International, 1985, Volume 2 Issue 1, pp 79–81
- Re Duncan, Garfield v Fay [1968] P 306
- Riddick v Thames Board Mills [1977] 3 ALL ER 677
- Shearson Lehman Hutton Incorporated and Another v Maclaine Watson & Co. Ltd. [1988] 1 WLR 946
- Three Rivers District Council and Others v Governor and Company of the Bank of England [2003] QB 1556
- Ventouris v Mountain [1991] 1 W.L.R. 67
- Westwood Shipping Lines Inc. and another v Universal Schiffahrtsgesellschaft MBH and another [2012] EWHC 3837
- Wheeler v Le Marchant (1881) 17 Ch. D. 675

France

- Bleustein et autres v. Société True North et Société FCB International, Tribunal de commerce de Paris (Ord. réf.), 22 February 1999, in: Rev. Arb. 2003, Issue 1, pp 189–194
- G. Aïta v A. Ojjeh, Cour d'appel de Paris (1ère Chambre suppl.), 18 February 1986, in: Rev. Arb. 1986, 583
- Société True North et Société FCB International v. Bleustein et autres, Cour d'appel de Paris (14e Ch. B), 17 September 1999, in: Rev. Arb. 2003, Issue 1, pp 194–197
- Société National Company for Fishing and Marketing 'Nafimco' v. Société Foster Wheeler Trading Company AG, Cour d'appel de Paris (1ère Ch. C), 22 January 2004, in: Rev. Arb. 2004 Issue 3, pp 647–657
- Uzinexportimport Romanian Co. c/Attock Cement C, Cour d'appel de Paris (1ère Ch. C), 7 July 1994, in: Rev. Arb. 1995, 107

New Zealand

- Television New Zealand Limited v Langley Productions Limited [2000] 2 NZLR 250

Singapore

- AAY and others v AAZ AS, High Court, Suit [Y], Case No. [2009] SGHC 142, 15 June 2009, in: Michael Hwang and Kevin Lim, AAY and others v. AAZ AS, High Court, Suit [Y], Case No. [2009] SGHC 142, 15 June 2009, A contribution by the ITA Board of Reporters, Kluwer Law International

Sweden

- A.I. Trade Finance Inc. v. Bulgarian Foreign Trade Bank Ltd., Svea Court of Appeal, Dept. 16, 30 March 1999, in: Stockholm Arbitration Report, Volume 2, 2000, pp 137–160

Switzerland

- ATF 91 I 200
- ATF 92 II 15, JdT 1966 I 526
- ATF 97 II 97, JdT 1972 I 242
- ATF 102 Ia 516
- ATF 108 Ia 197
- ATF 109 Ia 81
- ATF 111 Ia 259
- ATF 112 Ib 606, JdT 1987 IV 150
- ATF 114 III 105, JdT 1990 II 98
- ATF 116 II 695, JdT 1991 I 625
- TF 11.05.1991, in: ASA Bull. 266 (1992)
- ATF 117 Ia 341
- TF 4P.61/1991, 12.11.1991, in: ASA Bull. 264 (1992) as Moser v. BMY
- TF 18.10.1993, in: SJ 1994 106
- TF 11.04.1996, in: SJ 1996 453
- ATF 124 III 297, JdT 1999 268
- TF 2P.313/1999, 08.03.2000
- ATF 127 III 328, JdT 2001 I 254
- ATF 129 III 445
- TF 8G.9/2004, 23.03.2004
- TF 1P.32/2005, 11.07.2005
- TF 4P.154/2005, 10.11.2005, in: ASA Bull. 55 (2006) as La République du Liban v. Y. and Z
- TF 4P.74/2006, 19.06.2006, in: ASA Bull. 761 (2006) as X. Gesellschaft, Y. Gesellschaft v. Z. Gesellschaft

The United States

Bibliography

Aboul-Enein M (2007) The need for establishing a perfect balance between confidentiality and transparency in commercial arbitration. Stockholm Int Arbitr Rev 2:25–37

AMJUR POF (1988) American jurisprudence proof of facts, 3d series, Lawyers Co-operative Pub. Co/Blancroft-Whitney Co., Rochester/San Francisco

Aravena-Jokelainen A, Wright SP (2017) Chapter 16: balancing the triangle: how arbitration institutions meet the psychological needs and preferences of users. In: Cole T (ed) The roles of psychology in international arbitration. International arbitration law library, vol 40. Kluwer Law International, pp 391–418

Arnaldez JJ, Derains Y, Hascher D (1997) Collection of ICC arbitral awards 1991–1995. Kluwer Law International

Arnaldez JJ, Derains Y, Hascher D (2003) Collection of ICC arbitral awards 1996–2000. Kluwer Law International

Arnaldez JJ, Derains Y, Hascher D (2009) Collection of ICC arbitral awards 2001–2007. Kluwer Law International

Arnaldez JJ, Derains Y, Hascher D (2013) Collection of ICC arbitral awards 2008–2011. Kluwer Law International

Arroyo M (2008) Dealing with dissenting opinions in the award: some options for the tribunal. ASA Bull 26(3):437–466

Arroyo M (ed) (2013) Arbitration in Switzerland/the practitioner's guide. Wolters Kluwer, Law & Business, Alphen aan den Rijn

Ashford P (2014) Handbook on international commercial arbitration, 2nd edn. Jurisnet, Huntington

Augsburger TP (2012) Confidentiality in arbitration law, rules and practice – a Swiss perspective. Transnational Dispute Management, No. 3

Austen-Baker R (2011) Implied terms in English contract law. Edward Elgar, Cheltenham

Azzali S (2012) Confidentiality vs. Transparency in Commercial Arbitration: A False Contradiction to Overcome, published on 28 December 2012. Available at http://blogs.law.nyu.edu/transnational/2012/12/confidentiality-vs-transparency-in-commercial-arbitration-a-false/. Last visited 13 September 2018

Bagner H (2001a) The confidentiality Conudrum in international commercial arbitration. ICC Int Court Arbitr Bull 12(1):18

Bagner H (2001b) Confidentiality – a fundamental principle in international commercial arbitration. J Int Arbitr 18(2):243–249

Baizeau D, Richard J (2016) Addressing the issue of confidentiality in arbitration proceedings: how is this done in practice? In: Confidential and restricted access information in international arbitration. Jurisnet, Huntington, pp 53–78

Bärtsch P, Petti AM (2013) Commentary of Article 4 of the Swiss rules of international arbitration. In: Zuberbühler T, Müller C, Habegger P (eds) Swiss rules of international arbitration, commentary, 2nd edn. Schulthess Verlag, Zurich

Baudenbacher C, Planzer S (eds) (2011) The role of precedent. German Law Publishers, Stuttgart

Baudesson T, Rocher P (2006) Le secret professional face au legal privilege. RDAI 1:37–66

Beale HG (ed) (2015) Chitty on contracts, 32nd edn. Sweet & Maxwell, London

Beatson J, Burrows A, Cartwright J (2016) Anson's law of contract, 30th edn. Oxford University Press, Oxford

Bennett SC (2013) Confidentiality issues in arbitration. Dispute Resol J 68(2):1–9

Berger B (2011) Notification and deposit, publication, confidentiality and preservation of the file. In: Post award issues – ASA Special Series No. 38. Juris, Huntington

Berger B (2013) Rights and obligations of arbitrators in the deliberations. ASA Bull 31(2):244–261

Berger B, Kellerhals F (2015) International and domestic arbitration in Switzerland, 3rd edn. Staempfli, Bern

Berger KP (2006) Evidentiary privileges: best practice standards versus/and arbitral discretion. Arbitr Int 22(4):501–520

Berger KP (2010) The creeping codification of the New Lex Mercatoria, 2nd edn. Wolters Kluwer

Bernardini P (2012) Article 8 – confidentiality. In: The chamber of arbitration of Milan rules, a commentary. JurisNet, Huntington, pp 131–144

Bernet M, Gottlieb B (2016) Confidential and restricted data in the award: how do arbitrators draft awards without breaching confidentiality or restrictions? In: Confidential and restricted access information in international arbitration, Juris Huntington: p 79–93

Bertossa B (1981) Le secret professionnel de l'avocat, Note sur la jurisprudence de la Commission de surveillance. Semaine judiciaire, pp 321–324

Besson S (2011) Role of arbitrators and arbitral institutions in subsequent court proceedings. In: Tercier P (ed) Post award issues. Association Suisse de l'Arbitrage, Huntington, pp 93–112

Besson S (2014) Les mesures provisoires et conservatoires dans la pratique arbitrale – notion, types de mesures, conditions d'octroi et responsabilité en cas de mesures injustifiées. In: L'arbitre international et l'urgence. Bruxelles, pp 37–59

Besson S (2016a) Evolution of case law in international arbitration. In: The evolution and future of international arbitration. Wolters Kluwer, Alphen aan den Rijn, pp 47–57

Besson S (2016b) Confidential and restricted data: impact on burden of proof? In: Confidential and restricted access information in international arbitration. Juris, Huntington, pp 45–51

Besson S, Thommesen N (2013) Commentary of Article 31 of the swiss rules of international arbitration. In: Zuberbühler T, Müller C, Habegger P (eds) Swiss rules of international arbitration, commentary, 2nd edn. Schulthess Verlag, Zurich

Blackaby N, Partasides C et al (2015) Redfern and hunter on international arbitration, 6th edn. Oxford University Press

Bohnet F (2010) Les grands arrêts de la profession d'avocat, 2nd edn. Neuchatel

Bohnet F, Martenet V (2009) Droit de la profession d'avocat. Bern

Bond S (1995) Expert Report in Esso/BHP v. Plowman. Arbitr Int 11(3):273–282

Bondi BJ (2010) No secrets allowed: Congress's treatment and mistreatment of the attorney-client privilege and the work-product protection in congressional investigations and contempt proceedings. J Law Polit 25(145):145–178

Born GB (2014) International commercial arbitration, 2nd edn. Walters Kluwer

Borovsky M (2009) Das 'In-house Counsel Privilege' im Zivilprozess. GesKR, No. 4. Zurich, pp 449–452

Bortoluzzi S, Damien A et al (2018) Règles de la profession d'avocat, 16th edn. Paris

Boyd SQC (1995) Expert Report in Esso/BHP v. Plowman. Arbitr Int 11(3):265–272

Bredin JD (2004) Retour au délibéré arbitral. In: Liber amicorum Claude Reymond, Paris, pp 43–51

Brocker S, Löf K (2013) Chapter 8, the proceedings. In: Franke U, Magnusson A et al (eds) International arbitration in Sweden: a practitioner's guide. Kluwer Law International, pp 153–236

Brown AC (2001) Presumption meets reality: an exploration of the confidentiality obligation in international commercial arbitration. Am Univ Int Law Rev 16(4):969–1025

Buchanan A, Williams D (2000) New Zealand: the confidentiality of arbitral proceedings under the New Zealand arbitration act 1996. Int Arbitr Law Rev 3(2):24–25

Bucher A (1988) Le nouvel arbitrage international en Suisse. Helbing & Lichtenhahn, Basle

Bucher A (2011) Commentary of Article 183 of the private international law act. In: Bucher A (ed) Loi sur le droit international privé/Convention de Lugano, Commentaire Romand. Basle

Bucher A, Tschanz PY (1988) International arbitration in Switzerland. Helbing & Lichtenhahn, Basle

Bührung-Uhle C (2006) Arbitration and mediation in international business, 2nd edn. Kluwer Law International

Burckhardt P (2012) Legal privilege and confidentiality in Switzerland. In: Greenwald D, Russenberger M (eds) Privilege and confidentiality: an international handbook, 2nd edn. Bloomsbury Professional, Croydon

Burger L (1999) Observations – Tribunal de Stockholm 10 septembre 1998 – Bulgarian Foreign Trade Bank Ltd v. A.I. Trade Finance Inc. Revue de l'Arbitrage 3:670–684

Burn G, Pearsall A (2009) Exceptions to confidentiality in international arbitration. In: Confidentiality in Arbitration/Commentaries on Rules, Statutes, Case Law and Practice/ A Special Supplement to the ICC International Court of Arbitration Bulletin. ICC Publication No. 700, pp 23–38

Butler WE (2009) Russian law, 3rd edn. Oxford University Press, New York

Buys CJ (2003) The tensions between confidentiality and transparency in international arbitration. Am Rev Int Arbitr 14:121–138

Cairns DJA (2002) Confidentiality and state party arbitrations. N Z Law J, 3

Callens P et al (2014) Arbitrage et confidentialité. Brussels

Calvo Goller K (2012) The 2012 ICC rules of arbitration – an accelerated procedure and substantial changes. J Int Arbitr 29(3):323–344

Carlevaris A (2013) Confidentiality in ICC arbitration. In: Malatesta A, Sali R (eds) The rise of transparency in international arbitration/ the case for the anonymous publication of arbitral awards. Juris, New York, pp 123–136

Cavalieros P (2006) La confidentialité de l'arbitrage. Les Cahiers de l'Arbitrage 3:56–60

Chaix F (2012) Commentary of article 364 of the code of obligations. In: Thévenoz L, Werro F (eds) Code des Obligations I, Commentaire romand, 2nd edn. Basle, pp 8–54

Chaix F (2017) Commentary of article 530 of the code of obligations. In: Tercier P, Amstutz M, Trindade T (eds) Code des Obligations II, Commentaire romand, 2nd edn. Basle, pp 55–65

Chappuis B (2016) La profession d'avocat, 2nd edn. Genève

Chappuis B, Steiner A (2017) Le secret de l'avocat dans le CPP e le CPC: entre divergence et harmonie. Revue de l'avocat 2:87–94

Chen-Wishart M (2018) Contract law. Oxford University Press

Clay T (2001) L'arbitre. Dalloz, Paris

Collins M (1995) Privacy and confidentiality in arbitration proceedings. Arbitr Int 11(3):321–336

Comrie-Thomson P (2017) A statement of arbitral jurisprudence: the case for a national obligation to publish international commercial arbitral awards. J Int Arbitr 34(2):275–302

Coppo B (2013) Confidentiality in the arbitration rules of the Milan Chamber. In: Malatesta A, Sali R (eds) The rise of transparency in international arbitration/the case for the anonymous publication of arbitral awards. Juris, New York, pp 137–153

Corboz B (1993) Le secret professionnel de l'avocat selon l'article 321 CP. SJ pp 77–108

Craig N (2010) Arbitration confidentiality and the IBA rules on the taking of evidence in international arbitration. Int Arbitr Law Rev 13(5):169–170

Cremades B, Cairns D (2003) Transnational public policy in international arbitral decision-making: the cases of bribery, money laundering and fraud. In: ICC dossier, arbitration: money laundering, corruption and fraud. ICC Publication, Paris, pp 65–91

Croft C (2011) Recent developments in arbitration in Australia. J Int Arbitr 28(6):599–616

Dal GA (2011) Le secret professionnel de l'avocat dans la jurisprudence européenne/Legal Professional Privilege and European Case Law. Brussels

Daly MC, Goebel RJ (eds) (2004) Rights, liability, and ethics in international legal practice, 2nd edn. Juris Publishing Inc, New York

De Los Santos C, Soto Moya M (2011) Confidentiality under the new French arbitration law: a step forward? Spain Arbitr Rev:79–94

De Ly P, Friedman M, Radicati di Brozolo LG (2012) International law association international commercial arbitration committee's report and recommendations on 'confidentiality in international commercial arbitration. Arbitr Int Kluwer Law Int 28(3):355–396

Delvolvé JF (1996) Vraies et fausses confidences, ou les petits et les grands secrets de l'arbitrage. Revue de l'Arbitrage 3:373–392

Delvolvé JL, Pointon GH, Rouche J (2009) French arbitration law and practice: a dynamic civil law approach to international arbitration, 2nd edn. Wolters Kluwer Law & Business, Austin

Denoix De Saint Marc V (2009) Confidentiality of arbitration and the obligation to disclose information on listed companies or during due diligence investigations. J Int Arbitr 20 (2):211–216

Derains Y (2005) La pratique du délibéré arbitral. In : Aksen G et al (eds) Global Reflections on international law, commerce and dispute resolution: Liber Amicorum in honour of Robert Briner, pp 221–234

Derains Y (2009) Evidence and confidentiality. In: Confidentiality in arbitration/ Commentaries on rules, statutes, case law and practice/ A special supplement to the ICC international court of arbitration bulletin. ICC Publication No. 700, pp 57–71

Derains Y, Schwartz EA (2005) A guide to the ICC rules of arbitration, 2nd edn. Kluwer Law International

Dessemontet F (1996) Arbitration and confidentiality. Am Rev Int Arbitr 7:229

Diallo O (2004) La confidentialité dans l'arbitrage et dans les ADR: approche comparative. In: Zen-Ruffinen P (ed) Le secret et le droit. Schulthess, pp 371–397

Dimolitsa A (2005) Quid encore de la confidentialité? In: Mélanges en l'honneur de François Knoepfler. Bâle, p 249

Dimolitsa A (2009) Institutional rules and national regimes relating to the obligation of confidentiality on parties in arbitration. In: Confidentiality in arbitration/ Commentaries on rules, statutes, case law and practice/ A special supplement to the ICC international court of arbitration bulletin. ICC Publication No. 700, pp 5–22

Dotseth KA (2014) Confidentiality or confirmation: the complications of confirming confidential arbitration awards after Eagle Star Ins. Co. v. Arrowood Indemnity Co. Def Couns J 81(1):1–6

Drahozal CR (2015) Confidentiality in consumer and employments arbitration. Arbitr Law Review Yearb Arbitr Mediation 7:28–48

Dunand JP (2013) Commentary of Article 321a of the code of obligations. In: Dunand JP, Mahon P (eds) Commentaire du contrat de travail. Stämpfli, Bern, pp 52–75

Dupeyre R (2010) Arbitrators on the Witness Stand! Comparative Approaches, published on 3 August 2010 on http://kluwerarbitrationblog.com/2010/08/03/arbitrators-on-the-witness-stand-comparative-approaches/. Last visited 13 Sept 2018

Edwards A (2001) Confidentiality in arbitration: fact or fiction? Int Arbitr Law Rev 4(3):4–95

Engel P (1997) Traité des obligations en droit suisse : dispositions générales du CO, 2nd edn. Bern

Feder M (2009) Privilege in Cross-Border Litigation, ABA Section of Litigation Annual Conference, April 29–May 2, 2009: Privilege in Cross-Border Litigation: Will You Be Safe or Sorry?, Available at http://apps.americanbar.org/litigation/committees/international/docs/1009-materials-privilege-border-lit.pdf. Last visited 13 Sept 2018

Fernandez-Armesto J (2012) The time has come/A plea for abandoning secrecy in arbitration. Les Cahiers de l'Arbitrage, No. 3

Fischel DR (1998) Lawyers and confidentiality. Univ Chicago Law Rev 65(1):1–33

Fortier LY (1999) The occasionally unwarranted assumption of confidentiality. Arbitr Int 15:131–140

Fox R et al (2013) United Kingdom. In: Professional secrecy of lawyers in Europe/compiled by the Bar of Brussels. Cambridge

Franke U, Magnusson A et al (eds) (2013) International arbitration in Sweden: a practitioner's guide. Kluwer Law International

Fry J, Greenberg S, Mazza F (2012) The secretariat's guide to ICC arbitration. ICC, Paris

Furrer A (2008) The duty of confidentiality in international arbitration. In: Mélanges en l'honneur de Pierre Tercier. Genève

Gaillard E (2011) General principles of law in international commercial arbitration – challenging the myths. World Arbitr Mediation Rev 5(2):161–172

Gaillard E, de Lapasse P (2011) Le nouveau droit français de l'arbitrage interne et international. Recueil Dalloz 3:175–192

Gaillard E, Savage J (eds) (1999) Fouchard Gaillard Goldman on international commercial arbitration. Kluwer Law International

Galanter M (1974) Why the 'Haves' come out ahead: speculations on the limits of legal change. Law Soc Rev 95:95–160

Galanter M (1999) Comment/Farther along. Law Soc Rev 33:1113–1123

Gallacher N (2004) Confidentiality of court decision from an arbitration act 1996. Int Arbitr Law Rev 7(1):5–7

Garner BA (ed in chief) (2014) Black's law dictionary, 10th edn. Thomson Reuters, St. Paul

Geisinger E, Voser N (eds) (2013) International arbitration in Switzerland: a handbook for practitioners, 2nd edn. Kluwer Law International

Gilliéron P (2011) Les dommages-intérêts contractuels. CEDIDAC, Lausanne

Girsberger D, Voser N (2016) International arbitration, comparative and Swiss perspectives, 3rd edn. Schulthess Verlag, Zurich

Glover R (2017) Murphy on evidence, 15th edn. Oxford University Press, Oxford

Grégoire N (2016) Evidentiary Privileges in International Arbitration, A Comparative Analysis under English, American, Swiss and French Law. CG - Collection genevoise

Gu W (2004) Confidentiality revisited: blessing or curse in international commercial arbitration. Am Rev Int Arbitr 15:607

Haas U, Kahlert H (2015) Part IV: selected areas and issues of arbitration in Germany, privacy and confidentiality. In: Böckstiegel KH, Kröll SM et al (eds) Arbitration in Germany: the model law in practice, 2nd edn. Kluwer Law International, pp 963–980

Habegger P (2012) The revised Swiss rules of international arbitration: an overview of the major changes. ASA Bull 30(2):269–311

Habegger P, Bühler M (2009) Country Report on Switzerland. In: ICC international court of arbitration bulletin – 2008 special supplement: guide to national rules of procedure for recognition and enforcement of New York Convention awards. ICC Publishing, Paris

Hakeem S (2006) Confidentiality in arbitration proceedings: recent trends and developments. J Bus Law, pp 300–311

Hall JW (1987) Professional responsibility of the criminal lawyer. Lawyers Co-operative Publishing, Rochester

Hargrove J (2009) Misplaced confidence? An analysis of privacy and confidentiality in contemporary international arbitration. Disput Resolut Int 3:47

Hascher D (1997) Collection of procedural decisions in ICC arbitration 1993–1996. Kluwer Law International

Heitzmann P (2008) Confidentiality and privileges in cross-border legal practice: the need for a global standard. ASA Bull 26(2):205–240

Heuman L (2003) Arbitration law of Sweden: practice and procedure. Juris, New York

Heuman L, Jarvin S (eds) (2006) The Swedish arbitration act of 1999, five years on: a critical review of strengths and weaknesses. Juris, New York

Hill R, Fletcher C (2004) Confidentiality of arbitration in court proceedings. Int Arbitr Law Rev 7(4):48–50

Hodges P (2012) The Perils of complete transparency in international arbitration – should parties be exposed to the glare of publicity? Les Cahiers de l'Arbitrage, No. 3

Hoffet F (1991) Rechtliche Beziehungen zwischen Shiedsrichtern und Parteien. Zurich

Hollander CQC (2018) Documentary evidence, 13th edn. Sweet and Maxwell, London

Hollander P (2014) Confidentiality under Art. 44 Swiss rules. In: Voser N (ed) 10 Year of Swiss rules of international arbitration. ASA Special Series No. 44. Juris

Honsell H, Vogt NP et al (eds) (2013) Internationales Privatrecht, Basler Kommentar, 3rd edn. Basle

Hwang M, Chung K (2009a) Defining the indefinable: practical problems of confidentiality in arbitration. J Int Arbitr 26(5):609–645

Hwang M, Chung K (2009b) Protecting confidentiality and its exceptions – the way forward? In: Confidentiality in arbitration/ Commentaries on rules, statutes, case law and practice/ A special supplement to the ICC international court of arbitration bulletin. ICC Publication No. 700, pp 39–55

Hwang M, Chung K (2010) Confidentiality in arbitration. N Z Law J 4:153–156

Hwang M, Thio N (2012) A proposed model procedural order on confidentiality in international arbitration: a comprehensive and self-governing code. J Int Arbitr 29(2):137–169

ICC Report Working Group on Criminal Law and Arbitration (Doc 420/492)

Jarvin S, Derains Y (1990) Collection of ICC arbitral awards 1974–1985. Kluwer Law and Taxation Publishers

Jeandin N (2011) Commentary of Article 166 of the code of civil procedure. In: Bohnet F, Haldy J, Jeandin N, Schweizer P, Tappy D (eds) Code de Procédure Civile Commenté. Basle

Jolivet E (2006) Access to information and awards. Arbitr Int 22(2):265–274

Jolivet E (ed) (2011) Decisions on ICC arbitration procedure/A selection of procedural orders issued by arbitral tribunal acting under the ICC rules of arbitration (2003–2004), 2010 Special Supplement. International Chamber of Commerce

Jolles A, Canals de Cediel M (2004) Confidentiality. In: Kaufmann-Kohler G, Stucki B (eds) International arbitration in Switzerland: a handbook for practitioners. Kluwer Law International, The Hague

Jolles A, Stark-Traber S, Canals de Cediel M (2013) Chapter 7: confidentiality. In: Geisinger E, Voser N (eds) International arbitration in Switzerland: a handbook for practitioners, 2nd edn. Kluwer Law International, pp 131–152

Kahlert H (2013) Confidentiality in arbitration – a tale of doves, chromatics and European divides. Eur Int Arbitr Rev 2(1):27–40

Karton J (2012) A conflict of interests: seeking a way forward on publication of international arbitral awards. Arbitr Int 28(3):447–486

Kaster LA (2012a) Confidentiality in U.S. arbitration. NYSBA New York Disput Resolut Lawyer 5(1)

Kaster LA (2012b) Confidentiality during and after proceedings. In: Haklet TD (ed) Arbitration of international intellectual property disputes. Juris, Huntington, pp 271–324

Kaufmann-Kohler G (2003) Globalization of arbitral procedure. Vanderbilt J Transntl Law 35:1313–1333

Kaufmann-Kohler G (2007) Arbitral precedent: dream, necessity or excuse. Arbitr Int 23(3):357–378

Kaufmann-Kohler G, Bärtsch P (2004) Discovery in international arbitration: how much is too much? SchiedsVZ. pp 13–21

Kaufmann-Kohler G, Rigozzi A (2010) Arbitrage international: droit et pratique à la lumière de la LDIP, 2nd edn. Berne

Kaufmann-Kohler G, Rigozzi A (2015) International arbitration: law and practice in Switzerland. Oxford University Press

Kawharu A (2008) New Zealand's arbitration law receives a tune-up. Arbitr Int 24(3):405–422

Kinnear M, Obadia E, Gagain M (2013) The ICSID approach to publication of information in investor-state arbitration. In: Malatesta A, Sali R (eds) The rise of transparency in international arbitration/ the case for the anonymous publication of arbitral awards. Juris, New York, pp 107–122

Kluwer Privacy and Confidentiality in Arbitration Smart Charts. Available at www.smartcharts. wolterskluwer.com. Last visited 13 Sept 2018

Kucherena A (2013) Advokatura Rossii. Moscow

Kuhn A, Jeanneret Y (2011) Code de procédure pénale suisse, Commentaire romand. Basle

Kuitkowski D (2015) The law applicable to privilege claims in international arbitration. J Int Arbitr 32(1):65–105

Kunz C (2013) Dissenting opinions in international commercial arbitration proceedings in Switzerland. Selected Papers on International Arbitration, pp 1–22

LaHatte C (2008) Confidentiality in arbitration: the public interest exception. N Z Law J 9:1–3

Lalive P, Poudret JF, Reymond C (1989) Le droit de l'arbitrage interne et international en Suisse. Lausanne

Lambert J (2011) La confidentialité dans l'arbitrage international. Genève: Institut de hautes études internationales et du développement

Lazareff S (2009) Confidentiality and arbitration: theoretical and philosophical reflections. In: Confidentiality in arbitration/ Commentaries on rules, statutes, case law and practice/ A special supplement to the ICC international court of arbitration bulletin. ICC Publication No. 700, pp 81–93

Lew JDM (1982) The case for the publication of arbitration awards. In: The art of arbitration/ Essays on international arbitration/ Liber Amicorum Pieter Sanders 12 September 1912–1982. Kluwer, p 223

Lew JDM (1995) Expert Report in Esso/BHP v. Plowman. Arbitr Int 11(3):283–296

Lew JDM (2011) The arbitrator and confidentiality. In: Dossier of the ICC Institute of world business law: is arbitration only as good as the arbitrator? Status, powers and role of the arbitrator

Lew JDM (2013) Chapter 21: confidentiality in arbitrations in England. In: Lew JDM, Bor H et al (eds) Arbitration in England, with chapters on Scotland and Ireland. Kluwer Law International

Lew JDM, Mistelis LA et al (2003) Comparative international commercial arbitration. Kluwer Law International

Liu C (2005) The concept of fundamental breach: perspectives from the CISG, UNIDROIT principles and PECL and case law, 2nd edn. May 2005, CISG Database. Available at http://www.cisg.law.pace.edu/cisg/biblio/liu8.html#ccvi. Last visited 13 Sept 2018

Loquin E (2006) Les obligations de confidentialité dans l'arbitrage. Revue de l'Arbitrage 2006 (2):323–352

Loquin E (2015) L'arbitrage du commerce international : pratique des affaires. Issy-les-Moulineaux: Joly éditions

Lord Neill of Bladen FP (1996) Confidentiality in arbitration. Arbitr Int 12(3):287–318

Madsen F (2007) Commercial arbitration in Sweden, 3rd edn. Oxford University Press, New York

Magnus R (2010) Das Anwaltsprivileg und sein zivilprozessualer Schutz/ Eine rechtsvergleichende Analyse des deutschen, französischen und englischen Rechts. Tübingen

Malatesta A (2013) Confidentiality in international commercial arbitration. In: Malatesta A, Sali R (eds) The rise of transparency in international arbitration/ The case for the anonymous publication of arbitral awards. Juris, New York, pp 39–51

Malatesta A, Sali R (eds) (2013) The rise of transparency in international arbitration/ The case for the anonymous publication of arbitral awards. Juris, New York

Malek HMQC (ed) (2018) Phipson on evidence, 19th edn. Sweet & Maxwell, London

Marin J (1997) Invoking the U.S. attorney-client privilege: Japanese corporate quasi-lawyers deserve protection in U.S. Courts Too. Fordham Int Law J 21(4):1558–1605

Maurer P, Gross JP (2010) Commentary of Article 13 LLCA. In: Vaticos M, Reiser CM, Chappuis B (eds) Loi sur les avocats, Commentaire romand, Basle, pp 142–211

Mavromati D, Reeb M (2015) The code of the court of arbitration for sport: commentary, cases and materials. Wolters Kluwer, Alphen aan den Rijn

Mcllwrath M, Schroeder R (2013) Users need more transparency in international arbitration. In: Malatesta A, Sali R (eds) The rise of transparency in international arbitration/ The case for the anonymous publication of arbitral awards. Juris, New York, pp 87–106

Meier P, de Luze E (2014) Droit des personnes. Geneva-Zurich-Basle

Merkin R, Flannery L (2014) Arbitration act 1996, 5th edn. Informa, New York

Meyer O (2007) Time to take a closer look: privilege in international arbitration. J Int Arbitr 24(4):365–378

Meyer-Hauser BF (2004) Das Anwaltsgeheimnis und Schiedsgericht. Schulthess

Meyer-Hauser BF, Sieber P (2007) Attorney secrecy v attorney-client privilege in international commercial arbitration. Arbitration 73(2):211–231

Mistelis L (2005) Confidentiality and third party participation/UPS v. Canada and Methanex Corporation v. United States. Arbitr Int 21(2):211–232

Mooser M (2012a) Commentary of article 160 of the code of obligations. In: Thévenoz L, Werro F (eds) Code des Obligations I, Commentaire romand, 2nd edn. Basle, pp 1157–1163

Mooser M (2012b) Commentary of article 163 of the code of obligations. In: Thévenoz L, Werro F (eds) Code des Obligations I, Commentaire romand, 2nd edn. Basle, pp 1157–1163

Moreillon L, Parein-Reymond A (2016) Code de procédure pénale, Petit commentaire, 2nd edn. Basle

Morin A (2012) Commentary of article 1 of the code of obligations. In: Thévenoz L, Werro F (eds) Code des Obligations I, Commentaire romand, 2nd edn. Basle, pp 8–54

Mosk RM, Ginsburg T (2000) Dissenting opinions in international arbitration. Mealey's Int Arbitr Rep 15(4):29–36

Mosk RM, Ginsburg T (2001) Evidentiary privileges in international arbitration. Int Comp Law Q 50:345–385

Mourre A (2007) Precedent and confidentiality in international commercial arbitration/The case for the publication of arbitral awards. In: Banifatemi Y (ed) Precedent in international arbitration. International Arbitration Institute Seminar. Juris, Paris

Mourre A (2013) The case for the publication of arbitral awards. In: Malatesta A, Sali R (eds) The rise of transparency in international arbitration/ The case for the anonymous publication of arbitral awards. New York, pp 53–72

Müller C (2005) La confidentialité en arbitrage commercial international: un trompe-l'oeil. ASA Bull 23(2):216–240

Nesbitt S, Darowski M (2015) LCIA arbitration rules, Article 30. In: Mistelis LA (ed) Concise international arbitration, 2nd edn. Kluwer Law International, pp 558–560

Nisja OO (2008) Confidentiality and public access in arbitration – the Norwegian approach. Int Arbitr Law Rev 11(5):187–192

Nottage L (2017) Australia's International Arbitration Act Amendments: Rejuvenation by a Thousand Cuts? Kluwer Arbitration Blog, 13 May 2017, available at www.kluwerarbitrationblog.com. Last visited 13 Sept 2018

Nottage L, Morrison J (2017) Accessing and assessing Australia's international arbitration act. J Int Arbitr 34(6):963–1006

Noussia K (2010) Confidentiality in international commercial arbitration/A comparative analysis of the position under English, US, German and French Law. Springer, Berlin

O'Sullivan J, Hilliard J (2012) The law of contract, 5th edn. Oxford University Press

Oakley-White O (2003) Confidentiality revisited: is international arbitration losing one of its major benefits? Int Arbitr Law Rev 6(1):29–36

Onyema E (2010) International commercial arbitration and the arbitrator's contract. Routledge, London

Oswald D (2005) Pour une juridiction arbitrale spécialisée dans le sport. In: Bohnet F, Wessner P (eds) Mélanges en l'honneur de François Knoepfler. Basle, pp 355–374

Pair L (2012) Consolidation in international commercial arbitration: the ICC and Swiss rules. Eleven International Publishing, The Hague

Pallard H (2003) Déontologie juridique. Cowansville (Québec)

Pattenden R (2003) The law of professional-client confidentiality. Oxford University Press, New York

Paulsson J (1990) La lex mercatoria dans l'arbitrage C.C.I. Revue de l'arbitrage 1:55–100

Paulsson J (1995) The decision of the High Court of Australia in Esso/BHP v. Plowman. Arbitr Int 11(3):231–234

Paulsson J, Rawding N (1994) The trouble with confidentiality. ICC Int Court Arbitr Bull 5(1):48–58

Pendell G, Richards T (2009) Country Report on United Kingdom (England, Wales, Northen Ireland). In: ICC International Court of Arbitration Bulletin – 2008 Special Supplement: Guide to National Rules of Procedure for Recognition and Enforcement of New York Convention Awards. ICC Publishing, Paris

Perret F (2007) Is there a need for consistency in international commercial arbitration? In: Banifatemi Y (ed) Precedent in international arbitration. International Arbitration Institute Seminar, Paris

Philippin E (2013) Société simple. Not@lex, pp 125–126

Pic P, Léger I (2011) Le nouveau règlement d'arbitrage de la CNUDCI. Revue de l'Arbitrage 1:99–118

Pörnbacher K, Baur S (2016) Confidentiality and fundamental rights of due process and access to the file: a comparative overview. In: Confidential and restricted access information in international arbitration. Juris, Huntington, pp 21–43

Poudret JF (2004) Légitimité et opportunité de l'opinion dissidente dans le silence de la loi? Poursuite d'un débat amical. In: Autour de l'arbitrage, Liber amicorum Claude Reymond. Paris, pp 243–253

Poudret JF, Besson S (2007) Comparative law of international arbitration, 2nd edn. Sweet & Maxwell, London

Pryles M (2014) Confidentiality. In: Newman LW, Hill RD (eds) The leading arbitrators' guide to international arbitration, 3rd edn. Juris, Huntington, pp 109–160

Pshukov A (2008) Professionalnaya tayna advokata kak odno iz osnovnyh trebovaniy advokatskoy etiki. Biznes v zakone, Issue 2

Q&A with Professor Pierre Lalive, GAR Volume 3- Issue 5, 1 November 2008., Available at http://www.arbitration-icca.org/media/4/68645270843168/media01231910475880008_10_14_garpla_interview.pdf. Last visited 13 Sept 2018

Queen Mary University in Partnership with White & Case, 2015 International Arbitration Survey: Improvements and Innovations in International Arbitration., Available at http://www.whitecase.com/publications/insight/2015-international-arbitration-survey-improvements-and-innovations. Last visited 13 Sept 2018

Rachdi N (2014) Les mesures provisoires et conservatoires en matière d'arbitrage. Le juge et l'arbitrage, Paris, pp 69–86

Radicati di Brozolo LG, Ponzano F (2016) Confidentiality within arbitration. In: Confidential and restricted access information in international arbitration. Juris, Huntington, pp 1–20

Radjai N (2009) Confidentiality in international arbitration. ASA Bull 27(1):48–49

Rapport du Secrétaire général sur les éléments éventuels de la Loi type sur l'arbitrage commercial international, Annuaire de la Commission des Nations Unies pour le droit commercial international, Volume XII, 1981, deuxième partie

Rawding N, Seeger K (2003) Aegis v. European Re and the confidentiality of arbitration awards. Arbitr Int 19(4):483–489

Raymond AH (2005) Confidentiality in a forum of last resort: is the use of confidential arbitration a good idea for business and society? Am Rev Int Arbitr 16:479

Reid G (2000) Confidentiality – an algorithm. Stockholm Arbitration Report, No. 1, pp 53–60

Reiser CM, Valticos M (2015) Les règles professionnelles et les activités atypiques de l'avocat inscrit au barreau. Semaine Judiciaire 2015 II 191

Reymond JM (2007) Le secret professionnel de l'avocat dans les projets de code de procédure pénale et civile suisses: un droit fondamental du justiciable en péril. Revue de l'avocat 2:63–66

Ritz P (2007) Die Geheimhaltung im Schiedsverfahren nach schweizerischem Recht. Mohr
    Siebeck, Tübingen
Ritz P (2010) Privacy and confidentiality obligation on parties in arbitration under Swiss law.
    J Int Arbitr 27(3):221–245
Rivkin DW (1991) Restrictions on foreign counsel in international arbitration. In: van den Berg AJ
    (ed) Yearbook commercial arbitration, vol XVI. Kluwer Law International, pp 402–412
Rogers A, Miller D (1996) Non-confidential arbitration proceedings. Arbitr Int 12(3):319–346
Rogers CA (2005) The vocation of the international arbitrator. Am Univ Int Law Rev 20
    (5):957–1020
Rogers CA (2014) Ethics in international arbitration. Oxford University Press, Oxford
Rohner T, La Spada F (2013) Commentary of Article 44 of the Swiss rules of international
    arbitration. In: Zuberbühler T, Müller C, Habegger P (eds) Swiss rules of international arbitra-
    tion, commentary, 2nd edn. Zurich-Basel-Geneva
Roney DP, von der Weid K (2013) Third-party funding in international arbitration: new opportu-
    nities and new challenges. In: Müller C, Rigozzi A (eds) New developments in international
    commercial arbitration 2013. Schulthess Verlag, Zurich, pp 183–207
Rubino-Sammartano M (2014) International arbitration law and practice, 3rd edn. Juris, Huntington
Rudloff S (1995) Droits et libertés de l'avocat dans la Convention européenne des droits de
    l'homme. Bruxelles
Rüede T, Hadenfeldt R (1993) Schweizerisches Schiedsgerichtsrecht nach Konkordat und IPRG,
    2nd edn. Zurich
Sali R (2013) Transparency and confidentiality: how and why to publish arbitration decisions. In:
    Malatesta A, Sali R (eds) The rise of transparency in international arbitration/ the case for the
    anonymous publication of arbitral awards, New York, pp 73–85
Sanders P (2005) UNCITRAL's model law on international and commercial arbitration : present
    situation and future. Arbitr Int 21:443–482
Scherer M, Richman L, Gerbay R (2015) Arbitrating under the 2014 LCIA rules: a user's guide.
    Kluwer Law International
Schlosser PF (2005) Generalizable approaches to agreements with experts and witnesses acting in
    arbitration and international litigation. In: Aksen G et al (eds) Global reflections on international
    law, commerce and dispute resolution: Liber Amicorum in honour of Robert Briner. ICC
    Publications, pp 775–793
Schmitz AJ (2011) Assuming silence in arbitration. N J Lawyer 16(2011):269
Schneider ME (2016) The uncertain future of the interactive arbitrator: proposals, good intentions
    and the effect of conflicting views on the role of the arbitrator. In: The evolution and future of
    international arbitration. Alphen aan den Rijn, Wolters Kluwer, pp 379–392
Schöldström P (1998) The Arbitrator's mandate, a comparative study of relationships in commer-
    cial arbitration under the laws of England, Germany, Sweden and Switzerland. Stockholm
    University, Stockholm
Schreuer C (2014) Investment arbitration. In: Romano CPR, Alter KJ, Shany Y (eds) The Oxford
    handbook of international adjudication. Oxford University Press, Oxford
Schweizer P (2011) Commentary of Article 170 of the code of civil procedure. In: Bohnet F,
    Haldy J, Jeandin N, Schweizer P, Tappy D (eds) Code de Procédure Civile Commenté. Basle
Seibert-Fohr A (2014) International judicial ethics. In: Romano CPR, Alter KJ, Shany Y (eds) The
    Oxford handbook of international adjudication. Oxford University Press, Oxford
Seraglini C, Ortscheidt J (2013) Droit de l'arbitrage interne et international. Montchrestien, Paris
Shackleton SR (2003) Arbitration-related court proceedings and confidentiality. Int Arbitr Law Rev
    6(5):45–46
Shaughnessy P (2006) The Swedish approach towards arbitration. In: Heuman L, Jarvin S (eds) The
    Swedish arbitration act of 1999, five years on: a critical review of strengths and weaknesses.
    Juris, New York
Sheppard A (2003) Bermuda: confidentiality and issue of Estoppel in arbitration. Int Arbitr Law
    Rev 6(3):25–27

Sheridan P (1998) Privacy and confidentiality – recent developments: the divergence between English and Australian law confirmed. Int Arbitr Law Rev 1(5):171–177

Shirlow E (2015) Recent developments in Australia's approach to confidentiality and transparency in international arbitration. Kluwer Arbitration Blog, 19 December 2015, available at www. kluwerarbitrationblog.com. Last visited 13 Sept 2018

Sindler M, Wüstemann T (2005) Privilege across borders in arbitration: multi-jurisdictional nightmare or a storm in a teacup. ASA Bull 23(4):610–639

Smahi N (2016) The arbitrator's liability and immunity under Swiss law – part I. ASA Bull 34 (4):876–896

Smahi N (2017) The arbitrator's liability and immunity under Swiss law – part II. ASA Bull 35 (1):67–83

Smeureanu IM (2011) Confidentiality in international commercial arbitration. Kluwer Law International

Smit H (1995) Case-note on Esso/BHP v. Plowman (Supreme Court of Victoria). Arbitr Int 11(3): 299–302

Smit H (1995) Confidentiality in arbitration. Arbitr Int 11(3):337–340

Smit H (1998) Confidentiality/Articles 73 to 76. Am Rev Int Arbitr 9:233

Smit H (2000) Breach of confidentiality as a ground for avoidance of the arbitration agreement. Am Rev Int Arbitr 11:567

Smit H (2004) Dissenting opinions in arbitration. ICC Bull 15(1):37–41

Smith G (1999) Feature: confidentiality and the Attorney-Client Privilege: a few fundamentals. Louisina Bar J 326:47

Smutny AC, Young KM (2009) Confidentiality in relation to states. In: Confidentiality in Arbitration/ Commentaries on Rules, Statutes, Case Law and Practice/ A Special Supplement to the ICC International Court of Arbitration Bulletin. ICC Publication No. 700, pp 73–79

Stacher M (2007) Die Rechtsnatur der Schiedsvereinbarung. PhD Thesis at St. Gallen University

Steinauer PH, Fountoulakis C (2014) Droit des personnes physiques et de la protection de l'adulte. Bern

Stockholm Arbitration Report (2000) Volume 2

Stoudmann P (2008) Le secret professionnel de l'avocat: jurisprudence récente et perspectives. Revue Pénale Suisse 126(2):144–157

Sutton DSJ, Gill J, Gearing M (2015) Russel on arbitration, 24th edn. Sweet & Maxwell, London

Tashiro K (1992) Quest for a rational and proper method for the publication of arbitral awards. J Int Arbitr 9(2):97–104

Taylor N (ed) (1993) The guide to the professional conduct of solicitors, 6th edn. Law Society Publishing, London

Tercier P, Pichonnaz P (2012) Le droit des obligations, 5th edn. Zurich

Tercier P, Bieri L, Carron B (2016) Les contrats spéciaux. Zurich

Tevendale C, Cartwright-Finch U (2009) Privilege in international arbitration: is it time to recognize the consensus. J Int Arbitr 26(6):823–839

Thévenoz L (2012) Commentary of Article 101 of the code of obligations. In: Thévenoz L, Werro F (eds) Code des Obligations I, Commentaire romand, 2nd edn. Basle, pp 735–760

Thomson CR, Finn AMK (2007) Confidentiality in arbitration : a valid assumption? A proposed solution! Disput Resolut J 62(2):74–81

Timár K (2013) The legal relationship between the parties and the arbitral institution. Elte Law J 1:103–122

Tjio H (2009) The limits of confidentiality in arbitration/Emmott v. Michael Wilson & Partners. Lloyd's Marit Commer Law Q 1:10–15

Tompkins JJ (2017) The Loss of Confidentiality in NY Arbitral Enforcement Cases, Law360, New York, 27 February 2017, Available at http://www.shearman.com/~/media/Files/ NewsInsights/Publications/2017/02/The-Loss-Of-Confidentiality-In-NY-Arbitral-Enforce ment-Cases.pdf. Last visited 13 Sept 2018

Tweeddale A (2005) Confidentiality in arbitration and the public interest exception. Arbitr Int 21(1):59–69

Tweeddale A, Tweeddale K (2007) Arbitration of commercial disputes. Oxford University Press, Oxford

Villa F (2014) Le financement de contentieux par des tiers ("Third Party Funding"). Revue de l'avocat, pp 207–211

Von Goeler J (2016) Third-party funding in international arbitration and its impact on procedure. International arbitration law library, vol 35. Kluwer Law International

Von Schlabrendorff F, Sheppard A (2005) Conflict of legal privileges in international arbitration: an attempt to find a holistic solution. In: Aksen G et al (eds) Global reflections on international law, commerce and dispute resolution: liber Amicorum in honour of Robert Briner. ICC Publications, pp 743–774

Voser N, Fischer E (2013) The arbitral tribunal. In: Geisinger E, Voser N (eds) International arbitration in Switzerland: a handbook for practitioners, 2nd edn. Kluwer Law International, pp 51–71

Waincymer J (2012) Procedure and evidence in international arbitration. Kluwer Law International

Weber PC (1993) La responsabilité de l'expert à l'égard des parties et du tribunal arbitral. ASA Bull 11(2):190–209

Webster TH, Bühler MW (2014) Handbook of ICC arbitration, 3rd edn. Sweet & Maxwell, London

Werro F (1993) Le mandat et ses effets, Une étude sur le contrat d'activité indépendante selon le Code suisse des obligations. Fribourg

Werro F (2012a) Commentary of Article 41 of the code of obligations. In: Thévenoz L, Werro F (eds), Code des Obligations I, Commentaire romand, 2nd edn. Basle, pp 353–393

Werro F (2012b) Commentary of Article 394 of the code of obligations. In: Thévenoz L, Werro F (eds), Code des Obligations I, Commentaire romand, 2nd edn. Basle, pp 2369–2384

Wirth M (2000) Interim or preventive measures in support of international arbitration in Switzerland. ASA Bull 18(1):31–45

Würzburger A (2014) Commentary of Article 27 of the Law on the Federal Supreme Court. In: Corboz B, Würzburger A et al. (eds) Commentaire de la LTF, 2nd edn. Bern

Yong M, Chapman S (2009) Confidentiality in international arbitration. ASA Bull 27(1):26–47

Zuberbühler T, Hofmann D, Oetiker C, Rohner T (2012) IBA rules of evidence/Commentary on the IBA rules on the taking of evidence in international arbitration. Schulthess

Printed by Printforce, the Netherlands